Diary of a Drag Queen

Crystal Rasmussen

EBURY
PRESS

1 3 5 7 9 10 8 6 4 2

Ebury Press, an imprint of Ebury Publishing
20 Vauxhall Bridge Road
London SW1V 2SA

Ebury Press is part of the Penguin Random House group of companies
whose addresses can be found at global.penguinrandomhouse.com

Penguin
Random House
UK

First published by Ebury Press in 2019
This edition published in 2020.

www.penguin.co.uk

A CIP catalogue record for this book is available from the British Library

ISBN 9781785039508

Typeset in 9.98/16pt Latin 725 BT by Jouve (UK), Milton Keynes
Printed and bound in Great Britain by Clays Ltd, Elcograf S.p.A.

MIX
Paper from
responsible sources
FSC® C018179

Penguin Random House is committed to a
sustainable future for our business, our readers
and our planet. This book is made from Forest
Stewardship Council® certified paper.

This is for my families, biological and chosen – thanks for loving me.

This is for my community – thanks for teaching me.

This is for my thirteen-year-old self – thanks for sticking with me.

Prologue

What's the story of your life?

The story of my life is that I have more embarrassing poo stories than anyone I know. There was the time I shat myself during a kiss with a boy I fancied and he never spoke to me again. There was the time I shat my pants, a huge intact log, while giving a speech at a friend's birthday party in front of her dad who was a judge on *Dragon's Den*. Thank God I wasn't asking for funding. Another time, I got so drunk I shat my pants in the cinema in front of all my judgmental high school friends. Once, I was sick on a guy's dick after I'd had not one, not two, but three croissants for breakfast. Not an actual shit story, but a shitty story none-theless. There was the time I borrowed an American Apparel leotard from a friend of mine and gave it back, unbeknownst to me, with some pretty violent skid marks decorating the inside. We did speak again, but she made me buy her a new one.

I roll these stories out more regularly than my favourite leopard-print sequin pantsuit because I spent a lot of my life in the violent, painful clutches of shame, which manifested itself in various modes of self-harm, self-destruction, and other untenable, unsurvivable behaviours.

I learned, however, that the antidote to this shame is not pride, or honour, or even celebration. That comes later. The antidote to shame is honesty. Stark, crass, funny, powerful honesty. Honesty that smashes through notions of taboos and inappropriatenesses. I am not shameful, because I've done nothing wrong. It's the same with being gay, queer, femme, non-binary, a drag queen.

And so I tell my poo stories, because it's the only way I know how to free myself from the shackles of shame that would see us all bound for life. It's the only way I know how to survive.

But sometimes – rarely, but sometimes – it's not the right moment, in a social setting, to share one of my stonking shameless shit stories. And so I keep a diary.

December/
décembre

18th December / le 18 décembre

It was 1.15 a.m. last night, New York time, when, wrapped in a heavy Calvin Klein Egyptian cotton sheet, wet with my own cum, I realised I had to quit my first job in fashion.

It's a fairly usual first job in fashion: latte runs, bollockings for eating too much at a PR breakfast because I finished my eggs Benedict, constantly being reminded I'll never make it as I carry my boss up four flights of stairs while she's blackout drunk in the late afternoon . . . that kind of thing.

But there, last night, at 1.15 a.m., it all twigged. A sext from the boyfriend of my boss, Eve, arrived on her personal phone, which was by my bedside:

That was hot baby, wanna go again?

My job description was PA, which turned out to be a fairly loose catch-all term for a gig that encompassed a variety of descriptions: personal head-masseuse, scraper-of-dog-shit-from-bottom-of-Ugg-boot-person, boyfriend sexter. That's right: she goes to bed at 10 p.m. on the dot every night and makes me stay awake to keep texting her boyfriend while he works a nightshift. She told me very specifically that if I wanted to keep my job I would have to 'go with the flow with whatever Jared wants'. So when he sexts, I sext back.

When I arrived in Manhattan I was afresh with the naivety of a 24-year-old drag queen on the hunt for a big break and a series of big dicks. I thought my evenings would be the perfect time for an hour or so of writing,[1] followed by countless nights out with my swathe of queer, cool, self-assured American gal-pals.

None of that materialised and, instead, I've spent my evenings diving about a file of nudes of my boss on Dropbox. And, never fear, they don't run out – she constantly tops them up: butt naked at the gym, an exposed tit in the bathroom of a Hard Rock Cafe (wtf?).[2] She once sent me a close-up pic of her vagina and told me to study it so when I tell Jared that I'm 'touching my pussy'[3] I actually know what a 'pussy' looks like. Then she laughed. She doesn't pay me for this shit. If I'm going to do sex work I at least want to get paid.

And so, in order to survive this early career obstacle course, this nightly sexting ritual has moved swiftly from a place of trauma to a place of pure, unadulterated sex, because it had to. It has become a place in which I become my boss, my horrible boss, so horrible she could play a lead role in that horrible movie *Horrible Bosses*. This isn't that classic brand of gay male misogyny – something rife among many parts of my community – she's just a categorically dreadful person. And yes, if she were a man I would think she was even worse.

So, terrified, for three months I've sexted like a boss: aggressive, power-hungry, compulsively lying, with savageness coursing through my veins as I masturbate furiously in tandem with her partner, who is none the wiser.

1 AKA perfecting my begging emails to magazine editors to let me write for them to, thus far, literally zero avail.
2 By 'wtf?' I'm referring to the Hard Rock Cafe, not the bathroom tit, obviously.
3 Her words, not mine. Apparently Jared likes it.

I'm used to becoming 'her' after hours, but this is a different kind of her to the her I usually become. In drag I'm full of love, laziness, sensitivity, with a subtly promiscuous edge, but as my new virtual drag character, Eve, I'm all about the power fisting – something Jared has begun to love.

Truth is I like watching her do her job. I'm not quite sure what it is: producer of some sort, but she says things like 'unacceptable' and 'foreclose' and 'consequences' and 'Forbes list' all the time and it makes me feel powerful by proximity.

I appreciate how talented with targeted abuse she is. Honestly, she can out-savage anyone, and so many people are deeply terrified of her because she can make anything seem like it's your fault. It's power fisting, but in the boardroom. And I try to drink in her power, skimming off the severely abusive content that comes with it, there in her home office in a rapidly gentrifying neighbourhood in Harlem – her complaining about 'the number of chicken shops around here; it stinks', me wishing a near-fatal injury on her.

But, as anyone knows who has been obscenely mistreated at work – anyone who's been shouted at, bullied, underpaid, criticised for doing things exactly as you were asked to – it's impossible to take the good things without the bad. Instead it's all you can do to save the shreds of confidence you have left after a daily savaging.

I'd moved to New York using what was left of my pitiful overdraft, because I was moving here for a first job that would help me break into the closed-off, elitist world of high fashion. This was my break, I told myself, despite the pay and the perks being non-existent: I am Andy Sachs from *The Devil Wears Prada*;[4] these are(n't) the Chanel boots.

And, like any decent queer, I grew up watching fashion reality TV and, thus, assumed that, in order to succeed in the fashion world, all of this was simply a rite of passage: the constant barrage of abuse, sexting, near poverty. I was a northern queer who'd never left Europe and dreamt of working in fashion.

But, of course, the job wasn't what was promised, the terms of employment never arrived, and now all I have is mild PTSD, an overflowing canyon of fat-phobia, and a ban from every Union Market in the city because I was caught stealing an orange and a wheel of Brie a few weeks back, because I couldn't afford to eat.

Worse than all of this is that I am complicit in her violent behaviour, because I'm too poor and too scared to say anything when she takes another fist to the cat, or berates someone behind their back because of their weight, race, gender, shoes.

It's all for the Green Card: a golden ticket to lift me out of my regular life into a world of money, success, fame, glamour. Eve promised and promised, and I trusted and trusted, even though she's the kind of white person who wears a Navajo print poncho.[5]

With said Green Card I would finally become Carrie but not annoying, Hannah but not a racist.[6] I would be the 24-year-old who moved to New York, against all advice, and

---

4 Seriously need to find some non-gay references.

5 Honestly, where is she getting these from?

6 All white people are racist, but Hannah Horvath is the kind of racist who doesn't think all white people are racist.

actually made it. It wouldn't be long until I was one of those rich gays with a penthouse in TriBeCa who collect art and wear tortoiseshell glasses and go to Miami Basel every year and get a GLAAD award, and still, somehow, remain radically political.

It's now officially Christmas break, and Eve is flying to Australia with Jared, so my nightly sext duties are over, and I feel a little abandoned by him, to be frank. I decide now is the time to concoct a plan to quit and actually use my time to earn money a way I love. Time to follow my dreams: time to marry rich.

Gonna go to bed and wank over imaginary sext conversations with Jared.

21st December / le 21 Décembre

There are few things that make a queen twirl like vintage Madonna. I hate being reductive, because then I'm just the same as pretty much every single media portrayal of anything LGBTQIA+ or aligned.[7] For some queens (and also some queers, femmes, butches, bull dykes, trans women, transvestites, faggots, trans men, asexuals, leather daddies, fisting pigs, campy twinks, aromantics, bisexuals and radical faeries) their tonic might not be a Madonna: it could be a Judy, or a Lady Gaga, a George Michael or a Beyoncé, The

---

7 Lesbian, Gay, Bisexual, Transgender, Queer/questioning, Intersex, Asexual and + (not you, straight guy who loves glitter a bit but thinks bum sex is gross). Yes, it's a long acronym, yes, it's seven whole letters, but I learned the national anthem even though borders are constructs, so you can learn seven letters.

Cure, or a niche riot grrrl group who should be way more famous than they are, or Lou Reed or Alaska Thunderfuck.

But for me, a proud cliché, it's Madonna. She's always been an escape route when things feel uncertain: going back to this noise that set you aflame as a child.

Generally it's all Madonna, but right now it's 'Ray of Light', to which I've just finished spinning around in thigh-high silver lamé boots that chafe my thighs to within an inch of the bone. I'm wearing a red wig and a lime-green muumuu that has dried sperm down the back from a story for another time. And this kind of spinning has ignited a sensation I haven't felt for a while – a deeply sexual, emotional fury just south of my belly – and it reminds me of the first time I heard 'Ray of Light', aged seven, sitting on my dog-hair-covered lounge carpet, at home in the north of England while my siblings fought over the remote. I remember not understanding that deep-belly feeling.

All I remember is being both terrified and obsessively desperate to spin so fast I would hurricane through the roof and onto a giant stage with thousands of people watching me the way I was watching Madonna. Spinning the way I am now.

So much of the queer experience is spent spinning.

I remember the song being the soundtrack to my teen years, it blasting out on a yellow CD player that used to *skip-skip-skip* if you so much as inhaled, me sitting in my room flipping through *Glamour* or *Cosmo* or *Heat* with my one gay friend, Matt, who used to eat mayonnaise off a spoon, with whom I was silently in love for most of those teen years. Humming along would be our best girl friend Beth, who would get so rampantly drunk she would foam at the mouth and try to kiss any and all of my brothers, always revealing her giant, magnificent breasts at a moment's notice.

I remember, after fights with my parents – huge, hurtling rows full of terror and bile and homophobia and under-appreciation being flung like shit from both sides – running up the stairs and climbing out of a skylight onto my jagged slate roof and whirring around to 'Ray of Light', transmitted through the crappy earphones I'd kept from a flight my family took to Ibiza, our first abroad holiday ever.

I remember turning it up on the 555 bus home from Lancaster as homophobic, mean-spirited schoolkids pelted oranges at the back of my head or dropped fag ash into my hair from their endless Lambert & Butler Blues, me in a world light years away from the top deck of that bus, imagining being adored the way I had adored Madonna since I'd sat on my dog-hair-covered carpet years before.

I remember kissing a boy – who had a big beard that hummed with the scent of clever queer theory books and craft beers and vegan moisturisers, and who eventually moved to France with a much older guy to do a PhD in gender studies[8] – in my room at university while the song and my insides crashed hard like fireworks.

I remember all the times a song saved me as I twirl here on my own, spilling dollar-store rosé all over the dark sanded wood floors of this apartment I'm illegally subletting in New York. I'm in half-drag, a demi-lewk, about to go out to an infuriatingly glamorous club that once turned away Rihanna, but lets my queer friends and me in so the rich people can

---

8 Lol, who hasn't?

gawp at something interesting. I might not be on the stage, with thousands of adoring fans looking up at me the way I looked at Madonna, but I am twice as wondrous as the me watching that Madonna video two decades ago ever dreamed I could be. That me would be so, so glad to be this me.

When your identity is so fragmented, sometimes it takes an old song, *the* old song, to cram all the pieces into the same place at once.

22nd December / le 22 décembre

'I would totally die for you,' Ace told me over FaceTime. We were chatting before he went down to Suffolk with his family for Christmas.

Ace is my 'best friend', the kind of 'best friend' for whom you use air quotations whenever you describe them because the truth is we are both, dysfunctionally, in love.

Well, I can confirm that I'm in love with him, but I haven't gleaned whether or not it's reciprocated. Before I arrived here, in New York, in this noisy apartment on the Lower East Side with a puddle of cash in a city where you can only survive if you're swimming in wealth, into a job in fashion, which now has me never wanting to look at a piece of clothing again, we had driven around the south-eastern coast of the US together.

We ate packs of biscuits and splashed out on a Cracker Barrel to break up the long drives between states. We did stereotypical gay-love-movie type things like sitting in fields full of long grass and smoking and talking about shit like Why Gay Men Love Female Pop Stars and Will Lady Gaga's

New Album Be Any Good and Can Straight People Be Queer and Our Sexual History (testing the ground of our sexual future). Of course, we never arrived at that sexual future, and now our relationship is played out in a blur of crackly pixels three times a week.

'I would totally die for you.'

I'm not sure if it was true love or a manipulative technique to check my allegiances after I was clearly bummed out and turned cold by him telling me he had a date tonight. Who goes on a date three days before Christmas?

'Sure. I would die for you too, totally. But I wouldn't drown,' I replied, smugly testing his limits.

'Oh charming. Although, to be honest, I wouldn't think to save you first if a plane was going down. Like, I'd affix my oxygen mask before yours, and dive out onto the inflatable slide first. Removing heels, obviously. Dying in flight is just my idea of hell. But for the most part, I'd die for you.'

Then he hung up, bouncing offline to go on his date, which I decide is doomed, and also decide I'm being unfair because it was me who chose to move to New York 'for ever', air quotes.

Perhaps that's all I can ask for. For someone who could love me enough to die for me in all but one scenario. Maybe that's a better promise than monogamy, which will inevitably fall apart if modern dating statistics are anything to go by. Especially amongst the gays: we're allergic to intimacy.

Feeling bereft, I decided to take my sorrow onto the fire escape and smoke seven cigarettes, sitting in my loneliness. I miss Ace. I miss my friends at home, painfully, my heart hurting at the thought of them spread out across London, or

Lancaster or Manchester or Newcastle, sitting outside bars in Soho, or at the Sun, our old Lancaster haunt, or on their couches watching *Gogglebox*, chain-smoking and talking about radical queer politics or whether they want pasta-pesto or a takeout for dinner, sheathed in colours and sequins, dressing gown and slippers, no make-up, or make-up a few slicks too heavy.

I hope with a bursting wishfulness that they are thinking of me.

23rd December / le 23 décembre

I'm going out tonight with some friends, so I spent the better part of the afternoon getting into a full face. Day-to-day I've been wearing less face than usual – a lip stain here, a highlight there. But it's the big one before the scene shuts down for Christmas tonight, so I wanted to do full-drag-queen-with-a-beard realness. I left myself three and a half hours to do it in, and now, for the first time in my life, I'm ready early.

And so I'm sitting, staring at my make-up bag – messy, glitter-coated, jangled from coast to coast, up and down stairs, in the boot of countless cars. I love my make-up bag.

My make-up bag. That passport which contains a bunch of crèmes, potions, polyfilla and over-the-counter drugs that diminish the muscles of an overbearing gender binary. They allow me to cross it. They are the hardware that allows me to finally live out my childhood fantasies, every one. It's also a history book, connecting me to the radical queens, queers, butch dykes and trans folk who fought for me to be able to paint my face the way I want to paint it. In my make-up bag is a lifeline to an expression of my gender. In my make-up bag there are thousands of tricks for me to cover the scars of my teenage acne, or the slice on my nose from a homophobic attack that has never quite healed. I love the scars in some ways, but having the devices to cover them allows me to dictate their mark upon me.

In my make-up bag there are missing pieces and extra bits – given, received and shared between my drag sisters and me like heirlooms, like gifts from Christmas crackers. We are reminded of each other whenever we use them. In my make-up bag there are hairs cut from the long hair of a drag king friend to make a beard, strewn, unwanted, but so integral to the history this kit holds. In my make-up bag there's a kind of self-care that makes you omnipotent, even if just for a night.

In my make-up bag there's an ode to the women who gave me a femininity to explore, but not to parody (that's just terrible, lazy drag). In my make-up bag there's jewellery given to me by my friend who was so desperate for me to be kinder to myself that she found things to make me sparkle.

Indeed, there are a lot of things in my make-up bag. And while it's so easy to talk about colours, powders, primers, highlighters (yum! fave!) with a kind of Zoella level of soullessness and irrelevance, make-up to me, to many of us, is not an extravagant stockpile of excessive frippery, but something that bestows power. In a world where that power is only taken from us, make-up is a tool that cheers us on as we draw our battle lines, giving so much power back to ourselves. It's a secret language, misunderstood and disregarded by boring dudes who think make-up is 'gay', which allows us to communicate with each other both silently or with floods of Facebook messages about Kat Von D's new matte lipstick.

My make-up bag is not for anyone else. It's very much for me, as yours is for you. While people question whether the act of wearing make-up is anti-feminist (much like they question drag), make-up is, ultimately, about choice, about allowing yourself to choose how the world sees you. The same can be said for not wearing any, especially if you're expected to by society. Make-up gives us agency over our own image.

Above all, my make-up bag is a kit that allows me to create an illusion that is closer to the truth than most people ever reach. People bandy about terms like 'fake', but choosing how you want to look is the definition of authentic.

It's time to go out. I apply a blister plaster and sausage the thigh-high boots on to my signature chubby thighs.

24th December / le 24 décembre

I'm deathly hungover today, and I've been pricking a needle way too far into a blister I got on the ball of my foot after wearing those fucking heels, and I'm pissed off because I can't think of a single blockbuster gay movie that stars a gay actor.[9] I'm also pissed off because I've been scrolling through Netflix on a fancy TV, lying on a Calvin Klein couch, on Christmas Eve in New York. I've told everyone at home I'm having the most glamorous time, but here I am, alone,

---

9 Okay, just Googled and obviously there's people like Nathan Lane in *The Birdcage* but that was twenty-two years ago.

wearing Lonsdale briefs and the cum-covered lime-green muumuu, sweating a lot because this sack-dress is made of cheap polyester, and with nobody to speak to on this day of togetherness. After the big Christmas blow-out last night, all the queers have gone back on various buses to faraway places like Ohio and the Upper East Side.

I was supposed to spend the holidays with my New Yorker friend, Lily, but she's currently at home recovering from facial feminisation surgery – and she doesn't want to see anyone except her wealthy, married boyfriend who paid for the procedure to stop her getting attacked every time she walked anywhere after sunset. Fair, really.

It's sunset here and I've lit a roll-up fag, my last one scraped from a kilo barrel of Drum tobacco I bought two months ago in Nashville when I was driving around the south-east coast with Ace. For lack of anything better to do and anyone else to speak to, I've been leaning out of the window and onto my fire escape, smoking and chatting with the Empire State Building in the distance.

I'm lonely. It's always so embarrassing admitting you're lonely. I need to stop chatting to the Empire State because I've decided it's a patronising cis[10]-het[11] white man who, when I say something like: 'Isn't the fact that there are no big queer films starring big queer actors so representative of mainstream culture's desire to commodify, package and

---

10 For anyone out there who has missed the latest gender revolution, brush up your knowledge here. Cis = cisgender, someone whose gender matches their sex assigned at birth.
11 Het or hetty = heterosexual, someone who is attracted to people of the opposite sex/gender; many are very boring.

sanitise the queer experience by making the stars of 'queer' movies straight, white and beautiful and, ergo, acceptable to a mass heterosexual consumer who can't buy into anything if they have to imagine anyone involved actually taking a dick up the shitter?', replies: 'Film-making is storytelling, it's fantasy, dude. Let go; what's the obsession with identity politics? Aren't labels just so unnecessary, especially now when every straight man I know is basically queer? Like, have you read Kerouac? He's the ultimate queer. Look at my Varsity Jacket, bro, it's ironic – the name tag says Maud.'

I'm back on the couch, and I've landed on a cheap horror movie called *Would You Rather*. Its central premise is based on that game bored people use to pass time, but in the movie the 'would you rathers' are really violent and pointlessly bleak. Like 'would you rather shoot Brittany Snow (the lead) or gouge your own eyes out?' I mean obviously you'd shoot, because the grand prize is a million dollars – which Snow needs to save her brother who's dying of cancer, to whom she returns home after this traumatic night to find dead anyway. Sorry: spoiler.

Inspired by my profoundly dull two hours with Brit Snow, here is a game of 'Would You Rather':

Would you rather eat dog shit or cat shit?

Dog. Because you never know what a cat is eating because they spend 90 per cent of their time out of the house gumming at birds and rats and shit. At least with a dog you know what it's eaten.

Would you rather have teeth for toes or toes for teeth?

Teeth for toes – nobody can see them, and think how much it would hurt when you kick an abusive homophobe.

Would you rather be successful and miserable or unknown and happy?

Now, the self-care anti-capitalist in me reckons that success in the stereotypical sense – wife, kids, money, fame, matching socks, Diptyque candles – is a neo-liberal construct to get us all to buy into this idea of working tirelessly for something that is actually unobtainable. But the raging homo inside me who loves Barbra, Liza, Madonna and Gaga would totally opt for fame/success and misery. I mean is anyone really happy all the time anyway? Also, the question I set for myself doesn't stipulate whether I could get super successful, make loads of money and be really famous, and then one-eighty and step back from the spotlight to become a happy unknown who had an outrageous life and who says things like, 'That was then, this is now,' or 'Fame was killing me,' or 'When are *Hello!* coming to do the feature on my new life?' or 'Do I look rested?' after my latest botched surgery. Successful and miserable it is.

It's all hypothetical anyway. Because right now I am the most unfortunate mix of the two. Miserable and unknown. I moved to New York to be like a nu-age, politically engaged Carrie Bradshaw but I'm having infrequent and pretty sub-par sex and I'm not really doing anything in the city. Unlike Carrie and her mystery buckets of cash, I have no income, no savings. Come New Year I'll have no job.

I'm worried about quitting, because then I'll have even less reason to get out of bed and then I will literally be the queen who moved to New York – the city that never sleeps – to sleep.

It's 11.23 p.m. Time to go to sleep.

25th December / le 25th décembre

It's funny how so many Christian denominations (not all, I know) hate gays but love Christmas. Like, aren't they basically the same thing? Tinsel? So gay. Gifting? We invented it. A guy with major abs on a cross? That's gay BDSM 101.

It's a funny time for queers really, Christmas – the whole day, the whole tradition built around a religion whose central tenet (or one of) is that gays aren't chill. Love the sinner, hate the sin, you know. Add to this the fractious relationships so many queer and LGBTQIA+ folk have with their families and the Christmas turkey tastes much, much drier for us 'mos.[12]

I'm a lucky queer in that over the Christmases of recent years, after the spiral-of-existential-desperation-to-click-my-heels-and-disappear-dread that was my teens came to a close, I have actually developed a very special relationship with my very special family. But loneliness still resounds around these holidays for a lot of queers. While I'm fortunate to be tight with my close relations, the holidays proffer a different kind of loneliness: one brought on through everyone misunderstanding who you are now. It's nobody's fault, but the more I progressed into life as 'a full-on queer', the more it became evident that there were integral parts of me not to be mentioned at the Turkey Table. While we all chat kids and weddings, we don't chat HIV activism or the

---

12 I can say it, I'm gay.

powers of radical sex; we don't chat gender or whether RuPaul's transmisogyny renders her legacy obsolete.

All the burning queer politics or the nights spent in repeat motion unsticking your wobbly heels or battered Docs from the Red Bull and ecstasy-plastered dance floors of gay bars, hoping to suck anyone's dick, disappear around normative folk. A very Wizard of Ozzy kind of concussion. You feel infantilised and misunderstood, like you've got a thousand secrets scantily concealed just under the surface, because even though everyone knows you're the things you are, they don't know the things that come with them.

Many don't even have family to go to on account of severed ties, chopped messily by the homo-, trans-, bi-, queerphobia that often abounds from the families of people like me. For something so camp, so apparently joyful, Christmas for many of us is as emotionally tangled as the fairy lights you chuck in the bottom of the decorations box year on year. Only to spend three hours detangling them. Only to realise 65 per cent of the bulbs have blown out.

I miss my family, both biological and chosen. I especially miss my dad, and my mum and her Christmas dinner. Her four different types of potato, two types of carrot, parsnips, two types of stuffing, bread sauce and, even the worst bit, the turkey. One time, when I worked on a farm for pocket money, I had to wank off tons of male turkeys (or Toms or gobblers as we call them in the trade) in order to get them to spaff their loads into rubber tubes. Turns out fattened Christmas turkeys can't and/or don't have the energy to fuck, so we had to do it for them.[13] It sounds humiliating, but weirdly once you've wanked off one turkey you just feel proud to be part of the circle of turkey life, the wonder of the Christmas mass-slaughter.

I decided to send a few of my friends *Happy Queermas* texts, offering some queer solidarity on this strange old day. Glamrou – my sister, one of my best friends, and an Iraqi immigrant drag queen who hates Christmas more than me – responded with: *Happy Queermas baby! It's such a fucking white queerphobic day. Have been feeling lonely throughout. Thinking of you xxx*

I didn't respond and then, instead of texting back, I spent a while feeling guilty about not doing so. But it made me feel less lonely knowing someone else was feeling lonely too. Gonna go to bed and google 'Tumblr big dick windmill'.

26th December / le 26th décembre

This morning I smoked six cigarettes in twenty minutes and called my friend Lily, but she didn't answer.

It's Boxing Day, which feels like more of a thing in England than here. If I were at home, I'd be at a family gathering. Not the kind of close-family gathering where you can competitively argue, or fart, or fight over who'll do the dishes, but the kind of family gathering where your cousin

---

13 Other animals I have successfully retrieved sperm from include: goats, horses, pigs, dogs, a cat, cows. Animals I have fisted or fingered include: cows, goats, dogs. It taught me a lot about the art of masturbation, and gave me no sexual pleasure whatsoever – in case you were wondering. Except maybe the horses. But they're so muscular!

Alan – who is *still* trying to pass off gel-crisped curtains as a hair style – has come back from New Zealand for the Christmas period and you have to play 'Animal, Mineral, Vegetable' with him, and everyone else.

It's also the kind of family gathering where endless lies are told about 'how you're doing'. For many years with my family it was very much the order of service to avoid talking about my homosexuality and gender nonconformity. 'I mean,' as Mum would put it, 'why does Auntie Val need to know who you're attracted to?' In the parental world of protective logic, that might be you trying to keep your child out of harm's way, but as a gay kid, trust me, all we hear is: 'We're all deeply embarrassed by the fact you've failed us, and we want to look like we've raised you right, so shut your mouth and don't wear skinny jeans.'

I do my mother a disservice – she's now a veteran attendee of every and any drag show I do and in recent years has been possibly the most supportive and uplifting ally a queer person could know. But back then, at those family parties where you'd stand over a salmon mousse that Grandma had lovingly made, gurning at the idea of eating literal aerated creamy fish, I tried my absolute hardest to keep my queerness corseted in.

You have this huge secret, and you feel like everyone knows – because you're the little queen who has been wearing black sequinned dresses since your first day of school, crying daily to the warbles of Celine Dion's album *Let's Talk About Love* while glamorously lounging on a chaise longue your parents are storing for their friend who emigrated to Hull – but actually nobody knows because nobody wants to know. You try your hardest not to talk about how important Cher is to you, instead feigning interest in football and other boring shite like the number of barrels a whisky has been in.[14]

You wonder whether your louche-looking Uncle Col has a big cock or not, secretly fantasising that he and his step-son – the time-warped, crisp-curtained, New Zealand one – might like to bang you in Grandma's upstairs carpeted bathroom.

'Ah, Preston North End are doing well, aren't they?' Uncle Col drawls.

'Aye, Col, they seem to be doing so fabulously.'[15] My sibilant 's' ricocheting around the room like a giant 'I'm a fag' alarm. I'm sweating; can he feel what I feel? As I get hard in my bootcut jeans,[16] Col takes his finger and gouges a quivering slop of salmon mousse into his mouth, smearing the millennial-pink gunge all over his moustache . . . and I still have an erection?!

It's all so risky, febrile. While trying not to be gay all I can fucking think about is being gay and doing and saying the gayest stuff. Uncle Col is a blood relative, for fuck's sake – what am I thinking?

In retrospect it's all quite funny, but in the moment it feels terrifying: with everyone around you leaning towards the homophobic you start off from less than zero, believing

---

14 What on earth is that about? It all tastes like poison fag ash anyway.
15 'Fabulously'?? What was I fucking thinking – I may as well have handed out copies of *The Line of Beauty* and done a lip sync to Bonnie Tyler's 'I Need a Hero'.
16 Mother, I will never forgive you for those.

that what you are is totally wrong. It's pretty lonely and scary; it's dissociative, and – while it sounds extreme – it can be deeply scarring. It forever alters your self-perception. Here you are accepting Uncle Col's casual racism or your prick cousin's abject misogyny, under the orders of Mum who is squeezing your hand telling you 'not to make a scene', while you're just trying to be you, knowing that if they really saw you, you'd get the worst treatment of all. A kind of metaphor for society really. Even still, on a day particularly filled with homophobia, when I'm alone I sometimes fall into this idea that my queerness might in fact be *wrong* with a surprising level of alacrity for someone who's normally so vocal about how wonderful, brilliant and powerful queers are. I despise that the voices of people whom I don't respect constantly trigger crippling levels of self-doubt.

And really, for a lot of queer people that's how most gatherings populated by mostly heterosexual people feel: lonely and full of potential misunderstanding. I'm sure that's not the case for every queer person, but certainly for those of us from working-class backgrounds, or from com-munities of colour where homosexuality is disapproved of most overtly. When your lifestyle challenges the worldwide status quo, it's pretty hard to feel understood by people who live by that status quo.

That's why we gravitate towards each other; that's why queer and LGBTQIA+ spaces are so important in all of their flawed glory, and why we're always talking about 'com-munity': because it's mind-blowing how quickly you can connect to someone who you've just met but who shares an element of queer experience with you. At university I met some of these people – my queer family and my queer heroes. They instantly understood the pain of these micro-aggressions, and I found the beauty of this thing that makes us stand out, meeting people who mirrored that experience back at me.

Anyway, I've decided – with Lily being a no-show – to go about the rest of my day of reading, texting Eve about where I'm at with her taxes, avoiding doing Eve's taxes. I'll probably have a wank about that three-way with Uncle Col and Cousin Alan. Then I'll stop to consider how bleak it is to draw on past episodes of homophobia to get oneself off.

27th December / le 27 décembre

Sometimes when I'm on my own I eat my bogies. Of all the things in my life I think this is the thing I feel most shame about. And I once made out with my dog, in a genuinely sexual way, when I was eleven.

28th December / le 28 décembre

I'm doing extensive field work for a theory I'm working on at the moment: in order to really pound someone/take a real pounding, you kind of have to hate them, at least a tiny bit.

The perfect example for my theory of the hate-pound matrix is Laurie. Laurie is this guy I've been fucking for the last two days – since yesterday morning, when I got so bored that I trotted right to Grindr and met this guy who's a 'shoe designer', but between seasons. After gabbing about his shoes he showed me a series of velvet slippers with witty puns embroidered or appliquéd onto them, which I literally think are the most disgusting things I've ever seen.[17] He told me he loves 'African art', which visibly pains me because a) he's white, b) he's white, and c) he literally referred to Africa as a sort of general place, using words like 'primitive' and, I kid you not, 'muddy' and 'real'.

Everything about Laurie is everything I hate about people: he's incredibly self-involved, he loves craft coffee and honestly has fifteen different ways of making it, he can't design shoes for toffee but describes himself as if he's as important to culture as Samantha Mumba or Jenny Holzer. He has loads of tattoos – none of which are ironic, all of which he describes as 'pieces' with genuine earnestness – and he wears cycling hats even though he doesn't cycle. Pros, although few and far between, are: he's got a perfect 6.5-inch dick with girth that seems custom-designed to tessellate with my once-tight (now tight-ish) bum-hole; he has a nice dog[18] and an interesting collection of zines; he has enough money to order us takeout so we don't have to leave the house for literally two days; and he doesn't seem to take issue with the fact that I'm a drag queen.

Unsurprisingly, he doesn't really like me either. It's a hate-mance: he contests my love of identity politics, claiming that I'm 'the problem with the gay community – how can we escape our past if we are constantly putting ourselves in boxes?'; he scoffs when I suggest consent should be visual as well as

---

17 Apart from Eve's poncho.
18 Although he watches us have sex and that's weird.

verbal; and he thinks Meryl Streep wasn't very good in *The Devil Wears Prada* (a remark I had to genuinely take five to get over).

But the fucking. Neither of us can deny that the fucking feels better than your parents telling you they're proud of you. It's all so base: pissy, cummy, sweaty, pounding, and both of us cumming minimum five times a night. It's full of sexual aggression, to which we are both consenting: he asks, I say yes, he spanks me with a steel-toecap boot and I push back in a way that reads 'harder'. I've lost count of the times he's choked me with his perfect cock and punched me in the face while doing it.[19]

And there's no way I could do that with someone I like. In fact, actively getting pleasure out of being hurt by someone I dislike is the very heart of my relationship with subservience and dominance.

I decided to FaceTime Ace earlier, for the first time since before Christmas. I tell him I'm working on a theory.

Ace is charming and has a smile so heartfelt you can feel pink flowers grow every time his lips crack upwards.

'Go on . . . is it a sex one?' he said.

Our conversation was fucking awkward because all our exchanges are roundabout bush-beating in which everything uttered carries an underlying tension of me, and maybe him, wanting to scream I love you and want to marry you and have babies with you and make all your worries go away forever. It's the kind of dynamic that can only form between two best friends who are secretly in love with each other, but are in utter terror that if they pursue that

---

19 My safe word is 'goat', btw.

love they will fuck it all up and lose everything. And when your friends are your family you are terrified that something as potentially throw-away as a long-term relationship could jeopardise your absolutely certain lifelong friendship. Think Ross and Rachel but queer and more complicated.

I explained the Laurie thing, and it was fucking painful because I wanted to tell him that it means nothing to me and that all I want, really, is him, but even entertaining that idea makes my lip quiver like when old people have orgasms in movies.

'I think I get what you mean, but what about totally anonymous sex – like in a sauna or a quick Grindr in and out – when you don't even know if you hate the person?' he provoked.

'Well, I think that's the same but perhaps the hate comes from slightly hating yourself for being gay. So you put yourself in these painful and potentially dangerous situations in order to access the deep buried hate you feel for yourself because, as a gay person, you've failed in the eyes of society.'

Pause.

Weird, long pause.

'Wow, that's bleak. I disagree. But report back on that one.'

29th December / le 29 décembre

Okay, theory out the window.

Earlier this evening, the door clacked. It was Laurie, wearing a pair of his own shoes – one of which featured an appliquéd picture of a screw and the other of which was appliquéd with a giant letter 'U' (get it?). I looked at them trying not to gip, then looked him up and down, realising it was the first time I'd seen him dressed and he was wearing BOOTCUT JEANS. 'Get them off,' I said, 20 per cent because we were about to fuck, 80 so I wouldn't have to look at them any more.

We opened the wine he brought, a claggy red, and drank it from the bottle on the bed. Then things got weird. He undressed, I undressed, he asked if he could keep his shoes on. I said, 'Ah, I'm worried about the sheets'[20] so he flicked them off. I was hard, he was hard and I was getting ready to take his wonderful gift in my wonderful gift receiver, when he put a finger to my lips and murmured 'wait a sec' in his really nasal Ohio accent, and dashed to the bathroom.

I waited, as told, with my finger pressing on my bumhole, in truth thinking about Ace and not even a bit about Laurie.

And lo and behold, Laurie reemerged in the doorway to my bedroom in a grease-smudged head-to-toe gimp outfit[21] in deep black rubber, a funnel and tube to his mouth for me to – so he hoped – urinate into, and a zip from the belly button to the lower back offering access to all areas.

My first thought was that he didn't bring a bag. 'How did you get that here?' I asked, to which I heard a rubber-muffled 'hmm mmmmh cuhmmtp ppmmmkt' that I translated as

---

20 I wasn't worried about the sheets.
21 Like that guy in *Pulp Fiction* who lives in a box.

'in my coat pocket'. I then wondered why that was the first thing I'd thought about – the practicalities of the transportation of the piss-funnel-gimp-suit he hadn't even taken the time to polish, rather than the fact he wanted me to get gimpy with him. Disclaimer – I'm not shaming gimps here; I love a gimp suit. What I'm shaming is his audacity in not even checking whether I was up for a good gimping.

Before I knew it he'd launched himself onto my sheets, which I was at this point genuinely worried about, and was holding both of my legs up in the air like I was a roast duck hanging from a meat hook in a restaurant in Chinatown. How was he lifting half my bodyweight? Again why was I thinking that? And then his cock started poking out of the zip, like a snail from its shell, and he was about to ram it in me, no lube or anything.

I asked him to stop – 'it's all got a bit flustered' – but he carried on. I don't know if it's because he couldn't hear me through all the fucking rubber, but I asked him three times and he was still teasing my hole with his big purple bell-end ready to thrust it in there quicker than you can say any safe word.

Fourth time, 'stop'; fifth time and I was feeling really edgy. Sixth time, 'stop', and I felt his bell-end beginning to push through the tight-ish resistance of my now totally clammed-up butt hole.

I swiftly jerked backwards and started slapping his cock really hard while shouting, 'I!' *slap* 'Said!' *slap* 'No!' *slap* 'No!' *slap* 'No!', chasing him across the room as he backed out of the door, the sticky rubber pulling things with him as he went, his sight obscured by the two tiny holes in his gimp mask.

Then he left, really quickly.

I have no idea how he got changed in such record time, but I think I need to stop thinking about things that aren't immediately important, especially when I have a gimp coming at me.

Then he came back, knocking at the door – I shit you not – to get the remnants of his wine.

Shaken, shook, I immediately FaceTimed Ace. He was very sweet, and very concerned about my safety, but at the moment I feel more focused on the fact that Laurie was cheap enough to come back – after I'd literally dick-whacked him like it was a poisonous snake in the grass – and ask for his wine. I'm aware I'm doing that thing where I use humour to mask the fact that I'm feeling violated and I'm very aware that if I weren't as physically strong as Laurie I would have been in a potentially much worse position.

Looking back on all my close encounters of the anal kind and I can't remember any of their faces, names, bodies – dicks, I can remember the dicks – or any of their defining features.[22] What I can remember, however, is how I felt when I did the deed, and not much else. Like when I was really upset about this guy not texting back so I got hammered and swallowed the cum of three men aged sixty-plus,

---

22 Unless I kind of knew them at the time of fucking – like a priest at my university, or my six-week boyfriend when I was nineteen who I was certain that I was gonna marry (because he had a gorgeous dick, he was a lawyer-in-training and his armpits smelled literally like musty-man-heaven and even the thought of the smell of his BO-stained armpits still makes me erect to this day).

one after the other, in an alleyway near my house. Or the time I fucked a primary school teacher in Hong Kong who offered me 'ice' (which I declined) and then took me into a custom porn-making room (which I accepted) where we made a keepsake DVD of him fucking me doggy-style,[23] and I remember nothing about him or it; I just remember feeling particularly thin that day, and hence jumped at the chance to make a home-porno.

I think about the straight boys at university, high school, even primary school, who took advantage of my evident gayness to try and solve the puzzle of their sexuality, how I just felt glad to be someone's receptacle, that someone would want me in that way even though once one of them spunked in my mouth and eye during lunchbreak, then told me he'd 'slit my fucking faggot throat' if what we'd done ever got out. I still don't remember much about him, just the pleasurable mix of shame, power, and terror he left in his wake – feelings that stayed at the forefront of my wank bank for years to come.

Perhaps, then, this is my new theory: sex with strangers is about satisfying yourself, about playing out and projecting deep-set emotions you can't share elsewhere, emotions that are pushed down in order to survive the day-to-day, that rear their heads, and their subservient inflection, only when you know there's nothing to lose with a sexual partner, when you don't really care about them.

---

23 It's still in my wardrobe at my family home, and I constantly have night terrors about my mum clearing it out and putting it on because it just says 'Hong Kong' on it and she might think it's a DVD full of pics omg.

30th December / le 30 décembre

It was fucking freezing this morning so I smoked inside, which was a terrible idea because I then had to actually leave the apartment to buy air freshener, for which I had no money. But then I found a fucking ten! In the corridor outside the door. I thanked a God I don't even believe in. Lily finally picked up the phone. She was getting ready to go visit her 'academic friend in Boston', who is this Harvard PhD guy who's obsessed with her, and who wants to take magic mushrooms with her and have wild, trippy sex with her.

I helped her pick outfits.

'There's the black latex, which looks good with the purple marabou jacket?' she puzzled. At that I told her I was having a slightly off-moment with latex after what happened yesterday with Laurie.

She insisted on coming over. I protested, but she insisted.

We ate almonds and pears and half a Butter Finger (my favourite) and talked about different awful experiences we've had with sex – some hilarious, some heart-breaking, and what they each mean in context for her as a heterosexual trans woman, and for me as a non-binary homosexual drag queen.

'For me it's this constant fetishisation,' Lily complained. 'People on these dating apps are always obsessed with what I've got down there – which is none of their goddamn business. Like, if you get that far you should be so fucking lucky.

And the number of men I've had call me a "chick with a dick", or "their fantasy", or approach me to do porn . . . is . . . it's fucking outrageous.'

Lily is an incredibly beautiful woman. I don't know how she does it; she never seems to work yet always has the cash to buy the things everyone wants – today she was wearing thigh-high Balenciaga spandex boots in black, at which we both frequently stared in silence, interrupting our conversation. She has perfectly manicured nails, beautiful silky underwear, and her hair is always blown out. She's very aware of her passing privilege as a trans woman, explaining that she feels both overwhelming guilt and overwhelming pride at what her transition looks like. She has impeccable taste. I always wonder what it would be like to have grown up with impeccable taste – a wardrobe full of 'archive' this or 'S S 00 Prada' that. I guess to do so you need a little money, and my family was pretty cashless. I spent a good few years developing my personal style first through the prism of hiding my gayness, and then back through the other side. This resulted in a kind of 'Only Gay in the Village' style, there in my northern not-quite-a-seaside town.

'I feel like a trick – like I'm either tricking men into sleeping with me, or like I'm a trick they can bring up with their friends to prove how kinky they are. It's fucked – I want intimacy, like, not just a shag and a token pair of Miu Miu sunglasses as a thank you; I want to be touched, like, emotionally.'

'At least you get Miu Miu,' I gassed, before asking her about Jeremy.[24]

'He'll never leave his wife. She and the kids get daddy for the weekend, and I get daddy in the week – I get daddy in the office, daddy in the shower, daddy in the bedroom, bathroom, living room, in the pussy and in the butthole.'

We smoked a spliff. And then I was sick because we'd had wine and weed and I need to stop doing that.

31st December / le 31 décembre

It was 5.15 p.m. before I woke up today. I'm still claiming jet lag, but I've been here for four months. Lily must've slipped out a while ago as she had her train to catch from Penn Station at 3 p.m.

I met Lily on the street outside the Natural History Museum uptown, right when I first arrived in New York. She had just taken a bunch of mushrooms and was sliding out on a bench just off Central Park, and I was getting to grips with the city, which essentially meant walking around and

---

24 Truth is Jeremy's a homophobe and thinks gays are 'too loud about it', something I learned when Lily invited me to join them both for dinner at Eleven Madison Park (which isn't even that good by the way, it's just that a ton of good reviews and four Michelin stars means everyone croons over it because they think they should). He's good(ish) for Lily though, who has struggled a lot with the marriage of her trans identity and her sexuality. They met just after she had bottom surgery and he totally went at her pace before they started anything sexual. It shouldn't be applauded, obviously, but in comparison Lily has had a rough deal with a lot of the men, and women, in her life and so one must forgive Jez for his homophobia, but only on the count that he's good to Lily who is amazing to me. The moment he stops I'll have his balls for breakfast.

thinking about all the gays who'd had sex here, what scene in *Sex and the City* happened where, and trying for the life of me to work out why everyone thinks Bloomingdale's is any good.

As we sat there on a bench just outside Central Park, Lily spilled the tea on everything New York. 'The park is for rich people and tourists, unless you're a leather daddy who wants to bum or be bummed. Are you?'

'Maybe,' I'd said.

I'd been lying, of course. I was just trying to seem chill about everything, up for anything but, to be totally honest, I wasn't really searching for leather daddies because I was burning for Ace. Turns out, some weeks later, I would find myself getting ravaged in the ass in the park: in an unexpected twist I found myself on 'the Ramble' – that's what they called it in the eighties, I think – where I picked up a leather daddy (Lily was right) who took great pleasure in 'pounding that chub hole'. I was pretty slighted by his liberal use of the word 'chub' – 'c'mon chub, suck daddy's cock', 'c'mon chub, sit on papa's dick', 'c'mon chub, you want daddy's load?' – as I was actually feeling particularly thin that day, but I took it nonetheless because I was really living for the whole Louis-getting-bummed-on-the-Ramble-in-*Angels-in-America*-degradation-realness-vibe. Thinking the whole time: 'God, I'm so New York!' as this chub-loving daddy worked out his baby issues on my booty.

There on the bench Lily offered me a mushroom-truffle. I declined. I've only done hallucinogens once – I'm not majorly into drugs, sadly – but I was in Amsterdam with some university friends and we all thought we should go for the shrooms to really get 'inside' the culture of the city.

Turns out I just saw Anne Robinson in different all-black-everything outfits for, like, four hours then went to sleep.

Checked my phone, had a text from Ace:

> Hi my queen! Will have to miss FaceTime tonight as I'm going to a New Year's party with William of all people ... ! Unsure whether it's a date, will report back tomorrow. Love you lots, Happy New Year beautiful xxxx

William is Ace's ex of four years ago, an ex who seems to crop up everywhere we go. He's an incredibly handsome, thin, floppy black-haired, very cool east London boy whose demeanour flexes towards the masc, and he's read a lot of books. He's essentially the polar opposite of me: a northern drag queen with a flabby Lancashire accent and an even flabbier belly. Spiralling into delusion, the following thoughts ramble around my skull:

Maybe I've made this whole romance thing up? I've done it before.

Maybe I am just, at the heart of it all, completely unlovable.

Why would someone like Ace want to date me? He's got a six-pack, for God's sake.

Why didn't I take the chance to kiss him ages ago before I was, most definitely, friend zoned?

Am I mad? I'm mad.

Well, he doesn't deserve me.

William is fucking boring compared to me, so Ace can make his bed and fucking suck a dick in it.

I have a habit of doing this. Going from self-loathing to blaming all men for not seeing how iconic I am, a truly Joan Crawfordesque mood swing.

Anyway, I'm about to head out too, so whatever. My friend Cora has invited me to spend this evening with her at the Beaumonts, 'an incredibly Upper East Side family', as she puts it. 'Wear something glam!' she instructed, so I've decided to wear an entirely red outfit, like a red Smartie: red silky trousers, red-heeled canvas trainer things, a red shirt, and a giant red mohair jumper with a wide roll neck. I'll definitely do a red lip, and smudge it over my eyelids too, and then pin my red(ish) fringe into two victory rolls either side of a centre parting. I've done this look a few times, and general consensus among friends and mouthy passersby is either 'Mugatu from *Zoolander*'[25] or 'beef tomato'.

That's glam, right?

---

25 Not *Zoolander 2* though – that's a shit, transphobic movie.

January/
janvier

1st January / le 1 janvier

Here's a comprehensive list of my New Year's resolutions:

- Sort out athlete's foot.
- Read communist manifesto, and *Speaking for Myself: The Cherie Blair Story* to work out how she gets such bounce in that hair.
- Learn something new about drag every day – lol, def gonna fail this.
- Be woke, but also stop using the word 'woke' as it's been dislocated from communities of colour and isn't yours to use.
- Be better with money.
- Quit job.
- Buy Balenciaga boots.
- Wear Balenciaga boots while overthrowing capitalism/ white male dominance.

I spent yesterday evening on the Upper East Side with the Beaumonts, which was a genuine lol a minute if you enjoy feeling undermined by the rich.

The Beaumonts live in one of those buildings that I thought were a myth – the kind that have an elevator stocked with a waistcoated lift attendant. It turns out the Beaumonts are the kind of wealthy that's scary. Like they have a Monet . . . in their loo . . . which I clocked during a mid-dinner shit. There's two Warhols, a Brâncuşi sculpture, a Gauguin, and a family portrait shot by Annie Leibovitz, before she got shit. Phrases like, ' . . . and that was how Barb got her eighth skiing injury!' get thrown around. And, while

I downed their amazing Riesling, all I could do was cement my position as the evening's entertainment by rolling out much-censored stories of drag, which would be met with gasps and 'fascinating!' or 'what a fabulous friend you have, Cora!', said as though they'd found a rare jewel and stepped in dog shit at the same time.

Also turns out the Beaumonts have a yearly tradition. It's call 'DP Time' and at the very mention the whole family moans with orgasmic glee. I thought it meant 'Double-Penetration Time', which I found both hysterical and, of course, exciting: my mouth filling with saliva at the idea that things might get interesting. A cross-generational-cross-family orgy? Jackpot!

'Barb loves a good DP! When we got the house we DP'd! When the girls were born we DP'd! When Hanna turned thirty we DP'd! When Gammy died, we DP'd to celebrate her life!' Daddy Beaumont almost foams at the mouth, explaining the family's history and its irrevocable tethering to the DP tradition. I was hysterical, weeping with laughter, and their fabulousing and fetishisation of me switched swiftly to disappointment at my strange behaviour.

After much foreplay they brought out the 'essential tool' for this impending DP session, and I had an erection.[1]

Turns out a DP is a goddamn bottle of Dom Perignon and they have been shortening the name to D-bloody-P for years.

I tried to explain my hysteria at the gleeful embracing of family-wide double penetration, explaining that the one that got me the most was 'DPing in memoriam of Grandma!'

---

1 Honestly, who am I?

I was swiftly – before DP Time began – escorted to the lift by Cora as I smiled at everyone, telling them I couldn't wait to see them again 'for another DP extravaganza!', as Barb shook her head in unbridled, silent, shock.

2nd January / le 2 janvier

Today I discovered the word *triboluminescent*. Essentially, it's an optical phenomenon where light is generated when a material is 'pulled apart, ripped, scratched, crushed, rubbed'. I think this is a beautiful metaphor for queers, for our culture born from resistance to oppression. Sometimes I wonder if culture can exist without oppression, but then that answer is too hard to actually work out because to imagine a utopia would mean undoing loads of shit that's happened to us and I have too many receipts to tape into Eve's fucking tax book to take the time and envision a new future. Will have to wait for another day.

Instead, I'm just going to drink wine and watch reruns of *Buffy*, probably weep, and tape receipts into Eve's tax book.

3rd January / le 3 janvier

I decided to write a letter of apology to the Beaumonts – Cora's family are upset at the shameful fracture I caused between the families, but not really mad at me, all of them apparently admitting in the lift on the way out that the DP joke *is* very funny, and that they can't believe they didn't spot it themselves earlier. I decided, while I want this letter to be one of apology, I also want to offer up a new idea for ways of thinking about my ejection from dinner.

A Grateful Guest
Manhattan

The Beaumonts
Penthouse
Manhattan

To the whole family,

Firstly, I'd like to extend my thanks for your generous invitation to dinner some nights ago. As a visitor here, it's been so touching to be involved in any family rituals – and so to have me for New Year's Dinner felt momentous, like I belong. This, for a queer person around the holidays, is a pretty rare feat!

Secondly, I'd like to offer two kinds of apology. The first is that I made you all blush – at this point the wine had somewhat won, and I wasn't quite pacing my jokes at the well-put, perfectly-timed rate I was aiming for. For any offence caused I am very sorry.

The other kind of apology I would really like to make is this: I am sorry I am forced to send this letter because you deemed inappropriate and disgraceful something I deemed really rather brilliant and comic. While this isn't a criticism of you, it is in fact a criticism of the harsh binaries to which we tether our behaviour here in Western society, these binaries being an impossible assault course that changes all the time depending on the company you are in.

The binary at play over dinner, you see, was one of 'inappropriate' versus 'appropriate'. Once I had crossed over from the latter to the former, you all collectively decided that I was no longer fit company. However, riddle me this: can I not be multiple things at once? Can I not be someone who swims in a pool of appropriate and inappropriate? Shocking and dull? Good company and a little irksome? And all in between?

I propose a dinner soon; you can come to me! A dinner which shall be named 'Binary Soup: let's swim in the bowl!'.

I do so hope you can make it, and send lots of love and understanding that you, like me, have made multiple social faux pas and that we can perhaps put it all behind us!

All the best, and Happy New Year!

Now things sound a little strained here, but they aren't meant to be – I'm just trying to sound posh, so that the Monet-owning Beaumonts might take my queer questions a little better. Better to pose as not-a-prole and win them over for the queer cause. The letter I want to write, in full me mode, would read something more like:

Dear the Beaumonts:

Get the fuck over yourselves. It was a funny joke. See you never; you're boring as fuck anyway!

But that would probably tip from helpful to unhelpful in the behaviour binary system.

4th January / le 4 janvier

I arrived at Eve's, walking from the Lower East Side way up town as I had no cash for the metro, psyching myself up ready to quit as I promised myself a week or so ago. I did the usual of listening to a bunch of power songs and imagining I was Madonna or Lady Gaga or Tina Turner or a man.

But then, upon arrival, exhausted but ready to go full Britney Work Bitch, I heard Eve repeatedly smacking her cat very hard for lying on her Ugg boots[2] and I wondered if today was not the day to quit and be smacked like a cat.

I'm now sitting, still under her watchful eye, in bed, holding her phone, ready to sext her boyfriend and I desperately want to out her as a cat-beating, talent- and hope-sucking alien to this man I've weirdly become sexually intimate with.

I decide, just for tonight at least, that I won't tell him about the cat beating. Instead, I'll sext him unenthusiastically until 1 a.m. – *oh big boy you are so big, oh big boy wow I'm tired, oh big boy I'm touching myself are you close?* – goading him to the finish line.

---

2 A favour, if you ask me.

6th January / le 6 janvier

Had lunch with Eve at a new Danish restaurant in TriBeCa. She mentioned my Green Card over a sharing plate of tiny fish-centric starters, probably because she'd sensed a level of detachment from me since the holidays finished. I was all ears.

She'd cooked up a bargain.

'I'm happy to sponsor you for a Green Card. Just look over this contract before you sign, then initial each page and sign the back one, and date.'

I read, flicking pages, furiously, excitedly, steaming through the contract as if Eve had never told me I had no talent, or that I was useless, gratitude outweighing a hard-won hatred. I neared the end of it. The second-to-last page. All good. All in order. Then, there, at the bottom, it explained that any earnings I made while under the sponsorship of Eve must be shared, in a 60:40 split, with her – including any wage she pays me, doubling back from my account to hers the moment it's sent.

It's hard to be young and to know your worth, but I feel like I'm worth more than 40 per cent of a full salary.

'What? Oh, the sixty per cent thing. That's nothing to do with the Green Card side, it's just so I get what I deserve. Sign it,' she urged me, like Isabella Rossellini telling Bruce Willis to drink the potion in *Death Becomes Her*, 'sign it and you can stay here forever. There's so much opportunity here. Sign it.'

She was pushing so hard for me to sign it, yet all the while her whole approach has been to explain to me that I was never going to make it, that I'm untalented, and that I need her.

But, as my pen approached the paper, I remembered the time I went to a penthouse a few blocks over for a gay sex party. There were about forty men, all naked, the older ones magnanimously peering through an array of tortoiseshell spectacles, post-coitally enquiring about you after they'd just shot their load all over your back. It was all very civil, with actual fabric napkins on hand to wipe up aforementioned load. These men were an acceptable kind of successful, conventionally interesting, had all lived in New York for twenty-plus years. It felt gay in that very specific pink pound kind of way – not my scene, but good material for a story over FaceTime. There, I met this man called James who was born in Bolton – one city over from my home town of Lancaster. His accent was international, lilting from continent to continent, and it was only as he'd growled, 'Fuck me, you're tight,'[3] that I'd heard the northern weight of his vowels.

Sitting there in the restaurant, my eyes jittering around this clinical Danish box, looking for an exit, I remembered something James had said to me after we'd left the party and strolled to get happy hour oysters in Chelsea. 'Don't forget about England. Well, not England per se, but where you came from. Consider what you're running *to* and make sure that you're not running *from*. I've been running from things my whole life, and I missed my friends and their successes

---

3 Probably not true, but telling a bottom they're tight is the same as saying, 'Oh my God! Your cock's so biiiiiiig!', knowing full well it's average in size. Weird how telling someone they have a big cock seems to relax a man in bed. Quite a boring standard really – the whole cock size thing. What about: 'Oh my God! Your personality is so uniiiiiqueeee! Your character so generous! I want to suck it so bad!!!!' – that's better.

and my parents and their deaths. And for what? Always run *to* something.'

At the time it all sounded like bollocks, and in that moment I brushed off this advice as the mutterings of someone who had started off way more lost than me, someone who had it harder and perhaps had more to run from on account of his age and his being gay in a northern working-class town, someone who had spent a lot of money on therapy and a lot of time escaping. I definitely wasn't running *from*, I told myself. I had run to success, respect from my peers. There was no way being a drag queen was ever going to pay the bills, there was no way staying still was ever right for me.

But today, in the Danish restaurant shrouded by torrential rain beating against the windows, its duck-egg-blue walls closing in on Eve and me, I wondered why I had come all this way just to give both myself, my talent, and now it seemed also my livelihood, to someone so full of hatred for me. And in the process shedding my friends and my context, my community.

So, in a classically ill-thought-out move, I did what people spend the whole movie willing the goofy lead character to do and chose to run. But, this time, *to*.

I fucking did it. I tore up the contract. I tore it up into tiny little bits, at which point Eve nearly choked on a lump of charcoal that had been floating in her glass of water. 'This is the straw that broke the camel's back, Eve. It's a classic you move – a smoke-screened opportunity underpinned with deceit and betrayal. Sixty per cent of my own earnings? Is that what you think I'm worth?'

She went to answer; I raised my ten-dollar manicured hand.

'These are rhetorical questions. You know, when you gave me this job I was so excited – I had read about you in *Vogue* as the "producer of the now", I thought you would be a mentor, someone for whom I could shine.'

She rolled her eyes. Usual me would live for such apathy, but I was so close to those kind of tears that you get when you're being really strong that I had to simply focus on the task at hand.

'I'm done. You don't own me. And what's become painfully clear is that you need me. I'm smart, I'm charming, I am good at everything you ask me to do and I come up with, like, ninety per cent of your ideas all while keeping your sex life afloat – the split should be ninety:ten in my favour . . . of *your* earnings! And if sapping my talent with no return is your idea of sponsorship, then frankly I'd rather eat my, your, and your cat's shit while wearing one of your hideous ponchos. You'll never see me again.'

So dramatic. I'm obsessed.

As I pulled my scarf-cape[4] from the back of my chair with the flourish of a matador, I knocked over a fish platter – everyone watching while the slate plate clacked along the dark wood floor.

I gave her my parting shot. 'I'm a fucking drag queen, Eve – and that's what I'm gonna be. A drag queen. I'm gonna be a sensation!'

───────────

4 Yes, that sounds like a poncho, but it's a just a stunningly big scarf – huge difference.

And there it all clicked. I had an out-of-body experience and laughed hysterically at myself screaming 'I'm gonna be a sensation'. I put on my scarf. 'No. I *am* a fucking sensation!'

I pranced out of the Danish place, under a pissing sky. Then I realised I'd forgotten my wallet, which has my passport in it, so I had to Google and call the number of the restaurant, ask them to grab my wallet and keep it aside. I waited an hour in a doorway for Eve to leave[5] before I went back to collect it, blasting Martha Wash's 'Carry On' through my headphones on repeat, getting a little wet from the rain but rejoicing in how glamorous this whole thing was, how drag this whole thing was. Fuck Carrie, I'm a Samantha.

7th January / le 7 janvier

I awoke to a pretty curt email from Eve studded with a colourful array of compliments such as, *'I've never met a more ungrateful cunt'*, *'I'll be billing you for all the lunches'*, *'I pity your lack of direction'*, *'You'll never work again'*, *'Ponchos are in!'*, all of which reinforced all the reasons I quit in the first place – but, still, I'm having doubts – terrors, even – about quitting my job.

Terrors that I'm going to have to do the worst and admit defeat, call my mum, call my friends and everyone else at home who had waved me off and shed tears at my big 'Gone But Not Fag-gotten' party some six months ago.

Terrors that I haven't made it. In fact, what I now have

---

5 Literally, what was she doing for an hour?

to do is not only admit defeat, but also admit that I've been swimming in an uncomfortable pool of delusion for the last four months: not only have I failed at my 'dream' job, but it was never really a dream job in the first place. I have failed at New York, at fashion, at money, success, fame, a Green Card. I never even came close to succeeding in this city. Instead, I've had all the wonder sucked out of me. Such a stupid privileged problem.

I believe in this theory of celebrating things that would usually be deemed a fail. Like falling over on entering an exceptionally glam party[6] or reading someone's behaviour as flirtation and then spending months and months convincing yourself they're in love with you, unpacking their behaviour behind their backs with any sucker who will listen, only to watch them fall happily into a relationship with a girl as they tell you they were never gay anyway. The power you can find by repurposing that failure into humour has been a genuinely life-changing technique for me and loads of queers I know.

My friends and I call these things 'team'. Like if your mum catches you wanking it's 'team', if you shit on a hot guy's dick it's 'team', if you break your leg the day before running a marathon[7] it can all be made better by 'teaming' it.

But this right here – spending all my money, of which I really had very, very little in the first place, and lying to all

---

6 Done that so many times. Once I went to a *Dazed* magazine party and, while trying to glamorously drift down the stairs, my ankles gave way under the instability of my flatforms (lol) upon which I hurtled down the stairs and into a waiter carrying seven glasses of champagne on a tray. Iconic.

7 Hahahahaha.

my friends that this is the life I've always dreamed of while slowly decaying under the savagery of being cashless and emotionally battered by my boss – all this is really, really not team. It's too bleak for team. It might be team in a few months. But right now it's WAB – weird and bleak. Another term my friends and I coined when we went to Iceland and stayed with this person who had painted literally three hundred self-portraits and hung them all in the guest bedrooms.

It's actually a complete mess. I don't really know what to do.

I intend to reply to all my messages: *Sorry can't chat today! Mad day at work xxx*

Of course, it's not. But I plan to spend the day working on an escape route, finding the right way to be honest with everyone I'm lucky enough to have care about me, a right way to battle back my shame at failing before revealing it to everyone in my life. After all, I don't believe in shame.

8th January / le 8 janvier

Around this time last year Ace and I were talking about what it means to be 'yourself'.

The queer conundrum is knowing where yourself stops and the conception of what and who you should be starts. Judith Butler says that when you're alone you don't feel your gender because gender is brought about by the presence of others. Of course, as Judy says, when you're alone you can remember the presence of others and feel it. But when I'm alone, I don't feel my gender: I feel its absence, as well as the confusion at my body and the things demanded of it, combined with knowledge that none of the (male) things society demands of me fit. Sometimes that makes me feel standout, like a star; sometimes like a leper.

I remember all the years I spent narrowing myself down to a small stereotypical box of what others perceive gay people should be: fab, bitchy, promiscuous, reads *Chat* mag, good at curling hair. But that box is not me, nor is it Ace. I've learned so much how to 'be' through existing in my narrow gay box that I'm not sure where it ends and I begin.

I'm grateful for the box, in a way, because it helped me survive, but I'm also always unsure how to escape it. And when I reminded Ace of this year-old conversation over FaceTime earlier today he said he feels that too. It's taught many of us, I'm sure, to be funny, quick-witted, emotionally intelligent. But one can't help but wonder what we would be like without such narrow conceptions and representations of us.

'I feel like I'm fully myself when I'm with you,' Ace said as we chatted, our faces pixelated by a six-hour and 2,000-mile time and space difference. And then he played our favourite song on his laptop, holding his phone to the speaker: 'Love and Affection' by Joan Armatrading. And I knew I wanted to go home.

13th January / le 13 janvier

A good measure of how life is going can be achieved by taking stock of your friends. When, as queers, the world often makes you think your choices are terrible, like you're doing it all wrong, I look at my friends and think that I must have done something really right because I bagged these living icons as my family.

It's been five days since I wrote anything down because I've spent it with these friends. Friends on FaceTime, friends on the street who I met over the course of my final days in New York while eating pumpkin pie at Sugar Diner, friends over email, friends over Instagram messages, friends dancing with me all night at the Boom Boom Room, friends who skip the queues with me at every difficult door in town, friends who spend sun-downs getting glammed up with me while we drink rosé, beating our faces and telling each other we look fierce, friends to whom I send GIFs or have conversations with only in meme form, friends who roll out of taxis with me and get early-morning dollar pizza with me, friends who have sex with me or who kiss me in a rage of utopic queer power on the dance-floor, friends who wear my wigs, friends who lend me theirs, friends who stick their fingers down each other's throats when we've all drunk too much while holding back aforementioned wigs, friends who take you to their mom's house in New Jersey, who in turn give you three-inch long acrylic nails for free, all while reading your Tarot cards, friends of all kinds who didn't have a single thing to say about my failure other than a collective 'We're Proud of You, We Love You'.

For queer people (and for most people, I'm sure), friends mean family. Friends mean protection and understanding. They mean sharing the problem, the shame, the violence – among fifteen, or twenty, or two.

I've decided to leave New York, and I feel a sense of relief I haven't experienced since I got the results of my last STI test.

Worried about cash, though. Don't have enough for the flight. Maybe I'll swim – the first drag queen to swim the Atlantic.

14th January / le 14 janvier

Pak is a Filipino-Swiss very femme gay man, who comes from a rather conservative, wealthy family. He's someone I met at uni, someone who I coached through his coming out: a regular role in the life of a longtime-out queer person, a baton that you pass on: Pak is now helping his housemate do the same, while kind of getting with him too. Unrecommended, but gays have a propensity to fuck their friends and then forget about it. Kind of sweet really. Plus his housemate is very hot.

Pak and I weren't really friends in the beginning – in fact, I didn't think much of him at all: rich, judgmental, superficial and straight just wasn't (and isn't) really my scene. (It's funny how an identity as vast as 'gay' or 'queer' can unify you across borders you never knew you had the volition to breach.) But Pak turned out to be a grower, not a shower. An incredibly generous person – both with his time and his belongings – who, perhaps because of his pretty vicious family who all vote Tory, harnesses a rare ability to be unfazed by most things. With Pak you could slip up and he'd be unfazed. He's not apolitical; he's just more forgiving than a lot of my rad queer friends (me included).

He called today, with major anxiety about his career choice as a music producer. This confession of doubt was uncharacteristic for him, but since I made a Facebook announcement that I was coming home, and that I'd learned more by hating it here than loving it, people have been more forthcoming with the ways they're feeling worried about stuff too.

Pak opened the conversation with: 'I always thought I was going to be discovered.'

Same.

'Yeah, well, I had a thought, like, two days ago that actually we probably won't be. Like, while we read about all these people who blew up overnight, I reckon that their narratives have totally missed out the years of scrimping and saving and waiting days on end for emails back from people whose work you don't even respect.'

Thing is, Pak has his own house in south London, so he doesn't really know about scrimping and saving. I had to serve him the truth about our economic and class difference, something I've promised myself I'll do more.

Then, we spent an hour planning how we'd 'do it' – a plan which consisted of all that bleak shit about personal brand management and social media followers (Pak decided to buy a thousand on Instagram) – and then he said that he was going to go to Ibiza to relax (to which I said, 'Ibiza is tacky').

'When you're home, we can work on making it together!' he said before he hung up. At this I strangely got an erection: a kind of success erection, about two queens making it in the big city. It's every queen's dream.

Then I wandered around the Lower East Side, and I wondered what it's like to be rich: culturally and financially. I wonder about this all the time. I roamed past all these fancy places I've been to in the past, all these places totally out of my reach. Some nights, I would get dressed up and go to fancy restaurants, just so I could then sit there and watch rich people, miming to the maître d' that my friends were 'super late, sorry!', when in fact they weren't coming. Really I would be desperately waiting for someone to leave a smidgen of a drink so I could minesweep it (something I've truly mastered after months of not wanting people to discover just how broke I am).

And while waiting for the dregs of that sweet, expensive nectar in those sweet, expensive places I would think about how life would change so immeasurably if I was just gifted a mil by some Dickensian-style benefactor, it turning up in my bank account with nothing but a quill-written letter that reads:

> Here's a mil, huni!
> Xoxo Magwitch (aka: Charles Dick-ins)[8]

But then there's my working-class pride: my want to have built myself from the ground up; my want to have read the books because I had the time and the money and the inclination to; my want to own property and give handsomely to charity, all because I could and all because of me, not because of some windfall money but because I did it all, I worked myself from the shores of Morecambe Bay to the top office in the One World Trade, where Anna Wintour currently chills, her Clarice Cliff vases neatly lined on the windowsill.

---

8 Googled that. Have never read any Dickens because, let's call a spade a spade, Dickens is boring.

'Am I the next Margaret Thatcher?' I worry as I obsess over pulling myself up by my own bootstraps.

These feelings are at odds with my hatred for how capitalism oppresses minorities like me and mine. Were I to receive a huge sum of money, anyway, I wonder if I'd lose that belly fire that drove me here in a mad want for something 'big', even though that something big turned out to be something bleak. But perhaps this bleak is best.

Truth is, now I'm ready to leave, I can think of nothing 'bigger' than being home, in my own context. I have been transfixed by the idea that 'big' means 'different' and 'financially successful', but perhaps 'big' really just means 'full'.

The other truth is that I secretly still believe I'll be discovered like Bowie or Iggy or Madonna or Cher Lloyd – we all think we will be.

But I'm going to stop worrying about my flawed class politics and, instead, look at my shoes and think how amazing they are. A knee-high lace-up kitten heel, in black suede. Sounds gross but they're actually very fashion right now. They will be for the next five years, too, because, apparently, we're at the dawn of something called 'The Half-Decade Trend' according to Jess Cartner-Morley at the *Guardian*. She once won an award for a piece of journalism all about the trend of wearing cardigans.

17th January / le 17 janvier

Last night had been a final hurrah, a funeral for the partial life I squeezed out of New York. Attending were, mostly, drag friends, save for Cora and Lily, who I'd met in the queues, loos, on the dance floors, instantly coding each other as gender-skewed siblings who share a cultural DNA; one just as strong as the biological alternative.

We started at Le Bain, at the rooftop of the Standard Hotel, in which there's quite a bleak pool.[9] Next, a swing through Le Coq (a kind of nostalgic nod to seedy sex clubs of the Meatpacking pre-AIDS, which is a weird aesthetic to invoke – not because AIDS is weird but because associating it with shady sex is a little unhelpful, if you ask me), ending the night backstage at the Box watching a woman who pulls a corkscrew and a bottle of wine out of her asshole snort coke off a hotdog.

And we lived, clicking and tongue popping – our form of worship. We drank, and we lived, and we danced, and we lived, and some people took pills and we lived, some people didn't drink a drop and we lived, we loved and lived and outpoured our emotions onto each other about being separated and we lived: these queens and queers and trans women and club icons I've come only to know by the flash of their phone lights during the taking of an iconic picture and their varying postures as they all recline on the city's club couches like glistening panthers, raking in cash for simply appearing, living by night, between pay cheques, wearing heels to the gym and eating one meal a day while rhinestoning their next garment. The New York nightlife scene is like nothing else in the world: it's the American Dream, gone clubbing.

As I peeled myself away from the back room of the Box,

---

9 I NEVER go in pools in public because I had chlamydia once when I was seventeen and I was convinced I got it from a pool at Oceana in Warrington. Ugh, so bleak.

cuddling Lily and the bouncers who always let me skip the queue since my first night in town, knowing I'll see them all again, I hurtled down East Houston and picked up my case from the charmingly dated Remedy Diner. From the corner of there and Norfolk I walked to the subway, weaving my way through the appallingly signed city rail network that I never quite got the hang of.

I woke up pulling into JFK, which means I must have fallen asleep on the train. My head had pressed against a glass partition, and left there was my final, and perhaps most significant, mark upon New York: the waxy, oily print of the left side of my face, the kind that would stay there all day until some unwitting passenger accidentally put their hand on it and then thereafter feel incredibly worried about the germs on the subway.

Deep breaths as I entered JFK where I was about to attempt the biggest heist in my New York history: a free flight home. There are seventeen dollars in my overdraft and a twenty that Cora slipped into my pocket as I left. Not quite a transatlantic flight.

What ensued was sixteen hours of tactical begging at different flight vendors, all of whom said no with varying degrees of brutality.

On the verge of giving up, I connected to a Wi-Fi network somewhere near the hell that is Michael Kors, and checked my emails. Ace had responded that his parents are chill with me staying with them for a bit in Clapham, until I find my own place. At least I'm sure of my destination. With a newfound confidence, a reason to head home, it was time for one final push.

'What fragrance are you wearing?' the wonderful Wizz Air lady queried.

'Ah, I don't know – I've been here sixteen hours, had a strip wash in the loos and I think, probably, doused myself with something obvious and expensive: Tom Ford maybe?'

'Ooh, my husband wears Tom Ford,' she enthused. 'How can we help?'

I explained my predicament totally honestly, at which she made a phone call to the man at the end of the Wizz desk. 'We can get you to Reykjavik . . . any good?' at which I squealed so loudly that nearby armed guards tensed their hands around their giant guns like apes clutching their cocks.

She checks my bag, hands me a ticket, tells me she feels a 'connection' with me, and I respond 'ditto' with a smile of unbrushed teeth.

Now I'm flying. And as we bump through the clouds I catch a final glimpse of Manhattan in all its long, thin, morning glory and think about giving up on a dream life which was 40 per cent within my grasp. I press my head against the window and relax into the thought that giving up on stuff in my past has led me to better things, weirder things.

I scored a place to study veterinary medicine at Cambridge and quit and then I got to finish in philosophy and become a drag queen. I tried to be a heterosexual for a bit in my teens and quit and then I got to have way more salacious sex than the rest of my peers who were in serious relationships throughout high school. I signed up to DuoLingo to learn German once and eventually quit and then I got £4.99 more a month to spend on cigarettes. And, as I leave Eve and my Union Market ban behind, I'm starting to feel excited about what will be born from torching my most recent plan to ashes. Maybe I'll start going to the gym?

18th January / le 18 janvier

Still on the flight. Food gave me diarrhoea. Should've gone for trusty veggie option. Sitting next to a baby who has taken a liking to me, which is unusual, so the mum asked if I would hold it for five minutes. It fell asleep on me, then I fell asleep on it. Cute: a little innocent drag queen and a little innocent baby soaring across the world at thousands of miles per hour, asleep together. For a second I thought about stealing the baby after I woke up but then I realised it had done a shit and I've instantly gone off the idea. Probably don't want kids.

19th January / le 19 janvier

I landed in Reykjavik and couldn't get a flight for love nor a crafty blowjob. I fell asleep in an outdoor smoking room, bitter Icelandic air having now possibly replaced anything that produces heat in my body. Eventually I made the call I never wanted to make. Bless her heart, Mum sent me £200 that she certainly doesn't have.

Unfortunately I was unaware I could go over my overdraft limit. My card was declined by Norwegian Air for a flight costing £74; Mum's bail-out having been swallowed up by the debts on my debts. I then had to make a second call I never wanted to make. I FaceTimed Pak, who sent me another £200.

Got the flight.

On the flight I was lured by a shopping magazine and spent £56 on a bottle of Jean Paul Gaultier Fleur du Mâle, as an ingenious yet manipulative 'maybe this'll make you love me' gift for Ace when he picked me up at the airport. My guilt at borrowing all that dosh wore off pretty quickly, but love is more important than money, I reasoned.

But when I touched down in London, even after I'd spent some time smoking a few ciggies, Ace was nowhere to be seen. Turned out he was somewhere with William and we made a new plan to meet at his family home, into which I'm now moving.

I took the Piccadilly line from Heathrow to Leicester Square, emerging in Soho to drink in the glorious stench of what once was the best gay village on earth, reminding myself of this place I'm in love with but have never actually lived, although I know it well after countless visits during university holidays. I stopped for a quick coffee and six cigarettes at Bar Italia on Frith Street, watching all the gay men in their multifarious cloaks of masculinity gathered outside Caffè Nero, dishing the dirt on who's fucking who and who's definitely not fucking who. 'I'm doing it,' I thought, 'I'm moving to London.' For many this doesn't sound like a big deal, but for me – or anyone from where I'm from – London always felt like this gigantic thing that wasn't really real, or possible, and now it's both and for a split second I was impressed with myself, especially after just having been burned by the other big city I tried to move to. This one's different though: my friends are here, my family is here, and if it all goes awry I can blag my way onto a train back to

Lancaster, surely? I looked around and tears rose to my eyes, and I gave myself a split second to feel proud, proud that I hadn't simply stayed still.

I arrived at Ace's house just in time for family dinner, from which Ace was absent. I regaled Savannah, his sister, and his mum and dad – Lara and David – with tales of Eve, Laurie, the nights out clubbing, the time I met Kristen Stewart at the Box, the time I face-planted in front of Tom Ford himself because my heels were two sizes too small but too cheap and statement not to buy, Lily, D Ping with the Beaumonts, all of it, as they scrambled with laughter and listened sweetly.

Now I'm red-wine tired and in bed, but unable to sleep. I heard Ace come home. I heard two voices ascending the stairs and approaching my door. Outside I heard Ace and someone else – William, I think – bouncing through the upstairs corridor, smacking into walls and shelves as they kissed their way to bed.

Should've been me. My heart feels like it's splintering. They're having sex. I can hear them having sex.

It's my fault for not making a move. It's his fault for not realising I was too scared to make a move. 'I would die for you' – I reminded myself of him saying this, as I paced around my room weeping while listening to Celine Dion's cover of Meat Loaf's 'It's All Coming Back to Me Now'.

24th January / le 24 janvier

I've been going out most days, pretending I'm busy, sitting alone in cafés having one cup of coffee and staying all day while staff members grimace at me because I'm taking up a table even though their cafés are always less than half full anyway.

Most of these free days have been spent looking for jobs to apply to, prepping all the paperwork, and then chickening out before hitting send because I don't want to get it wrong this time around. I am trying to think of slower approaches, more careful.

I'm also looking for drag gigs.

It can be extremely intimidating: entering a city's scene. Upon each scene you'll find stacks of drag kings and queens with specific skills – looks, sewing, lip syncing, dancing, singing, reading, reading to children, being in pantos, more looks, very specific looks, being funny on social media. You'll find queens who are very protective of their families, and kings who (rightly) don't want you around because queens, historically and still, get all the attention, all the priority.

But these people, these performers, often dedicate their lives to the scene. They throw nights, dance on bars, do make-up, all while working countless other jobs. Thus, it's a natural site of contention if a performer barges into a scene and takes the jobs and the slots other queens and kings and non-binary performers have worked tirelessly to build. We are protective of our scarce income and of the few spaces we are able to run, and be safe in. One wants to think of a big, loving scene centred upon one family, but practically you have to eat.

28th January / le 28 janvier

I've always been quite popular. At school, I had no real sexual value and was the target of many of the frustrations of the men around me who loved to explore their raging masculinity by either bullying me or forcing me to suck their dicks, then bullying me. So I used comedy, outrageousness, gossip, good fashion sense, and an unusually adept knowledge of relationships[10] to claw my way to the top of female-led social circles. I was easily the funniest, most 'fabulous' person on the teenage circuit, because I had to be in order to gain some sort of respect, and not die of the unrelenting homophobia or, worse, invisibility.

Then at Cambridge I had very little intellectual or cultural value due to my bookshelf-less background. But what I could provide, by the bucketload, was humour and honesty, a knife with which to cut through people's poncey bullshit. And they, too, loved me for it. I became very skilled at knowing how to make the right friends and the right enemies in social situations. It sounds manipulative but, as most queer folk will confirm, it's one of the keys to our survival.

But there's this odd feeling that parks up and unloads in your early twenties if you're someone who's used to being popular-ish. It's a feeling of being forgotten about. It's a feeling of waking up to no texts or tags or plans, thinking everyone around you is going to work, dinner, lunch, theatre, clubbing, and they're forgetting to invite you.

10 Which I learned from *Sex and the City*, God help us.

It's exacerbated by moving to big cities where all your friends are spread out and desperately working to survive before rent robs them all on the twenty-third of every month.

I've spent a week catching up with those friends here and there, but it always feels like they have somewhere else better to be. My university friend Violet says she feels the irrelevance setting in too. But then she has to go, 'meeting the man!' – while I finish the dregs of a bottle of white wine, squirming until the card machine reads *'accepted'* when paying for it.

February/
février

2nd February / le 2 février

'Well, this is a joke!' is probably the worst response a prospective employer has ever given me when looking at my CV, the nineteenth I'd handed out today.

'Turkey farm manager? Drag queen? Oh, it's this bit that kills me, under "social skills": intelligent, canny, a fantastic listener and an even better friend.'

I cringed at myself. But then, as the guy put his glasses on and stood up, I had an odd feeling that I'd slept with him, some years ago, a last-minute Grindr meet during a visit to London.

'Is your husband a jewellery designer?'

He lunged towards me.

Yes, I'd definitely slept with him – I remembered the shoes he was wearing being kicked off before he'd pissed on me in the shower.

It's hard to find employment in London.

6th February / le 6 février

It's been a futile series of days searching for jobs and catching up with friends, all telling me how hard it was for them to find a job. Some are working in coffee shops and late-night boozers; one in a gay sex bar in King's Cross, where he has to mop used condoms and bits of poop up at closing time; others with full-on salaries at theatre production companies and law firms. I like these lawyer ones the least; they don't offer to pay for dinner even though they are rapidly rocketing towards the 1 per cent with their £95k starting salaries and secondments to Hong Kong.

Something I've noted among my friends after university is that the playing field is no longer equal. Now, we are divided into two stark sub-groups: the rich ones who are stingy with money and the ones on minimum wage who earn pittance and still offer to buy you a drink.

Today I went to Mediterraneana Café on Berwick Street with my friends Cecily and Ellie. We spent the day watching the old-school Soho set stumble over the cobbles in all their faux-opulence, wigs or tattered coats, guarding an array of (most likely) filthy secrets. Cecily and Ellie are two of my best friends from university whom I met one gay night out, during which we invented a cocktail we now call 'Gava: gin and cava!' It's only to be consumed if undergoing a breakup/post-surgery/death in the family, or if there's any lying around.

Ellie is taller than average with a small waist and giant boobs that make her look like a vintage burlesque lesbian – despite the fact she's a power bisexual – queerlesque is a style she's really leaned into. Cecily is cool but doesn't know it. A proud dork, so proud that everything she loved at school, and was constantly ribbed for, has now become ultra in. She sends links to viral videos before they're viral, and often provides some of the most incisive input at the times you least expect. They are both part of the minimum-waged generous set.

Ellie said she can get me a job at this art-space-studio-space-gallery-space-yoga-space-restaurant-space-concept in east London. 'It's really niche but my bosses are looking for drag queens to sort of "spice up" the place. I know it's bleak, but you'll get to perform and they'll pay you all right.'

I've decided to go for it. Although Ellie warned me the boss will probably be high on coke and he's definitely fucking the girl who's head of marketing right now. His wife has just had a baby. *Can you believe?*

We erupt into cackles knowing we would probably all do the same. Cecily adds that if it were us, we would be better because 'we'd be honest, and like probably have an agreement re: polyamory or something, right?'

I sometimes wonder if our laughter at those on the more normative end of the spectrum comes from a place of being terrified to admit you want in to a system which has only caused you hurt. From an early age we are conditioned to want this stuff – marriage, kids, good job, money, house, car, to vote in the interest of what is good for you and yours and nobody else. When you come out as anything that strays from this norm you feel like you've failed those who wished you an easy life. 'What about grandchildren?' homophobic family members cry. 'It's a phase! Once you find the right girl you'll forget all this.'

But the very nature of being queer is questioning what society wishes on us. Queer is always the horizon, never the shore, as sexy theorist José Esteban Muñoz says.

And then what if we do want in? Around my radical queer friends – the butches who wear thick belts squeezed into the dark denim belt loops of their jeans, the ones who are the first on site at any and every protest, and the queens who have given up so much to be able to blister themselves in a pair of heels – it can sometimes feel like you lose queer points if you admit to liking the idea of getting married, or that one day you might want children. The truth is I tread the line – I want a life full of gender nonconformity, promiscuous sex, political resistance and cocktails in the morning, but I also dream of a big house in the country with kids running around in high heels, and a wedding ring on my finger. Perhaps one can have both, blended into one: perhaps if the content stays queer then the form doesn't matter?

9th February / le 9 février

Went out last night with Glamrou, Aphrodite, Elektra and Shirley to a big night at the Troxy in east London: Sink the Pink. These queens are my sisters with whom I'm in a band called Denim; Ace is one of them too. We were pretty big at uni, although I guess that's not hard when uni was a tiny enclave of repressed students desperate to find an ounce of subversion in their routine of interminable study and painful normativity.

It's probably a year since any of us performed together but, while drunk last night, Glamrou announced that there's a gig on the horizon, and she's in talks with Bethnal Green Working Men's Club – the same place that launched the sequinned ships of a thousand drag careers, including that of Sink the Pink.

We all decided that we were desperate to reunite, like the Spice Girls, so in the middle of the beaming disco we pulled up our diaries on our phones, all of which were alarmingly empty, and scheduled a meeting next week to 'lock it down'.

The rest of the night consisted of being pushed and shoved in a sea of topless muscular torsos, the gays taking this would-be queer space and making it into one big homogenised IRL Grindr meet.

I, unusually for me, ended up getting with a guy in the loos who whispered, sexily, 'I don't have a dick.' Obviously it wasn't an issue, and one knows not to enquire as to why or how, knowing that he was most likely trans.

We left the stalls to get a drink, at which point he offered me a bump of MDMA. I obliged – but as an infrequent drug taker I've never snorted anything and so I just gummed a tiny bit to be polite.

After I bumped the bump, Sivan (his name) took my hand and shoved it down his pants, guiding me to his clitoris. He took it out again and licked my fingers, asked me if it was okay. 'It's wonderful,' I said.

He guided my hand in ovular motions around his junk, new territory for me, and we made out and he quivered as if he was climaxing, him doing all the work, my hand a mere joystick. He took it out of his jeans and we both kissed my fingers. It felt glorious and brand new for me, like gender and sexuality could be anything in the world as long as all parties were consenting.

'That's the best orgasm I've had today,' Sivan breathed out.

From ecstasy to agony. On the night bus home, Ace was sobbing. William hadn't showed up and I felt disastrously smug and like a terrible friend all at once. I comforted him, as best I could, but then Ace revealed it was because 'William doesn't like it when I'm in drag', at which I lost it and asked 'Why the Fuck Would You Want to Be with Him?'

It's so distressing, these stupid masculine gays. I get it's complicated for men like William, who can conceal their gayness at a second's notice, who can 'pass' in a straight world. Femininity scares them; it represents something that has been used as a tool to attack them, us, our whole lives. 'But an explanation is not an excuse,' I wager.

'Sure, but I really like him.'

I didn't reply. The desire to be a good friend was outweighed by my jealousy of this man who most definitely doesn't deserve Ace. And the hope that Ace might also like me back was sucked out through the loud, open, hydraulic doors of the London bus like so many of my 'relationships' past in which I dreamed up a far more elaborate entwinement than was ever on offer from the other party. Growing up a lonely gay, my terminal issue was mistaking proximity for romance once I met other gays, assuming that because we were close we had to be an item.

Back home, we made some toast and had a vodka. Ace fell asleep in my bed as we watched the start of *Devious Maids* – a show we'd promised to watch together, so I lied and told him I 'haven't even started', not wanting to hurt his feelings even though I'd watched the whole season since I got back to London[1] to the muffled soundtrack of him fucking someone else so loud it felt like he was trying to assure me we were never going to happen.

As Ace drifted off, I went to the loo and had a wank about Sivan. Best orgasm of my day. I went to sleep disappointed I never got his number, but elated that I got to spend one night sleeping next to Ace. I think I might have to start getting over him tomorrow.

---

1 Fuck, almost a month ago; need to get a job.

12th February / le 12 février

Today is my mum's birthday. Happy birthday, Mum! I am proud of you, and grateful for you. You are, more than any man, the love of my life.

I called her to wish her happy birthday, but of course I didn't tell her this.

It's also just over a decade since I came out to her. I hear other stories of people's parents saying, 'We know, and we love you.' But as I stood in my fluffy polka-dot dressing gown holding a mug that read *I love shoes!*, revealing my homosexuality to my mum couldn't have felt further from that. Her exact words were, 'We'll see,' in a stroke negating any agency I had harnessed in deciding to de-closet myself at age thirteen.

For years thereafter, we undulated between subtle disapproving digs to monumental fights because I'd wanted to wear a decorative Venetian mask to a masquerade party and she'd hated the idea that I might 'parade' it around. 'It' being my gayness. These things may seem innocuous, but when they're really about who you are, the slightest disapproval from someone who should love you unconditionally burns like a hot poker searing into pig's skin, a brand of shame for life.

For all those years I was full of blame toward my mum: bitching behind her back about her confusing disapproval of my sexuality and gender identities. I held things back and built things up. She in turn misjudged and angered and grew frustrated with this kid of hers who wasn't exactly what she'd expected, especially after she'd dedicated so much energy and all the money she could muster to making me happy, safe, protected, empowered and intelligent in the ways she knew how.

One of our biggest arguments ever, brought about by something unmemorable now like her not wanting me to wear skinny jeans, erupted in a statement I still believe to be true today: 'If you're going to have a child you'd best love it for who and what it is. Any other shit is on you and your judgments.' Enough of these stories of people kicking out and disowning their children because they're gay or trans or queer or something which doesn't fit neatly into a suffocating plan laid out for a child by a parent: the number of friends and LGBTQIA+ siblings I have who still have gaping hang-ups and constant therapy because of their parental disapproval is appalling.

The other day I was telling a friend, Jessie, about all of this, explaining the details of those painful memories. She couldn't believe it because my mum and dad are now exemplary parents, and even better allies. I would, in a heartbeat, call them for anything: an HIV scare, a bad date, a particularly homophobic comment made, a question about work or love or sex or anything else that I wasn't sure of. I would tell them anything, pushing them to understand ever more about what it means to live as queer.

'Sometimes I have group sex with loads of people' gets less than a batted eyelid from a mother once so disapproving.

'How did you get here though?' Jessie asked.

'Hard fucking work,' I replied, sipping a cosmopolitan like the wealthy city slicker I am.

The work is different for each person, and it doesn't

always pay off. There are some instances where blame is jus-tified and the effort isn't worth it for an undeserving loved one or relative. But for me it was about being uncompromis-ing about aspects of my life that Mum might have me change: 'I am a drag queen, I am wearing these clothes, I am having sex in this way and if you want to be a part of it then I will tell you it all. If you don't, then I will tell you nothing; I won't even be in your life.' My siblings roll their eyes at my honesty with her, but I can't understand the harm in telling her: she has lived a life longer and fuller than mine in many ways, and her understanding of my experience only seems to proffer even more acceptance.

I worked hard early on to recognise that she really owed me nothing, and that a lot of her hurtful actions and words were because of fear and miseducation, and mine were because I was hurting and scared. It's a weird moment when you realise your parents are flawed humans whose knowl-edge doesn't encompass everything, whose opinions aren't always right. After all, I was the first gay person they'd ever met. Where I'm from nobody really talks about it.

From my mum's perspective, getting over her hurtful behaviour came when she let go of the desperation to pro-tect me, learning to see my world as something blossoming with culture and love and not as something that would bring violence and judgment. She doesn't 'feel pride, because that's somewhat patronising' – a quote I always remember her saying as she was getting the shopping in Aldi, looking after my poorly grandma and doing another hundred things at once. Instead she feels 'grateful', grateful that me and my friends have opened up a whole culture to her and my dad and welcomed them in. It makes her excited and moved. It makes her feel full.

In Catholicism you pay penance for your sins by action. I fucking hate Catholicism, bar the campy visuals, but if anyone has paid penance it's my mum. There's no need for forgiveness on either side because we both worked hard to move beyond what was there before. We burned down our relationship and built a new, greener one on the ground that was left. Both of us have learned how to blossom together, with much hard work and mutual education.

She's taught me so much, as any true love does. But mostly she's taught me the power of learning and unlearning, and working hard to do it.

13th February / le 13 février

People think drag queens are stupid.

This is misogyny in action: they think that because we feminise ourselves, because we spend a lot of time on make-up and hair and getting exactly the right look, we are vapid, bitchy and stupid.

People are wrong to think drag queens are stupid.

We get fluffed off: called 'darling', 'fabulous', coded as frippery before foxy or smart. We get underpaid and exploited, but we're aware; we're just too broke to lose the gig. We make a living off laughing at you laughing at us. We know exactly what we're laughing at, what structures we're punching at, what strings to pluck at to make you gasp with shock or huff with laughter.

We created a culture which the world marvels at, wishes

for, sponges off. We know how to navigate cities and spaces in the smartest of ways, mapping out routes to escape people's stupid, ailing masculinities. We know how to wear heels all night and not feel the burn. We know how to make a mockery not of women, but of what you (men) think women should be, whereas you (men) just, simply, mock women.

It's stupid to think drag queens are stupid.

14th February / le 14 février

It's now become the kooky, intelligent position to be anti-Valentine's Day, right? Every year there are viral tweets, memes, think-pieces about how Valentine's Day is for sucky assholes who are obsessed with capitalism and single-shaming.

I agree, in some ways, that needing a day to celebrate being coupled up with someone is stupid, because I want a man who celebrates me *every single day!* Amirite ladies?!

But it twigged to me this morning that, like all things, a queer reading of this idea of couplings might be more pro-ductive than another year of hurling anti-couple propaganda at people on Facebook all day. No, queen, that was last year. This year, alternatively, I've decided to dedicate Valentine's Day to my genitals.

Strange choice, perhaps, but that's a subject that hasn't always been so easy for me.

I don't remember much about being a young child, like an astoundingly small amount actually, but I remember grow-ing my first armpit hair. I remember seeing it and feeling jubilant as, ever since I could remember, I had courted a feeling that my insides were ill matched to my outside. But, here was puberty: and I was jubilant because I was becoming male. Finally the confusion would stop. I would like girls. I would hate dresses. I would play football. I would be normal. Now that word sends shivers down my spine. Then, desperate hope for normality kept me alive.

And in pushing out this tiny armpit hair, my body confirmed my maleness, my normality, and herein I would be free of all of these doubts and dysphorias. I willed more to grow – every day I used shampoo and conditioner on my one armpit pube in the hope that such brilliant care would coax more of these sticky little hairs to prick out.

Eventually more grew, and I hated them.

More grew on my chest, and I hated them.

More grew on my face, my ass, my legs, my arms, and I hated them.

Then the worst happened – not only did my hair grow, the other thing, the other piece of conformation that confirmed my maleness grew. And I hated it.

I toyed with changing it; I hid it between my legs and stared in the mirror for hours, pulling sleek fabrics over my body as if I were a wealthy woman with fine taste, who had lots of time for preening herself and saying 'oooh-la-la', and, most crucially, who had a stunning vagina.

I did drag in my bedroom and, eventually, drag on stage. I had sex in the receiving position – for years ignoring the urge to have my genitals touched, pleasured. I felt they weren't mine; my penis an appendage that got in the way of my role as pleasure-giver in the bedroom. When I think about that I feel disappointed that I thought the 'femme' position in bed meant to receive no pleasure.

Last summer I gained a lot of weight. This isn't unusual for me: and what usually follows is a usually winding spiral of self-loathing, crash dieting, and painful punishment on my body that has always seemed to fail me.

In the same summer I also came out as non-binary. For the first time I had said what I really felt about my body – and it wasn't how much I hated it, how much I wanted to change it, how much I wanted to hide it – no, for the first time I was offering it the care it had always deserved. For the first time I had really seen it.

Through starting to accept a gender I'd always been, looking back on those forgotten years as a child, I finally gave my mind the tools to reframe the way I thought about my body. A body that had previously felt like a lost cause, like a wreckage built of cigarettes, blisters from heels, years of violent homophobia; one constructed of all the ways I'd failed being male, and all the ways society had punished me for that.

But being non-binary offered a place to depart the pains of maleness and masculinity, and look at my body – penis included – and see it first as mine, and not as society's.

I don't see my hair as man, my fatty-boobs as woman, I don't see my small feet as female and my cock and bollocks as a big lumbering justification for structural dominance. My body is just mine. It belongs to me. My penis is femme, my penis is masc, my penis is an alien, it's soft, a flower, it's hard, it's anything I wish it to be. It is a site for pleasure. Pleasure that I deserve, that I am learning to receive. I don't have to make my pleasure smaller for someone else's to be bigger.

So, this year Valentine's Day is dedicated to my penis, my flower, my junk, my thing that doesn't make me male or female because it's mine and I am neither. And thus ends my queering of Valentine's Day. I'll take a table for two at Carluccio's – one for me, and one for Brenda, my penis.

17th February / le 17 février

Last night I had dinner with Ace, Lara, who was on iconic form, and his godmother who is a living icon. She's perhaps the most cutting person I've ever met, and routinely throws boulders mid-conversation, things like: 'Aren't you a little fat for that top?' or 'This story's offensively dull.' It sounds vicious, but once you allow yourself to bathe in those acidic waters it's remarkably refreshing.

Naturally, as is often the way of these drunk dinners when there's a drag queen present, things progressed to talk of drag.

'It's misogynist,' Ace's godmother rattled. 'You're allowed to do so many things that women aren't allowed to do because you're "brave" enough to sacrifice your maleness and put on a dress.'

It's a difficult question – the one about drag being anti-feminist. Sure, a lot of cis male drag queens do exploit femininity and femaleness in ways women wouldn't be allowed to. The most common portrayal of drag in mainstream culture is of one which is by and for cis men only – look at *RuPaul's Drag Race*.

But labelling all drag misogynist – and don't get me wrong, a lot of it is – reduces gender and identity down to a deeply boring and limiting binary in which men are men and women are women and any transgression from these oppressive posts is misogynist. It leaves no room for exploration.

'I disagree,' Ace responded to his godmother. 'I'm not a woman so I can't know what it feels like, but do you not think drag, when done cleverly, smartly, can actually undermine the way femininity is loaded with so many expectations from society?'

We all swilled back our red wine. It was all frightfully middle class, the kind of dinner I shamefully revel in.

'For me, all I know is that drag saved my life,' I piped up. 'When I put on drag I'm never thinking about becoming a woman, I'm always thinking about disentangling myself from the concept of maleness that has always brought me pain – both from the outside and inside – because I was too feminine for it.' Ace agreed.

And yes, it's likely that most drag queens and kings have at some point done something offensive, said something offensive, worn something offensive. Most queer people have, too, and probably most minorities, because we aren't born as the beacon of political brilliance we might be now. Sitting at society's fringes doesn't make you instantly a human rights specialist/oracle. But I have noticed within queer communities people are more often ready to learn their wrongdoings, apologise and move on than those who have more privilege. 'My drag definitely started as misogynist – empowering me to act slutty while women around me were shamed for it. But I think a lot of us, whatever gender, are having these conversations now,' I said.

We're all learning. Well, everyone except the powerful, stuffy men who go on and on about Political Correctness Gone Mad (such a nineties debate, literally get over it). But while they drone on, we're here spending time learning how to get it right, do it better, fight for inclusion and as broad a range of nuanced viewpoints and opinions as possible. We are, simply, progressing beyond the tiny minds of the tiny men who, for centuries, made us feel tiny. The picture is shifting, albeit slowly.

We talked all of this through over, like, three more bottles of wine; I lost count. 'I think I was wrong actually, perhaps drag isn't *always* misogynist, just most of the time,' Ace's godmother retracted. Even she was a little shocked at herself.

Then we had Viennetta and talked about whether football was homophobic.

It defo is.

21st February / le 21 février

This morning I woke up to find this guy from high school[2] had gone through every Facebook profile picture of mine and commented 'fagget' [sic], which I found weirdly funny. This random guy, one I literally forgot existed, took the time to misspell faggot under 267 of my profile pictures, one of

---

2 I reckon this rogue commenter is probably gay. (Although not all homophobes are secretly gay, and I think when people say this it's actually removing accountability from the person dishing out the abuse. We wouldn't say all arachnophobes are actually spiders.)

which he's actually in (!). It's truly comical to imagine someone sitting in their bedroom obsessively copy-pasting such a
non-insult beneath every image. It should be noted I'm not
laughing at him for misspelling—that's just classist.

I am a faggot; I got the memo way back when I watched
Christina Aguilera's 'Beautiful' video and saw those two
men being stared at for kissing, realising to my terror (and
eventual joy) that they were me. Being a faggot is not a
problem for me.

I find it oddly validating for two reasons though, and
both of them make me laugh somewhat smugly. One – if
you've got this much time on your hands your life is certainly not as exciting as mine. Two – if you think this is
something that will offend me, because you obviously think
it will, I'm glad I don't fit inside your worldview. It's way
better where I'm standing.

Anyway, off to the dry cleaners to pick up three
sequinned gowns that had started to really stink. I love
being a faggot.

22nd February / le 22 février

Today was all about Denim. We had our first meeting in ages,
now we've all taken time to try different things, subsequently
failed, and are committing to the original girlband.

So, there we were, pulled back together and in need of
the nourishment that is our drag family. I like to think of
drag and queer families like quilts: all patched together from
different places, offering different things. We all play roles
of mothers and children, make-up artists and cash machines:

each stepping up when another might be in need. It's reciprocity in the most beautiful way. It's fighting, and forgiving, the way you do with siblings.

We spent the day excited, talking about the things we want to say and do and portray, and who Denim are now (now we're in London and not at university, where it all began). We agreed that the way forward was to launch a full-scale attack of delusion: 'From now we are the biggest band in the world,' Glamrou explained.

Fake it till you make it.

We spent a while budgeting and came to the realisation that it's no good budgeting if the money doesn't exist. Glamrou decided they could afford a grand on their credit card – an offer we all softly protested but eventually took because we all knew it was the only option. Bless her.

As for the show: we've decided it will be about gentrification and Soho losing its queer spaces because of a strange life cycle it seems that only queer places undergo, a life cycle that seems particularly accelerated right now, which looks something like this:

1. It opens.
2. Queers have it for about a month, in which time it becomes a little pop-up utopia.
3. A subculture magazine writes an article about how amazing it is.
4. Straights get a whiff, stampede the place, queers stop going: paradise lost.
5. It's no longer cool in the way aforementioned subculture magazine decided it was.

6. Custom declines.
7. Rent goes up.
8. It closes.

It's been pretty buzzed over as an idea, but people have kind of stopped talking about it – except the amazing activist group Friends of the Joiners Arms. The fight for the future of the LGBTQIA+ spaces in London and the world over has felt like a losing battle. These community spaces are more important than just being venues for a drink, a dance and a hookup. They're populated by people who experience a plethora of shared oppressions; these clubs and club nights are an emergency room for people who can't otherwise express their sexuality, their desire, their gender and their dance moves anywhere else for fear of violence.

It's our job, as the biggest band in the world, to make a literal song and dance about this.

25th February / le 25 février

Today was my first day on the drag job Ellie promised me would be 'on my own terms'.

'Oh my God, what was it like?' Ellie laughed down the phone to me.

'Well, I thought it was going to be like street performing, which I found pretty bleak as an idea anyway. But turns out I'm selling spiced cider and putting on an "old cockney fishwife accent" – how your boss described it – and saying things like, "Yar come for mama's awwwd spiced cider, the best in awl the land!" I even blackened out a tooth.' Ellie was literally howling.

Given the number of guys I've shagged in east London, all of whom I've told I am a successful journalist – something I've decided I might try to have a go at, proper, now I'm back in London – meant that every time some bearded bear who looked like I might have sat on his dick went past, I had to put my face to the wall.

As I peeled off an eyelash on the Overground home, recounting my day over the phone to a hysterical Ellie, five queer femmes looked over at me in full solidarity – they too understanding what it feels like to be a shiny queer token.

At least it paid in cash – forty-five quid. Although I spent £6 of it on a spiced cider. Which I would've stolen but the boss was watching me with his bastard cokey hawk eye.

Welcome to the worst part of drag: the money jobs.

27th February / le 27 février

The tradition of the nightly family dinner is fairly new to me. My family, because of my mum and dad's work schedule, would scoop dinner (made by one of my parents) off the breakfast bar (which was cluttered with piles and piles of ironing from which we'd excavate a singular garment and iron it in a rush were it needed) and then we'd crowd around the TV. All four siblings squished on one sofa, punching each other so hard we bruised, to win control of the remote. The worst nights were when my dad got it and would make us watch the fucking news which was, back then, unimaginably boring and insignificant to a group of teens who just wanted to watch *Will and Grace* (my sister and I) or *The Simpsons* (my brothers).

But at Ace's house the family dinner is a very important part of their bonding ritual. Every night, around 8 p.m., we set the table, the plates, the rock salt in a beautifully decorated pot, and sit on plastic school chairs painted by Ace's mum in different motifs that all mismatch in that perfect unified way I could never pull off. One a landscape, one a person, one a still life of a pink flower. She's very cool.

A bottle or two of red wine is shared about as a starter, and we'll graze olives and talk about our days. And then Lara will present the table with something made in one pot and delicious – perhaps her famous bolognese, or a hunter's stew or something chicken. We all tuck in, salivating. It feels too trite to tell the family how much this inclusion means to me.

Most nights there's a guest – a friend of Ace's mum's from a School of Art back in the day, or a friend from his sister Savannah's group, which is really merging into mine and Ace's group – all of us hitting the gay clubs in a gaggle every Saturday, sharing tinnies of Red Stripe and cheap bottles of wine. Sometimes a tequila shot if someone's been paid.

Anyway, tonight William came for dinner.

I tried to make other plans but it seemed like everyone in the world was busy at a theatre opening or a gallery opening or opening their legs. Annoying. Why do all my friends have to be so sex positive?

'Have you guys met?' Savannah asked, unaware how many times I've plotted William's 'tragic', 'accidental', 'whoopsie' death, me ending up as the shoulder for Ace to build a relationship on.

'I don't think so?' William replied, knowing full fucking well how patronising that is, because we met about seven times back when they first starting dating. Having my name forgotten is something that infuriates me more than anything. I always say that if I don't have my memorability I've got squat. That's like my thing. At university people used to come up to me and say things like, 'I know you don't know me . . . but . . . omg . . . I'm obsessed with you.'

I really need to let those days go.

Anyway back to dinner: there's William pretending he doesn't know me, which has tipped me over the edge. So I said to him, 'What's your name, again?' and it obviously infuriated him too.

One point to me.

'I thought Ace would've mentioned it? We've been spending so much time together recently,' he smirked, dimples deepening in his cheeks (which would make a gorgeous punchbag).

One point to him.

Round one – Crystal the Queen versus William the Posey Douche-bag. Ding ding ding.

'Nope, Ace hasn't mentioned it at all.'

Point to me.

It was tense in the ring. Everyone else watched like we were upper-cutting each other in slow-mo. (Obviously, I was Hilary Swank in *Million Dollar Baby*.)

'We don't really talk about this kind of stuff though,

right, do we?' Ace offered meekly, trying to diffuse the fight between his best friend and his boyfriend(ish?).

'Oh, so you're not as close as I thought then?' William said, feigning innocence.

Point to him.

'We're closer than you can understand, probably. I think romantic love at such a young age is doomed, it's a dead cert, there's statistics and everything. Platonic friendships, especially among queers: that's true love.' I honestly can't believe I said that in front of Ace's family. I felt deeply childish, like I was back in my thirteen-year-old bedroom with my friend Leyah fighting with boys from other schools over MSN. I feel really bad for Ace. I'm aware I'm being fully shit here, not considering his feelings at all.

Two points to me though, a good burn. If a little pathetic.

'Dinner! Chicken! Just for you, William!' Lara shrieked as she plonked a shredded roast bird in our shared eyeline, mine and William's gaze fixed like a savage lioness's on its prey, both of us unsure who will be the victor.

Round two – Crystal the Great versus William 'I'm so cool I grew up in London blah blah I love literature blah blah blah'. Ding ding ding.

'Ace told me you're unemployed at the moment?'

The bastard. One to William.

'I thought you didn't know who I was, William?'

Big point to me.

He fumbles.

'Anyway,' I cut him off, 'I've actually just got an amazing new job! Someone heard about what a good singer I am and they've hired me to sing at the weekends in this brilliant, really niche but well-respected jazz bar in east London. I'd say come but you need a membership.'

Wow. Lies. More points to me though.

'We'd love to, but I'm taking Ace away this weekend!' He grabbed Ace's hand and stroked it while he said it, and Ace, in his shock, could do nothing but squeal like a ferret being stepped on.[3]

I felt a weird quiver down my spine, like the one you feel when you're wanking and your parents pop into your head.

'Barcelona.' William looked around the table as the family's eyes lit up. A barrage of questions: 'Where are you staying?'; 'What's planned?'; 'That's so romantic!'; 'Oh my God! You guys are so cute.'

So many points to him. So many points my nose is broken, I'm on the floor and I'm about to be tapped out.

One final try: 'I'm not a fan of Barcelona.'

A swing and a miss; everyone ignored me. I fell to the floor, as the family crowded William and gawked at his wonderful generosity, his amazing romantic skills.

It's a KO for Crystal.

28th February / le 28 février

I often like to think I'm in a movie. One of those films that has a really inspirational lead who, despite a life of rejection and heartbreak, somehow goes on to, like, walk on the moon and cure cancer and everyone who rejected them is watching

---

3 If you've ever stepped on a ferret you'll know the sound I'm referring to.

on TV as their own boring lives play out around them. Like that song 'Sk8er Boi' by Avril Lavigne.

For so many queer people, dressing up our emotions in fabulous guises is a coping mechanism for a reality so often punctured by pain. It's a mechanism I used all the way through high school to deal with endless instances of physical and emotional violence. Instead of being the boring upset one, you dress it up in stereotypical sass and glitter – trying to make these experiences survivable by showing yourself, and those around you, that you are a strong, self-sufficient person who finds it funny when the third rock of the day pelts you in the back.

I still use this mechanism to cope with things beyond my control. I bury my feelings, and instead of asking people to be better or for more, I simply come at them with a read, or an overtly self-aggrandising comment about how fierce, fab, fun I am. What would I do if I were in a movie? Rise above it all, of course.

Tonight I have no plans, and Ace is on another date with William. They have just moved into the phase of posting mysterious pics of each other on Instagram – the silhouette of one of them with a backdrop of the raging club they danced in all night, atop the caption 'London nights with this one . . .'

I've decided to leave the house, put on my headphones, a floor-length leather coat, and Christina Aguilera's saddest song,[4] full blast, coaxing the inevitable tears to fall.

---

4 'Hurt', from the album *Back to Basics*.

Blockbuster rom-com style. I'm Katherine Heigl. This is my twenty-eighth dress.

29th February / le 29 février

After I left the house last night, I wandered around Wandsworth Common, tears spluttering from ducts, as I soundtracked my heartbreak to a selection of Spotify's bleakest songs until 10.30 p.m.

After two hours, I found myself alone, in the park, distraught and with one of those awful headaches that can only be induced from running out of tears.

I decided to wallpaper over my emotions, doing what so many of my queer peers do in times of loneliness, and turned to Grindr: the home of muscular torso pics, the graveyard of emotional intimacy.[5] Frantically, I messaged the first twenty men on my home screen[6] the same 'you up, fancy some fun?' message, one after the other after the other, literally copy–pasting.

Transactional sex has always been a stronghold in the gay community – for many years, while we were outlawed, and classified as mentally ill, sexual promiscuity was a political act. Beyond politics, it actually built much of this community – our way of finding touch and feel when there was little elsewhere. It's something we could do which

---

5   Disclaimer: I know a bunch of people who wound up in happy relationships from Grindr, not that it's always the end goal.
6   I can't afford Grindr Xtra – it's £3.99 a month – so I can only see the twenty guys closest to me.

others – who had unquestioningly slipped into a life of normative marriage and monogamy – couldn't.

So I started listening to Rihanna's sexiest song,[7] waiting for my knights in shining Grindr to message back, feeling 50 per cent turned on, 40 per cent aware of the gaping lacuna left by Ace's Instagram happiness, 5 per cent aware that a Grindr meet will in no way fill this gap, and 5 per cent terrified I was going to meet a murderer[8] who would stab me to death on entering his house, lured by his promise of penetration.

I paced furiously across the common, so turned on I was shaking – the tension between my extreme sadness and extreme sexual desire proffering an incredibly vulnerable brand of arousal where I either wanted to cuddle someone all night or get pounded at knife point.

I had two replies (from twenty messages, what a blow) and I instantly replied to them both. They asked for a dick pic, so I went behind a bush and took one with the flash on my phone so bright that the image looked like a Juergen Teller original. They both loved it.

I scheduled a shag with one, down the road, for an hour's time, and another for which I got instantly into an Uber.

I arrived at door number one, knocking patiently and waiting, shaking a little – 'the Pre-Grind Shakes' as they're affectionately termed. His name on Grindr was 'Top4Bottom':

---

7 'Skin', from the album *Loud*.
8 While it's an awful stereotype, every hookup or dating app user has been scared by unavoidable *Daily Mail* headlines that tell shocking tales of murder and catfishing. It's our primal instinct to expect danger, and it's all part and parcel of the thrill.

radically imaginative. I was greeted by a sixty-something-year-old, fairly fat, very sexy man with a bald head, wearing slippers and underwear, a rolled-up fag hanging out of his mouth.

I hadn't done this in months; I'd forgotten procedure. I entered. He pulled me into the lounge and ripped down my pants, shoving his dick in, no condom, even though my party line on bareback is that I don't do it. But sometimes, secretly, I let it happen. He fucked me on the sofa, over a computer desk, and eventually he put me on my back in a kind of beige orthopedic chair, as he pile-drived/drove (?)[9] me, eventually withdrawing and coming all over my face from above.

Before I could clear up, he threw my stuff at me and told me to leave. For some fucked-up reason I found this incredibly hot, and did as he said, leaving his house covered in his cum.

En route to Fuck Number Two's house, I found a pub bathroom to clean up in. I tried using some leaves but they just spread the seed instead of sopping it up. On the way I kept thinking about something Top4Bottom had said to me when he was in me. 'Cover your nails, they're so faggy.'

In the moment I did it, and I hate that I did. I love my three-inch-long neon green and gold acrylics, something Top4Bottom obviously wasn't into. I'm used to this kind

---

9 A pile-driver is when the receiver lies on their neck, hips up, while the giver stands up, squats and thrusts. According to Urban Dictionary, most porn stars can't do the pile-driver for long because they pass out when too much blood rushes to their heads. Top4Bottom and myself manage just fine.

of femme-phobia from self-hating gay men who can't stand to be associated with anything but masculinity, but I never actually listen to it, and I don't really want to have sex with it.

Fuck Number Two went much the same as Fuck Number One, if a little less throw-down, and he wore a condom upon my asking. He also didn't have a problem with my nails and we chatted afterwards about what we both do. He's a plumber and nobody knows he's gay at work. He's forty-four.

I told him I was a drag queen. And joked that *everybody* knows I'm gay at work.

He was absolutely stunned, unsure how to take this really quite basic information. 'But your pictures were so masc?'

I was literally naked, gagged, readying myself for Act 50 in the life story of any Grindr user: 'Latent Homophobia from Gays Who've Just Bummed You'. I've been in this exact situation too many times – gay men, who have just been deep in your ass, spouting their issues with 'drag queens' and 'gays who rub it in your face' and 'femmes'. I got dressed and decided to leave. He didn't protest or apologise, even though he'd just pissed in my mouth. In fact, as I was leaving, I saw the orange glow from Grindr reflected on his face; he was looking for his next (fingers crossed more masculine!) hookup, before I'd even left the house.

I'm over it. Am I over it?

This is why I keep falling in love with my fucking friends: because they don't have a problem with my nails; they love me because of them not despite. I go back to

Grindr in times of sadness, hoping desperately to find some-one who is looking for the thrill of an alternative approach to having sex too. And every time I leave with a feeling of disappointment, rejected for some facet of my personality, and with a more deeply ingrained sense of disassociation from the gay male community. I'm sure my partners feel the same too.

Grindr – which was built on the promise of an 'easy way to meet other gay men' – has made our sexual appetites incredibly specific. On the app you can select your preferred height, weight, age, race – presenting your profile as a faceless body beholden to none of the social etiquette it would be in physical space. The app is rife with blatant, seemingly acceptable homo-, femme-, and transphobia and tons of racism. 'No fats, no femmes, no Asians' is the usual tagline. And so this radical site for sexual potential has become, for the most part, a hunting ground for the classic masc-on-masc shag and nothing else. Now we have the chance to be 'normal' and get married, it feels like a huge swathe of gay men no longer want to engage with aspects of our culture that gave us our 'freedoms' – one of which is most definitely drag; another is gender-nonconformity, and another, damn it, is these acrylic nails.

I feel bored with my brain for whirring constantly over Ace. I feel numb about the blisters on the ends of my little toes because of my new trainer heels I'm wearing at the moment. I'm going to get undressed, get into bed and furi-ously masturbate.[10] And so the cycle continues.

~~~~~~~~

10 Neither Grindr meet finished me off, I should add.

March/mars

1st March / le 1 mars

I couldn't decide on what to wear today. My go-to is over-accessorised with crap, but some days I want to preempt people staring at me, like today, and so I opt to tuck the more garish side of myself away for safekeeping.

And, yet, when I left the house and walked down towards Clapham Junction station, my first encounter with another person was a guy who kerb-crawled me for about three minutes, calling me a 'faggot'. Such effort! Probably wanted to fuck me.

The thing is, all my life people have stared at me and I never really knew why. Because to you you're just you and you don't really stare at yourself. Unless you have a spot you need to squeeze.

These stares vary in their feeling: sometimes it's like 'woah, there's a freak on the loose' and, on the other end of the spectrum, it's like, 'I see you, oh beautiful gender non-binary body, and I accept you.' I prefer the latter, but they often come with a pinch of the patronising, too, because I wasn't asking for anyone's approval in the first place. I think it's an issue that we congratulate people for *not* being homophobic, for *not* being transphobic, for *not* being a mis-ogynist. We say things like 'God, your boyfriend is amazing' because he does the washing up and believes in equal pay; or 'Wow! Your parents are so supportive' because they didn't kick you out when you revealed your homosexuality. But you don't applaud a fish for swimming, so why applaud someone for being a decent, non-violent human being?

With expressions of gender, we're so often punished for

how we transgress out of a role – because we're excessive, over-the-top, attention-seeking, we're regarded as the rightful recipients of abuse because 'you brought it on yourself'.

When I dress up it's always for me, even though I've amassed so many stares because my very presence challenges other people's beliefs about what bodies should look like, which makes them angry. But if those beliefs can't withstand questioning, then they aren't structurally sound.

When I dress up I feel authentic, like I've really questioned my beliefs and this is the result. I take ownership of the could-be wreckage of my body, after it's dodged the insults of countless people, and cover it in things that tell people who I am in the way I want to say it.

On days when I get kerb-crawled, when the energy in the air is febrile, I remember that it is me, us, who are lucky. Because we have been lucky enough to peek behind the curtain of life's binaries, which are more of a lie than anything I'm putting out there. Isn't it more authentic, more 'real' to fall wherever you want, rather than to fall into a preset, artificially constructed category that you had no agency over creating?

2nd March / le 2 mars

Today I'm obsessing about four things:

1. The fact I couldn't get into my larger dress for the spiced cider stall gig tomorrow, and I have trawled every Internet shopping site and there's literally zero options for a 'plus-size drag queen'. There's one site for larger queens but I kid you not they are all called

'sacks' – like 'The Georgy Girl Sack Dress' or 'The Miley Sack Dress'. There's nothing that makes you feel sexier than being relegated to the sack section.

2. The fact that last night I had a really intense sex dream about Ace, and the whole thing was like a stop-motion movie of his six-pack tensing and relaxing. In the dream he was consenting to the sex. In reality he's in a relationship with William, officially, and I'm working on getting over it.

3. The fact that this is weird, because my type was never the six-pack type. I'm finding this specifically confusing because for much of my life I was really into sleeping with big, fat older men who I often termed 'Daddy', in return for their calling me 'son'. Weird, I always thought, because I actually have a truly glorious non-sexual relationship with my own wonderful father and both of my male siblings, and so it confuses me that I spent almost all of my free time from the ages of fourteen to twenty-four – a decade – seeking out the oldest, fattest, ugliest men I could find, saving them as 'Daddy 1' or 'Daddy 2' in my phone and then riding them like a donkey on the Blackpool seafront: tired, low stamina, but so much fun.

Back when it all started I was also very fat. I'm still fat, but my body has grown so the fat looks more 'big', less 'puppy'. In Lancaster, there was little opportunity and no gay scene. I only ever had one friend who was gay, and had never knowingly met a gay person before I came out at the age of thirteen. Catholic school was full of homophobes (who later turned out to be gay). So all in all, not exactly the soil from which a healthy sex life blooms.

My parents weren't sure what to do with a gay kid, let alone a non-binary drag queen, and no amount of booze will let me forget the look on my mum's face when she found me at thirteen, in a sequinned dress, singing along to Celine Dion on the chaise longue in the dining room.

My best friends both adored me and fetishised me, and the Internet barely dialled up in those days, let alone allowed a space for me to find like-minded people. The only thing in my life, for a very long time, that was constant, supportive and provided me with an escape from a fairly fear-filled existence, was food.

Greasy food, cheesy food, sloppy food, doughy food, heavy food, rich food, unhealthy food, fizzy food – any food that would make me feel full to bursting, on the brink of being sick, so that in that moment I was simply alone feeling my body, filling the space that was usually occupied by the gut-wrenching terror of life as a pre-teen drag queen, exhausting myself by putting up a ferociously fab façade. A child who grew into a teen, who on the outside grew bigger and bigger, who took up more space, and who was eventually only bullied from afar because, although I was incredibly effeminate, I was bigger than everyone else.

Now, my extreme eating and my obsession with being fucked by old men are of course linked. I refute the idea that my sex with old men can find its entire basis in shame. However, over years of proudly gobbing about these experiences, and as my circle became more emotionally intelligent, conversations eventually moved from 'Yassss queen, get that grand-daddy dick!' to 'Why do you think you have a desire for older, fat men?'

I used to say that older men are good in bed; they've been there and they've done it all. In part reductive, but in part true.[1] But also I was fat. I had built my body to be both invisible to desire, but big enough to crush a bully; undesirable to my own peers, but suitable for older men who I always felt would take whatever they could get. I always thought of myself as the worst possible option – I was fat, gay, femme, and pimply. So, as the embodiment of undesirability, my only option was desperate old men.

But what's confusing is that these very fat, often un-showered, older men genuinely turned me on. They still do. While I believed them to be my only option, I still wanted to them to fuck me, and I wanted it so bad. So I'm attracted to bigger men, I know that fat people are no less attractive than thin people, and it's the person behind the body who makes you want to be sexually or emotionally intimate with them: that's like sex 101. I understand society's pressures, the pressures that force us all to consume in excess but tell us never to show any external markings of said consumption.

So, with this in mind, why all the constant self-loathing?

---

1 Especially with Stan, who has unfortunately passed away :(

Well, there's the desexualisation of my body as a fat person, and also its fetishisation. Thin bodies equal attractive, and fat ones are taboo. But whatever, I'm smart enough to know that this is just society's problem, not mine.

But being aware of the societal structures around us dictating how we respond to our bodies – fashion, advertising, lads' mags, men's health mags, the body-fascist gay community – is not the same as ridding yourself of the feelings of self-loathing and learning that, in fact, someone might want you: in all your fat, femme, gay, spotty glory.

Capitalism hates everyone, but it really hates fat people: we remind others of the effects of all this consumption, and we take up space in a world that is obsessed with keeping people small and invisible. So the journey to accepting your fat body as something wonderful and powerful and sexual is more than just bandying about the terms 'self-love' or 'body-poz'. It's about constantly pushing hard against set-ups that desperately want you to fail. It's about upending literally everything you see, everywhere you go, by proving to yourself that the entire world is wrong about your body and you are not. It's about making outfits look good even though you saw them modelled on a tiny body, it's about remembering how much your body does for you even though you've never seen yourself in a fitness ad, it's about really looking in the mirror and remembering that what's there is you. You're the only you, so how can you not be perfect?

I'm slowly trying to remove the negativity from the word 'fat'. That's what I am and why can't that be a descriptor? Just like thin. This makes so many of the things you see feel instantly less barbed, instantly less painful.

I'm not yet at the place where I feel empowered enough to show my body publicly in a tight top, for example. As a drag queen, that's hard – and my looks have come under criticism, which is fucking annoying when the person telling you this is some random from uni's straight boyfriend who works in a hedge fund, and is definitely wearing a mark-down suit from Debenhams. But those words hit. Right now there's a tab open on my computer that says 'WikiHow: Burn away stretch marks'.

But I forgive myself for this. We are all learning to love ourselves all the time – and there's no end to it because every time you manage to chip away at the internalised hatred, you clock another ad or read a statistic, and you internalise yet again. It's not about the five-step guide to loving your bod whatever its shape. No. Instead, it's about learning to just be in your body. Not to fill it up with food, or grand-daddy dick, or compliments from a loving partner. It's about learning to let go of feeling full of, and hence distracted by, something external; it's about dropping comparisons between yourself and other bodies; it's about having the courage to sit with your body in its reality, for a moment, as a body, that exists. I have never done that, but I'm trying.

4. The fact that I had K F C for lunch and dinner yesterday, and I really want it again today.

3rd March / le 3 mars

'It's called Wally. Annoying word in itself, but basically a radiator fell off the wall the day after I moved in and it had "Wally" scrawled on the back of it in blue permanent marker so I just thought it was a sign. Like woah, "this is a sign," I thought. And then, that night, I had to sleep under a table under a bunch of cardboard boxes because the lock on the door wasn't working and I couldn't afford a bed and so I used the radiator to prop the door shut like in a crap action movie or something and then I felt invincible and that's the power of Wally. So we named it Wally. Do you think it feels like it's called Wally? I want to respect the space by getting its name right, you know. I mean, to me it feels like Wally.'

This is Hatty. I've never met anyone like Hatty. She's tiny-framed, flat-chested, with a head that she describes as 'a pea', and hair that is accidentally bigger than any drag queen's I know because she cuts it herself and rarely washes it so tufts stand up. Like a budget mullet that's way more visionary than your standard east London mullet.

But Hatty can pull off a budget mullet better than you or I can pull off a crew cut, black jeans and a T-shirt. I don't know Hatty very well, but in the same breath I feel like I've known her for hundreds of years, in past lives, which I don't believe in but Hatty tells me are definitely real. She's an over-sharer, like me, and talks faster than anyone might believe is physically possible. From what I can glean, all of her clothes are various items of nightwear layered over each other in absurdly random patterns that look absolutely genius in combination. She has two pairs of shoes – one awful pair of brown boots, which she once pissed in when she was trying to break into Glastonbury and felt bad urinating on farm land, and another huge pair of iridescent creeper boots, which are way cooler than they sound.

She's remarkably queer, very artistic, and considers things in ways I genuinely would or could never. Like if you ask a question about her shoes, Hatty, instead of answering, will spend the next four minutes pontificating about the importance of shoes as a signifier of the internal self. She's right, when I think about it, and I'm obsessed with her, with all of this.

But she's not patronising; she's just managed to unbridle her brain from normative modes of thinking that all of us still get caught up in. Hatty feels like the future. Like she's seen past today and has arrived into a new place where everything and anything can be radical and queer. When you're with her it's like having synesthesia – all words becoming colours and moments becoming images and sounds becoming emotions.

Wally is her home. I use the term home sparingly because it's a total mess and the walls are filled with asbestos and they might bulldoze the place at a moment's notice. We met because we've been rehearsing Denim here for the past few weeks. Wally is this giant warehouse on the Commercial Road, 'the most polluted road in Europe', Hatty told me, enshrining her narrative in the artfulness of being poor – which she is, very.

It's an old office building that has had all its fittings gutted out. The brown-carpeted, yellow-stained-walled, asbestos-laden skeleton was what remained. Until Hatty covered the place in her: it is now bestrewn with chiffon and artwork she found on the street that has deep gouges she scratched into it while doing her 'wanking art: which is where I wank with one hand and then scratch paintings with another because I want to see what a visually realised wank looks like. It always looks really bleak and cloying, and kind of painful – never pleasurable, even though I can have up to twenty orgasms a day, it still hasn't translated onto the painting. Sometimes I wank and scratch about things that aren't even sexual: like playing the Pyramid stage or being a notable musician and then writing a book called *Just Queens*, à la Patti Smith but more real. I always get really bored the moment they start to "make it" in that book. Maybe that's my problem. I don't know.'

I think Hatty is the most unpretentiously artistic person I've ever met. I feel like a baby queer in her presence – my flawed politics abounding as she sets me straight (not in the het way) about things I find confusing, like how sexuality can be so rigid when gender is so fluid. 'I think it's about masc and femme and words we don't have for everything in between, them all swirling into a big spiral when you're attracted to someone. We're all everything, or we can be, so genitalia is as much of a lie as the Tory government working hard for everyone, or the fact that you told me that blonde is your natural colour. There's no need to lie – hair dye is my favourite invention.'

Much like herself, in this house, this Wally, she's created a utopia: since we've been rehearsing here I've seen queer photographers come to take queer photos, I've seen queer barbers chop people's hair into queer hairstyles, I've seen a group of trans women rehearsing a dance they're hoping to perform for International Transgender Day of Awareness. I've seen Hatty naked about thirty times.

I'm going to be moving in with Hatty. She asked me when I stayed for dinner one night after rehearsal.

'Rent's thirteen a week, ridiculous I know, and there's loads of spare rooms on account of everyone moving out because they all wanted real jobs and real stability. How boring? We'll have to pack away the beds every morning in case there's a random inspection – the property guardianship people assume it's just me living here, which is why the rent is such a steal. All three toilets are broken so you have to pee in the sink. But there's a loo in the café over the road, which they let you use if you need to poo.'

I need to tell Ace.

5th March / le 5 mars

What you up to tonight? A text from Ace.

> Am supposed to be seeing Ethan. You?

> Oh, Ethan. I thought he was in Berlin. Was supposed to be seeing William, but he cancelled, says he needs some time apart. Hope it's nothing serious. Would love to catch up with you ... feels like it's been ages x

I find this exchange frustrating. A month ago I would have, and did, drop everything to spend any time I could with Ace. But since I got back from New York that changed, unexpectedly and dramatically.

In New York we'd speak most nights, and wouldn't go a day without contacting each other. I'd cancel dinner plans with friends out there just so I could account for Ace's schedule, so I could see his face, so I could firmly keep half of myself in London, shutting out the potential of a fuller picture in New York. He never asked me to, of course, but I did it nonetheless. They say love is blind: I say it's anti-social.

But here, in London, even though I've been living under his parents' roof, we're more distant than we've ever been. Still, of course, hyperaware of where the other is in a room however, or what they're doing most nights – fully entangled in each other in microscopic ways that take more than a series of weird Grindr hookups to obliterate.

I was always told that in matters of the heart it's a waste of time trying to diagnose the other person, where they're at, what they're feeling. But if I *were* to diagnose, hypothetically, I would say that the potential promise versus potential risk of what seemed like a budding romantic relationship between Ace and me all became quite overwhelming for us both. Then, when William reappeared, he provided Ace with an easy out – a way to escape complex emotions and, instead, tread old, safe, risk-free ground.

But that's my hypothetical diagnosis. That's not helpful, is it?

Retaining shreds of hope here, holding on to the subtle wording of texts there, reading every smile or cup of coffee as a secret code that screams, 'It's you, Carrie, it's always been you,' without him actually saying it.

I'm bored of myself and how pathetic my devotion is. So I replied:

> Yeah, he's back! And he just broke up with his boyfriend so we're going out-out! Sorry, we must catch up soon though. When are you next free? xxx

> Sure thing, have fun then! Maybe tomorrow night? We could go to that Italian in Peckham everyone's said is really good? Or to Zeret Kitchen – your fave! x

Truth is I'm supposed to be having dinner with friends from my new, awful job but I see them all the time and I find their enthusiasm for this pitiful job deeply jarring. And Zeret Kitchen *is* my favourite.

> I would love that. Zeret Kitchen, 8pm? Should I book?

And, as ever, I caved.

6th March / le 6 mars

It was a lovely dinner at Zeret Kitchen, which featured a many-layered conversation I didn't think I'd be having.

So, Ethan is this guy I was once very much in love with. He was my best friend (I've always been one for a pattern of destructive behaviour) at university, where, for the first two years until he moved to Berlin and swiftly shacked up with a thinner, cooler, smarter, more masculine version of me, we spent every waking minute together. We used to do this thing where we'd get grotesquely smashed on the cheapest red wine known to man – Sainsbury's Basics, which came in a plastic bottle – and then dance for each other in his bedroom. He would perform full lip-syncs to the oddest songs he'd heard at his favourite club night in London, Horse Meat Disco, and every time term started he'd arrive with a whole new arsenal of bangers to which he'd spend the night showing me his choreographed dances – my clearcut favourite routine being Raquel Welch's 'This Girl's Back in Town'. I would lip-sync diva ballads to him – Celine, Shania, Mariah, Bassey, Tina, Cher, the lot – and we would move closer and closer and closer, stripping to our underwear and dancing more and drinking more, but never actually kissing. I used to walk home from his house at 4 a.m. in the pouring rain and listen to 'Beautiful' by Christina Aguilera and imagine us being together, reading books, with lots of houseplants and an ailing dog. So normative. Funny how hindsight makes you feel so dumb.

Over dinner I told Ace about a conversation I'd had with Ethan the night before in the dingy smoking area of G-A-Y – a place I'd vowed never to end up in again on account of the owner being a racist, but soon realised there wasn't anywhere else to end up in that didn't comprise of mostly pushy bears – a category into which Ethan and I both fit, but refuse to engage with. Anyway, in the smoking area Ethan and I were, for the first time, completely honest about the feelings we'd once had for each other: we'd once loved each other but we weren't in love any more.

As I told this to Ace, I wondered if he thought I was

dropping hints. But I wasn't. I realised, though, that I needed to get to that place with Ace, too. To decimate these feelings and end up a best friend, the way we'd always promised.

Ace did open up to me about William. He told me about the worries he was having – 'once a cheater, always a cheater,' I thought, it being my motto on most men, even though William hadn't cheated to my memory, and thus I held my tongue – and I removed myself from my position of 'in love' and offered him advice as a best friend. Frankly, I was proud of myself. In that moment, I really did want their relationship to work out because it hurts me more to see him sad than to see him with someone else.

As we left the restaurant to get the night bus home, I told him about Wally and moving out. I think we both sensed it was the end of a (relatively short, disappointing) era, one which was originally imbued with so much potential, potential which was never explored. But, in these moments, I felt emotionally closer to him than I had in months.

Maybe it's better, in the end, to be close to him than to be with him. Of course if he knocked on my door right now and said he wanted to be with me, I would jump at the chance.

I just waited for three minutes to see if he would. He didn't.

So for now we are back to being best friends who would die for each other again. The best feeling I've had since I realised I was in love with him.

12th March / le 12 mars

Today, I dragged my one broken suitcase from the doors of my first house in London to the asbestos utopia in the east.

When I was packing I found a note in the bottom of my studded clutch bag (lol) that I'd made on a napkin on the flight from New York in half-drag, after borrowing Kathleen the air steward's pen. It read:

> When he looks at me I feel valuable because I see what he sees in me.

As with most of the notes I make I don't really know what it means. I often jot things down to look and feel like I'm fancy and have ideas, and then when I go back to them I realise I'm either too cheesy for words or that I drink too much and need to stop making notes when I'm having a 'revelation' in a women's bathroom cubicle in the club.

But this one seemed to chime today.

Ace helped me to pack up my room: he folded bits of fabric and hole-filled T-shirts, collected all the cigarette filters I'd scattered across the floor and put them in a little leather smoking pouch he was donating to me as he had decided to give up smoking. All my friends are doing that. Such sheep.

I went downstairs to make us a both a coffee, and when I got back he'd set up his parents' record player on the chest of drawers in my room and dropped the needle on a vinyl of my favourite album, Celine Dion's *Let's Talk About Love*. I used to feel so shameful about how uncool it was to love

Celine Dion. But when I realised that you're only cool if you're not pretentious, I wrote a Facebook status[2] coming out to the world as an obsessive Celine Dion fan. And I never felt more cool.

This move from Ace was significant because he loathes Celine Dion and he's never been good at organising surprises. He often forgets birthdays or Christmas presents, but makes up for it by delivering all of his wondrous charm and presence when in your company, or getting you a present when you actually need it. People let him off because when you're with him you're with him. Ace is very present, and in today's distractible, virtually obsessed, world, that's a rarity.

We listened through the tracks that made me. This was the album I played so much when I was twelve years old and terrified of who I was that it melted under the heat of the CD player. It was the album I bought four different times. The limits of language don't stretch far enough to express my gratitude to Celine Dion for all she's done for me.

Ace and I spent the first few tracks stifled, cricking around each other, not really looking at each other, me visibly moved by this moment sound-tracked by Celine, Ace similarly moved but trying hard not to show it.

When track nine came on ('Tell Him', a duet with Barbra Streisand), I blushed at the number of times I'd listened to it, playing out the different ways I might 'Tell Him' – Ace – how we could be together.

---

2   I found it: 'Dear Friends, I have been meaning to get this out in the open for a while. I am a die-hard Celine Dion fan. There, I have said it. I am out of the closet. And it feels so good. Thanks for your support in this difficult time xxxx'

Instead I asked him to dance with me.

He led, even though he's smaller than me, and we slow danced. And for a micro-moment we were together, and there was no world outside the three-minute-and-twelve-second song. As it reached its climax, Ace bleated, 'I could, you know.'

'I know,' I responded.

'It just feels too risky. I don't want to limit what we could be. Or the future. Or something like that.'

'I know. Let's just listen to the song. Let's just see how it all goes.'

Then he kissed me – both of our lips covered in tacky shades of pinkish lip gloss we'd been messing around with while packing. It wasn't a kiss full of promise or sex, or a kiss testing our potential. It was a kiss full of respect. A kiss that made me feel like all those nights and all that time wishing wasn't wasted; a kiss that made me feel my value.

15th March / le 15 mars

Since I moved here, I've been awash with new feelings, phases, spaces. Last night, some members of the trans dance group Hatty hosts came and hung out and we talked about passing and being trans – opinions differing with some of us wanting to absorb into the category of passing and others wanting to be known and seen as trans or visibly non-binary.

'Am I trans?' I had addressed the table.

They all laughed. 'We can't answer that.'

'Probably not,' one of them added. 'Plus there's no way laser will remove all of that chest hair.'

Then we erupted into a conversation about surgery and how it does not define the trans experience.

I love my new home.

Hatty's boss also came over later on, after the dancers had dissolved into the sunset. He's a big, surprisingly camp, gay bear who works in a coffee shop and wears the signifiers of his leather and fisting fetish all over his body – ring tattoos on his arms, a handkerchief in his back pocket as a hieroglyph of the old gay hanky code, hi-shine polished leather boots with thick soles that he evidently takes pride in and polishes 'every Sunday' after they've probably been covered in piss, shit, cum and lube after a night down the hole of some fisting-bottom twink.[3]

We drank tequila. When Hatty left to get some more from E2 Local, the leather bear bent me onto the table with the forcefulness of a stern maths teacher and started fingering and rimming my hole, consent agreed upon the moment he walked in the door earlier that night after exchanging one of those exhilarating 'oh . . . this is *on!*' looks. He fingered it for near twenty minutes – one finger, two finger, four fingers and loads of lube (which he keeps in his backpack). He teased my hole with his erect penis, but we both knew he was more into hands in the ass.

Hatty walked in on us and didn't bat an eyelid.

Ten minutes later, he pulled my head back and asked if I wanted him to fist me. 'Well, it doesn't hurt right now, and that's four fingers, how bad can it be?' I asked naïvely.

---

3 Twink: gay slang for 'thin, white, into no kinks'. We all know one.

Turns out it was bad, real bad. And the moment he got knuckle deep I yelped at him to 'get out of my hole'.

Today, I spent the day at Shoreditch House,[4] my arse red-hot all day. I've gone from trans to fisting pig to yuppie in the space of a day. East London, while somewhat manic, feels like everything I've always dreamed of.[5]

16th March / le 16 mars

You know what I really fucking hate? I hate the terms used for people with large social media followings. Disrupters. Influencers. And the worst: zeitgeist shapers.

Off to work on the pissing spiced cider stall this afternoon and I'm pissed off. Why can't I be an influencer? How stunning would it be to just post a pic and get cash in the old account? I once heard that Kendall Jenner charges $100,000 to post a picture of her wearing a brand, and she doesn't even have to tag it.

I don't know how inspiring an influencer I would be, I guess, which is maybe why I still haven't hit 3,000 followers. Like 'here's a pic of me hungover at my spiced cider stall dressed as a fishwife' or 'here's a pic of me asleep on the loo' – don't know how much Kurt Geiger would be into sponsoring that post. Although now I read it back, that's the

---

4   The east London version of Soho House: its vibe is much more about having a good body and swimming in the roof pool on a Monday and pretending you're successful and hot enough to not have a job.

5   Bar the yuppie bit: turns out that category is full of men who think craft beer is a revolution and go to gym classes where they get called 'rebels'. Hahahahaha I'm laughing at you.

kind of prime content I'm desperate for. After work I've got a Denim rehearsal because it's our big comeback show at Bethnal Green Working Men's Club tomorrow night.

Got to run – need to black out my front tooth before work.

18th March / le 18 mars

Last night was Denim's first London gig ever and honestly there were more gays there than on Ticketmaster when Gaga drops tickets.

Our vocals were a bit wobbly, but the joyful thing about being a drag queen is that you really can get away with a shit ton of mistakes. The whole point is that you're already offering a service of empowerment – you're showing people there can be an alternative way of being powerful, happy, joyful, smart, and that you don't have to be an oppressive douchebag to achieve this – and in that powerful space you're also showing people that perfection is not the ideal.

Anyway, it's become our tradition to end our sets singing 'Spectrum' by Florence + the Machine because it's really fucking good.[6] And when we started verse one, the room erupted into screams as Florence Welch herself walked on stage, grabbed a mic and sung it with us. We promptly all died; none of us had spotted her in the crowd, and we teetered on the edge of hardcore fan-girling but also wanting desperately to impress her.

---

6 And of course gender and sexuality are both a spectrum.

After the show we asked everyone to clear their chairs to make a dance floor, and then our beautiful soft butch friend, who goes by the moniker DJ Soft Butch, played back-to-back Emma Bunton and that song 'Sweet Like Chocolate' by Shanks & Bigfoot. Then we did a party set – and we invited some amazing drag kings and queers to perform.

As we filed out, 3 a.m., I probably heard about fifty people saying it was the best night of their lives. For me, it was the second best. The best was the time I saw Celine Dion in concert. Then this.

24th March / le 24 mars

'We'll try really hard, but we might get it wrong,' my parents say over breakfast. They're in London visiting.

Now, I've come out to them a bunch of times – as gay, as a drag queen, as a failed vet.[7] They are, at this point, regular, perhaps even eager, spectators of me fumbling my way out of the next closet into something new. I had entered it once again around seven months ago, when I decided to openly change my pronoun to they/them/their, and couldn't find the words to tell Mum and Dad.

I was oddly nervous about this one. Once they'd got over me being a drag queen, they quickly settled on calling me 'she' when I was dressed up, on stage, trying to present as a her. But this non-binary business is less traditional for them: nothing has changed about my day-to-day appearance, not

---

7   Although the worst was the time I came home, and thus out, with blue hair. God, my mum freaked.

outside of the ways it usually changes with how I'm feeling at least, and so this is more steeped in concept, and they'll wonder about things like whether this is the first step on my journey to transition. In truth I think it's not, but I also didn't think I was non-binary a few years ago so one can never say never.

But when it came, the decision to switch my pronoun required little thought and I've known for about four years that using 'they' fit me as perfectly as cheese fits on toast, I just felt ceaselessly worried about asking those around me for even more consideration. I had spent a long while secretly anxious about being a burden, confusing people too much, worrying whether it would put me in the line of more violence; but when I told my friends it was like telling them I'd topped up the milk in the fridge, or bought more detergent – welcomed, necessary, not a big deal.

With my parents, however, I felt twelve again. I felt like I had a secret that would be blown wide open and cause my family dismay; I felt like I couldn't ask any more of these two people who have been through the big queer wringer in learning to understand me; I felt selfish. But after a week of them being in London and misgendering me – through nobody's fault – I launched it at them over a casual breakfast on the last day of their visit.

'I go by a "they" pronoun now and I really want you to both try to observe that.' There came a pause, followed by a few questions. While indeed it's not our job as queers to be everyone's educators, my mum pushed me out of her vagina and my dad once scooped my poo out of the plughole in the bath when I was eight, so I thought they'd earned the right to ask. Eventually they said, 'We'll try really hard, but we might get it wrong.'

Sometimes I think people see the they pronoun as a rejection of gender, or being 'gender neutral', when that is very much not the case. It's just that a commonly used pronoun doesn't exist for what my gender is. I definitely have a gender, but it's defined by its fluidity between thousands, no, millions of factors – so how can there be one name for it?

Glamrou complained over a drink last week how they feel about being misgendered and it really resonated. 'It annoys me, because my external body doesn't always match with what I feel inside – I mean, around four nights a week we're in drag, and I often feel more myself in drag than I do out of drag.'

What does drag say about gender? Well, annoyingly, loads of stuff. What's striking in the context of pronouns and drag however, is that some people are super quick to match pronouns to their external reading of you – and instantly, even though I have a beard, most people are au fait with gendering me 'she'. Sometimes you get men who can't cope, don't know where to look, so they'll call you 'lad' or 'pal' or 'dude' vigorously, as I'm stood there in a floor-length red sequinned dress, and say 'you're so big you should try weight lifting', because they are trying to push you into a narrow conception of gender. People are obsessed with doing that; I don't understand.

Surely the very ability to flip and flit between categories because you, I dunno, dragged some make-up over your chops belies just how flimsy the whole binary structure is. This is lofty, sure, and works in theory, but sometimes it can be hard to communicate this flimsiness, or to survive within the system. So that's why a 'they' pronoun works as a general rule, as an easy in, as a simple way for people to let you know they respect you.

That's why pronouns matter. It's about respect; about people deeming you worthy enough to try and understand you. When you're misgendered, or somebody purposefully disregards your preferred pronoun, it hurts; it jars with your notion of yourself – a self that is harder to preserve when people won't even call you something you asked to be called. When somebody does try, however, it feels like people see you. And that feels wonderful.

25th March / le 25 mars

It's better to regret the things you've done than the things you never did.

I once read that in a book and memorised it. Or maybe Lily Allen posted it on Instagram. I don't know.

Anyway, it can apply to so many things: like today, I ate seven slices of Daim cake. Then, as I finished the eighth and final slice, after agonising over it for an hour, I regretted it but quickly agreed with myself that it's better to have eaten it, because I don't want to look back on my life and think, 'I should have eaten that,' you know?

Off to work again. Last night my parents came to see me on the stall – cute – but then my mum nearly choked on a piece of dried star anise that was floating in her cider. It was all a deep blow – both the near choking and the actual absurdity of this job and my parents seeing me in it. They must be so proud of their little fishwife all grown up and making it in the big city.

26th March / le 26 mars

From my diary, a few years ago:

Ace and I were lying on a wheat field, or something like wheat – long, brown, with sheaths and ears and a rustling sound when the wind blew, which it did, quite excessively. We smoked about fifteen cigarettes before we left the field to go back to the cottage our friends had rented before exams kicked off. He asked:

'What's the perfect relationship?'

And I said: 'Emptiness?'

And he said: 'Well, that's an annoying answer. Emptiness. Come on, this isn't a philosophy exam. Emptiness?'

'No, seriously, emptiness. That's what I think a perfect relationship is.'

He was confused, and obviously thought I was being slippery.

'Right, so I'm lying here – with you – in the middle of a field and I'm not feeling anything, but in a good way,' I said – I'm paraphrasing after the fact here, but it was something like this. 'I have no worry, no excess, no anxiety and I don't feel as if I'm performing for you, which I do a lot, for other people. I feel, in the best possible way, nothing. Comfortable, empty, baseness. Just like I could say anything, at all, that comes into my mind. That's what the goal of a perfect relationship is. Right? Emptiness. Or maybe I mean fullness.'

'I think you're right.'

And then we lay there for seven more minutes, emptiness abounding, but my heart brimming with hope as to how mine and Ace's relationship is so perfectly full of emptiness.

Anyway, some years on and our relationship has taken on a different kind of emptiness. One in which we have basically stopped communicating. I'm all for a little distance, but cold turkey quitting each other feels like the wrong thing. I wonder whether I miss the anguish of it all, or whether I just miss my best friend.

31st March / le 31 mars

I made a promise to myself to not write one more word in this diary about that heinous job on the spiced cider stall in all of its fucking bleak hipster glory. And I think I did pretty well. Frankly, there's been nothing to report bar a bunch of dicks taking Insta pics of themselves with a real east London fishwife-drag-queen. If I'm ever famous I can't wait for that moment in the biopic.

Yes, it's all been pretty non. Until last night. At the end of my shift, an intimidatingly handsome brunette bear plus big beard (so my type[8]) came over to enquire about what I was doing. Furious, I handed him a spiced cider and asked

---

8 Literally the only thing that's more my type is a KFC.

for six pounds, which he paid, but explained he didn't actually ask for. And still he paid. What a charmer.

We got to talking, and then we got to kissing, indescribably fast. He was smart, with one big snaggle tooth that was soon covered in my lipstick, and we laughed as I licked it off, my padded ass pressed against the creaking trestle table that supported the machinery for my spiced cider side-hustle.

Kissing turned to canoodling, and as I closed the shop he fingered me up the ass, using olive oil from one of the tables inside as lube. Sometimes, when things like this happen, I completely jump out of the moment and take a second to appreciate what an icon I truly am.

Fingering turned to him buying me a slice of artichoke pizza at Voodoo Rays, turned to us hopping on a bus back to his flat in Dalston and having full-on sex three times in one night, watching reruns of *America's Next Top Model* in the interim, and bits of *Basic Instinct*, naked and wrapped in each other, each of us trying to do the Sharon Stone interrogation moment, opening our legs, our big bellies and flaccid willies hanging between them, and closing them in the blink of an eye.

In the morning we fucked again, this time really, really hard. So hard in fact the condom broke and he came inside me. He'd been relaxed all night, but suddenly the easy-breezy-beautiful-covergirl charm slid from his face.

'I'm HIV positive,' he gulped, obviously worried at how I'd take this. 'I'm undetectable, but I'm still positive.'

I collected my thoughts.

HIV is something that casts a shadow on sex between queer folk. It's a mixture of both a very real potential that at any moment you might contract the virus – this virus which is responsible for the death of 35 million people worldwide, a truly incomprehensible figure, since it pierced the world in roughly 1983 – combined with the other, darker part, of the shadow cast by HIV: the stigma. He's undetectable – which means the viral load in his bloodstream is so low it's practically impossible to contract HIV from him, or anyone who is undetectable.

'You're undetectable? How up to date are you with your bloods and meds?'

'Very. I'm at about 7 copies/mL. I'm so sorry about this.' He was in bits, and I sensed that disclosing his status in the past had been met with some real clangers that had left visible scars. That's the stigma.

'It's okay. I'm not on PrEP[9] because I don't have so much bareback sex. But if you're undetectable,' I touched his hand, 'then that's fine. Would you recommend I get a test?'

The truth was I was a little worried. I don't know this man well, although I do trust him. But I had a niggling feeling, as with any new lay, that he could also simply be lying about his undetectable status. That's the stigma too: something inside me mistrusting this man now I've learned of his positive HIV status. I didn't tell him this – the last thing he needed was to be made to feel like a morally bankrupt trickster. Society does that to people living with HIV quite enough without me replicating it.

---

9   PrEP is a little blue pill that has unbelievable success rates in reducing the number of new HIV transmissions between people living with HIV and those who are negative. There's also a big Tory wanker fight over who should fund it. Obviously they don't want to. What absolute douchebags.

'I mean, sure, you should go to the clinic. Explain what happened. There's no need to worry I don't think, but this has never happened before. I can come with you? I'll just call work and—'

'No, no, honestly it's okay. You go to work, this'll be totally fine – probably nothing; at worst I'll be on PrEP for the month. Give me your number though, I'll let you know what happens?'

'I was planning to, anyway.'

As we left, he asked if he could kiss me. I obliged, more than happily, not remembering the last time a one-night stand had asked to kiss me after the deed was done. And on the street too, which always, no matter what anyone says about gay progress, feels like a radical act of bravery. He jumped on a bus, blew me a kiss goodbye – another bold, gay move – and wished me luck at the clinic. I phoned them immediately.

Later, I checked my email on my phone. One, surprisingly, from him.

Hey, I found your email through Twitter and thought it was classier to communicate this way.

I just want to thank you for being so generous with your response to my disclosure this morning. It is something which remains a site of difficulty, and being undetectable usually makes it less complicated to have one-time, risk-free hookups.

Anyway, this wasn't as risk-free as I thought because I actually enjoyed last night more than I usually let myself, especially since intimacy has been a strange world for me to navigate since my *HIV* status changed.

Whatever's next, it was, really, my pleasure. I've
never done it with a drag queen before. Am I a chaser?

Warmest wishes, and let me know how the clinic
goes xxxxx

And there, in his signature, the game-changer: *an important person in online media.*

This could be my in. I've been complaining to all my
friends for years now that there's no way a working-class
queer writer could ever make it in a world of journalism
that uplifts only the voices of those who claim to have
built themselves from the bottom up but have Daddy, trus-
tee at the *Times*, getting them all their bylines.

I waited to reply. I ran into Soho and spent a while on the
loo in Balans trying to poo out his cum[10] while thinking
about what I might say.

My potential HIV worry was then quelled by a lovely,
but very direct, sexual health nurse,[11] and the day rolled into
sunset.

I've now written my reply:

Hey, how are you?

Sorry for my delay – been busy swabbing myself all
day. Lol. All good at the clinic, nothing to worry about.
Thank you for your candour, though; I felt very reas-
sured by you. I hope you're okay, too.

---

10 Iconic!
11 She recommended PrEP but left the decision up to me, and so I
left it.

Now, this is rather forward, but there are two things I'd like to ask:

1) Would you be interested in a second date? Perhaps we can watch *Fatal Attraction* this time, and spend the night flicking lamps on and off à la Alex Forrest?

2) I notice your email bio – so fancy. I know I didn't mention it last night, but I'm a writer. Would you be open to helping me get published as a journalist? I have been trying to write for various people forever, but I'm about as unconnected as it gets. Of course, mixing business and pleasure is quite tricky but I've learned that if you don't ask you don't get. Plus you've been inside me, and we had an intimate *HIV* scare together, so I figure we're definitely mixed up already.

Hope this finds you well. I would say 'best', but that feels so clinical. So – lots of love xxx

Now I'm hovering over the send icon wondering if my joviality about H I V is really the most professional tone in which to start my career.

But this is it: step one on the road to becoming a bollock-busting journalist: reporting from the front lines of anal sex, make-up bags and other queer protests.

April/avril

1st April / le 1 avril[1]

> Hey, it's been ages. Sorry we've both been so *AWOL*. Have
> loads to tell you! Let me know when you're free, and we
> can meet in the middle. Love you, miss you always xx

While I've been trying to escape Ace, busying myself with
my new career as a Pulitzer-winning journo-type (no reply
from the media bear, by the way) and a new life in east
London, he's always part of most of the things I do, or think,
or say, or feel. He's had such an imprint on the way I navigate the world. It's been two weeks since the Denim gig and
it feels like there's a gaping hole in my life where he would
fit. It's making me sad that it feels like this world, here in
east London with Hatty and all the wank-art and the fish-
wifery, and that world, with the family slant and the drunken
walks on Wandsworth Common and a deep understanding of each other, are disparate things – like the two don't
quite gel.

A reply:

> So odd. I dreamt of you last night! We were in a
> butterfly garden, drunk together? Missing you always
> too. William and I kind of over. Will explain when I see
> you. We have the Denim meeting on Friday, want to get
> dinner before? xx

---

1 Lavigne xxxx.

We plan to have dinner and I sent my condolences, secretly jubilant about William.

2nd April / le 2 avril

I awoke to a response from the media guy: both a text and an email. One, the text, explained that while he'd had a really great time with me he isn't in the 'place' to date. I don't buy it, and feel utterly baited by his whole 'what a special evening, I finally let my guard down' shit. Also, I asked him on a second date, not *to* date. Big distinction. But of course it's in his interest to shut me down, before I can shut him down because I'm so indescribably stunning; he was obviously just scared of my sacred lightning power and pulled out before he was left rejected by the love of his life. Yeah, that's it. The brutal tennis match that is gayting.

Or he just wasn't that into me.

No, definitely the former. My friend Pak confirmed over text that it's the former.

Then the email which, according to the time stamp, was sent three minutes after the text:

> hey, sure i can help. cc'd is my colleague jen who will take care of you. see you x

The real brush off. Handing me to a colleague. One kiss. He didn't even capitalise. 'See you'?? It's like taking a bullet.

I remind myself there are wars and poverty and pull myself together.

> Hey, thanks so much for this!
>
> And hey Jen, nice to e-meet you. Will send over some pitches today or tomorrow.

Send.

I've just checked Jen's Twitter – it says she's an editor at a big online newspaper, and three years ago she tweeted that the phrase 'nice to e-meet you' was among her most hated.

Texted Pak again to see if he wants to go to Golden Dragon in Chinatown for dim sum. I'm shirking responsibility[2] and choosing dumplings and a day overspending and talking with Pak about our brutal rejections.

Diary update: I was on the money. I'm home from lunch (which ran into dinner and then drinks) with Pak. Like me, like every *Sex and the City* fan who has been taught to be incapable in matters of the heart, he's having boy trouble too: living with his kind-of-ex, who just came out, and kind-of-dumped him, on the same day. They're also best friends. Classic.

I'm white–wine wasted and can already feel my hangover, but am being too lazy to walk to the sink to get a glass of water knowing this will only worsen my hangover. It's time to fuck shit up, and I've decided to email Jen with a list of fifteen pitches. The best, in my opinion, are:

> Piss perfect: meet the people who drink their own urine
>
> If my gender is fluid, why is my sexuality not?

---

2 Not sure what responsibility but I'm shirking it.

Are these the foolish ramblings of drunk drag queen (yes) or are these the theories of a nu-age prophet (also yes)? Only time, and Jen, will tell.

3rd April / le 3 avril

On the back of advice last night from Pak – who, as he paid for another of my meals, told me I have to learn how to budget – I've decided it's time to use this diary for a purpose beyond my emotional outpouring. For a week, only a week, I'm going to track my spendings. I have never, ever done this before. The aim here is to shock myself so intensely at how much cash I waste that I push myself into pits of turmoil and never spend again.

The problem is that drag queen and savings aren't words that usually find themselves in the same sentence. This applies, heavily, to me. I spend my life skirting over what I spend, never making any money and constantly dodging stuff I need while paying out extortionate amounts for deeply unnecessary things, like the sequinned eyebrows I just ordered, bespoke at £17 a pair (x 3). Yes, like most interesting people I have a terrible history of saving money, but a colourful history of spending it. One time I got a Raf Simons hoodie on finance (it was £550) and it took me seven months to pay off.

I have lots of incredibly loose theories about spending cash that really don't stand the test of reality, but I live by them nonetheless. Some of them are:

1. Why move to London – the epicentre of amazing food – to eat packed lunches?

2. What am I saving for right now anyway? A house? As if.
3. You can't take it with you. And I'll be damned if my kids get it.
4. Extravagance is next to godliness (I just made that one up).

I went online to find out the right way to do this, so the first thing I have to do is list my monthly incomings and outgoings, something I was, until now, totally unaware of.

Job: (in my head) drag performer, freelance journalist; (in reality) spiced cider seller/fishwife (I'm just so violently done with this job).

I'm a 24-year-old in London, and I've just projected that I'll be bringing in anywhere between £6–9,000 this year. Thank my drag stars that I only pay £52 a month in rent, and often skip the barriers at the tube.[3] I'm finding this quite distressing to be frank. Now this online budget generator is asking me whether I have savings.

I called Hatty in to ask if she has savings just now. We laughed for a solid twenty-five minutes. 'Don't worry,' she said. Hatty always calms me. 'We'll be famous soon enough. We have to be.'

Will report back later with findings.

Later: I've recorded, in a notepad with an eyeliner as I couldn't find a pen once I'd left the house, what I spent throughout the day and now I'm transposing it here.

10.35 a.m: For breakfast, I always get the same coffee and croissant from the same place because I'm disorganised with

---

3 Is this bad? It makes me feel bad.

my personal food habits so I literally never have breakfast at home. Even if I do, nobody would undergo such carbohydrate sacrilege as to have, let's face it, two bagels *every* morning so I usually just skip that, get hungry, and buy breakfast out. Obviously if Hatty has bought bagels I'll steal, let's face it again, two and have both that and a croissant. Anyway. £4.80.

12.15 p.m: My friend Cecily is having a tough time, so I took her out for a cup of Earl Grey. Turns out she's never tried it before. So I read her a bit, and then we enjoyed the tea . . . and spilled the tea. Yes hunnnnni. £2.52.

1 p.m: As I mentioned, I don't ever pack lunches. I decided a few years ago that I'd rather be broke than be someone who packs lunches because it's the ultimate sign of adulthood and I'm a drag queen so why should I not be glamorous? There is genuinely not one possible glimmer of glamour to be found in and around the world of Tupperware and Ziplocs. If you are a person who takes a packed lunch to work with you, I admire you but we can probably never be lovers, sorry. Anyway, a classic Pret was the lunch du jour today: halloumi and falafel wrap, sweet and salty popcorn, honey and yoghurt granola pot. £6.93.

2.09 p.m: Another coffee. I sat down to check my email (singular) in a bougie café in Angel. There's was no fucking plug socket and my laptop was out of charge so I had to move. £2.80 (wasted).

2.35 p.m: Finally find a Starbucks, even though chains are the devil. Bought an orange juice so I'd be allowed to work in there. On day one of budgeting I decided to quit the spiced cider job via email. Then I went to the loo and had a sit-down dance to M People's 'Movin' On Up' through my headphones as I took a poo. £2.80.

7.39 p.m: We had a Denim rehearsal/meeting tonight, and nearly every night this week, because we have a gig in a niche gallery and queer wrestling centre (obsessed) later this month. Ace has cancelled the dinner we were supposed to have beforehand. A blow. Scanned the streets of Angel, where we scammed a free rehearsal room from a dancer Glamrou's sleeping with, for anything decent to dine on. Swiftly settled on a glorious, girthy burrito. Obviously I also would never dream of packing dinner. That would be impossible to return from in my eyes. £7.70.

Total: £27.55.[4]

4th April / le 4 avril

9.10 a.m: I had a work meeting with a make-up brand who reached out two days ago on Instagram. Wasn't really into them, but then they gave me loads of free make-up! And they paid for breakfast as they're a literal multinational company and I'm a struggling queen. Had an organic muffin

---

4 Realised there was a calculator on my laptop but don't dare go back to work out monthly budget – at this point that just feels cruel.

which was, frankly, dry as hell. And an iced black Americano. £0.00

12.25 p.m: Had lunch alone, job-hunting at magazines and newspapers to zero avail. I decided to do what I always do and stupidly not check the prices on the menu. I ordered a coffee, a sausage sandwich and a side salad (that's a lie, it was a brownie) at a really expensive place in Soho. £16.10 (oh God, what have I done?).

5.15 p.m: Saw my friend Rina for a quick coffee because they'd just hooked up with a super great girl they've had a crush on forever, and we wanted to debrief. We talked, also, about bi erasure a lot and I am checked on sometimes erasing the experience of bi people, or assuming it's not as hard for them as it is for me, which is a very easy pattern to slip into and I promise to do better. I paid because, despite my harsh judgments on those who use Tupperware, I'm really a kind-hearted queen. £5.20.

8 p.m: Dinner out again, before Denim rehearsal. It was either another burrito or a Pret. So a Pret it was. Same again: halloumi and falafel wrap, sweet and salty popcorn, granola pot. So uncreative. Also realising now I haven't had one vegetable today. Omg or yesterday . . . unless pinto beans count? Anyway. £6.93.

Total: £28.23.

5th April / le 5 avril

9 a.m: Coffee no croissant, as I was in a rush and the croissants looked particularly dry today anyway. £3.20 (for a fucking coffee, I know . . . London).

11.30 a.m: Coffees for me and my friend Amelia, a journalist, because we wanted to catch up, and smoke loads – there's nothing better than a cigarette and a coffee. I paid even though she's employed by *Vice* and has just scored another long read in the *Guardian* because part of me likes to pretend I'm as rich as my successful friends. £6.08.

12.23 p.m: Bacon sandwich. With a fried egg. Oh my God, I'm gonna get scurvy. £4.95.

1.24 p.m: Ran out of rollie tobacco and now it's so pricey because of new laws that are supposed to stop us all buying it. But we're still buying it, Theresa, we're buying it for sure. £13.99.

2.20 p.m: I totally forgot I'd agreed to meet with a friend for lunch, and I'd already had lunch with that bacon sandwich earlier. But we went to Wagamama, and I love Wagamama even though I hate their corporate pinkwashing around Pride. Got a chicken and prawn yaki soba and a ginger beer. I made the decision to eat again on account of there being some (very few, but some) vegetables in the noodle dish. £12.25.

8 p.m: One of the Denim's bought me dinner because the spiced cider stall have delayed their payment. Probably because I quit. But I had to, as Marx would say, lose them chains. Anyway, we left rehearsal and had another burrito. At this stage I'm questioning who I am and whether, in fact, I will soon just be a burrito . . . with scurvy . . . and no money. £0.00.

Total: £40.47.

6th April / le 6 avril

8.58 a.m: Today I'm dead broke. Of course, I refused to pack a lunch, or eat breakfast at home. I bought my morning coffee as ever. Wincing, waiting for a 'DECLINED', I tapped my contactless card over a reader that said £3.20 . . . for a coffee . . . again. £3.20.

1.35 p.m: Lol, McDonald's for lunch. I truly mean it when I say that I literally never, ever have McDonald's for lunch. Except the one week where I'm writing this bloody budgeting shite. It was a double cheeseburger, three Chicken Selects with sour cream dip, fries and a DIET (!!!!!) Coke. Not gonna lie, it was a pretty special lunch. Paid in floor change. £6.00.

7.07 p.m: Received a text message notification from my bank telling me I'd breached my overdraft limit and am now spiralling into debts on my debts upon which Santander, the nichest of the banks, are applying charges. Spent about sixteen minutes seething, wondering how poor people are supposed to get out of poor situations when they're literally charged for being poor while fucking posh moneyed douchebags get tax breaks and rewards on their rewards. Make a note that the problem with capitalism, or one of, is that people think that the only limit to their personal income is how much or little effort and labour one's willing to put in, which arms all rich people with this fucking irresponsible moralising power that they are harder-working than people on minimum wage. If this was the fucking case my parents would be trillionaires, and all the mothers in the world would be both the breadwinners and the child carers at once. Fuck capitalism, truly. Decide to get an artisanal coffee to take of the edge off capitalism with £3.00 I found in my backpack xxxx

8.18 p.m: My invoice has been paid! I'm rich! As a celebration I had, of course, another burrito. I would like to talk candidly here for a sec: I urge you not to rehearse for any shows in Angel, dear friends, because – unless you're willing to trek to Upper Street – there honestly is only a Pret and two burrito shops. It's literally a joke. Anyway. £8.60.

Total: £20.80.

7th April / le 7 avril

11.33 a.m: Another friend is having a difficult time at the moment. We decided to meet for late breakfast at that place in Soho I went to the other day that cost me too much, but I was feeling flush. I had granola and apricots and loved feeling fleetingly middle class. She had a green tea; I had one coffee. I paid. £20.81.

3.25 p.m: Pret lunch. But, shocker (!), this time I had a banana and a ham and cheese sandwich. Feeling very proud of myself for eating fruit! £3.80.

4 p.m: I've been wheeled out for a drag gig tonight somewhere in Soho for a £40 fee and I was bored of my look. So I made a snap decision to go to the most iconic shop full of sequins and glitter, Taurus, and buy a headdress and some Lycra elbow-length gloves. Spent the fee before I'd made it. £55.00.

7 p.m: I sat on a panel at the Tate Modern about queerness and metal health, which my friend Amelia asked me to be involved in after someone else dropped out, then had to rush back to Soho to get in drag for the show. I grabbed a duck bahn mi from a street vendor and ran to the tube. Then I dropped the bahn mi on my right foot. I screamed a curse word and carried on running like the trouper-queen I am. £7.00.

7.30 p.m: Needed more cigarettes if I was ever going to be able to sing properly for the show. Bought a big bottle of water too, and a newspaper as a prop. £19.00.

12.30 a.m: Three beers. So. Many. Beers. All free for performers. I live my life on drinks tickets. £0.00.

Total: £105.61.

8th April / le 8 avril

1.44 p.m: Slept till 11 a.m., then rushed to Hackney to sing in a DIY gig in mine and Hatty's new band, which we aren't sure what to call. Maybe Fantasy Ice? It was pouring down and we were genuinely playing in an alleyway. Anyway, we had to wait around for literally four hours. So Hatty and I bought beer, bagels and the saltiest prosciutto and it was joyful. We sat in a leaky warehouse in Hackney Wick, where we watched some straight dudes play instruments on loop (with the aim to do so for ten hours). Visionary . . . £12.00.

Afternoon: We ended up getting quite drunk and time went somewhat hazy. But we found an in at the café near where we were playing and got loads of free beers. It was great. We played the gig and headed home, soaking wet. £0.00.

9 p.m: We are having a party tonight in the warehouse, and so before it all kicks off I cooked a fresh carbonara for a few friends – Hatty, Ace, Ellie, Cecily, Glamrou – with delicious salad. I also bought beers for the night. £22.25.

Total: £34.25.

9th April / le 9 avril

1 p.m: I was heinously hungover, and also on deadline for a piece for Jen! She responded and I'm writing the article about

being non-binary, but having a sexuality affixed to a gender. This is it. I'm a journalist now. I had coffee and a bagel at home. I felt remarkably proud of myself. £0.00.

6 p.m: Pak and I went for ritual hangover KFC. It's the best thing in the world. I felt alive again, until a man in the park near our house started screaming homophobic slurs at me. Happens all the time. £6.80.

9 p.m: Hatty cooked a roast, which took ages but was amazing when done. We had chicken, potatoes, broccoli, asparagus and honey and mustard carrots. We drank wine and watched reruns of *Friends* and the *Spiceworld* movie. It was literally the best hangover cure ever. Although I missed my deadline; will send tomorrow. A great start to my budding journalism career. £4.00.

Total: £10.80.

10th April / le 10 avril

Turns out I spent £267.71 in the week. That adds up to £1,000 a month(ish) and I haven't even accounted for rent and if my maths A level serves me well I'm spending way more than I'm bringing in. In fairness, I didn't count the cash I bring in and keep in a ball in my bag.[5] It must be that that keeps me afloat. My mother did it, unfathomably, for all our lives, and she had four kids to look after. So ends the

---

5   Still unsure whether I have to declare tax on this?

money diary. And what have I learned? Nothing. What am I going to change? Nothing. What am I? Everything!

Anyway, there's a lot to catch up on in the world outside of money.

First of all, I'm never doing a budget again. I'm sick of everyone moralising at us millennials (although I categorically wish to reject that label) that we need to save and be better with money. If we hadn't been so utterly fucked by the people telling us this we'd be fucking rolling in it. Socialism, not budgeting. That's what I say. Expunge the baby boomers, that's what I say. Universal wage, that's what I say.

A week of Denim rehearsals has been somewhat transformative for mine and Ace's relationship. There's a specific brand of brutal honesty that mounts as a show nears, as the tension rises: one where you can say things you wouldn't usually, if time weren't so pressed.

At a quick dinner, four nights ago, eating a chicken burrito, a conversation:

I said I was sorry about him and William breaking up; he said I obviously wasn't as I hadn't mentioned it all week, even though we'd seen each other every night. We were eating said burrito and my hands were covered in mulch of sour cream and rice and sauce that made my hands smell for the rest of the night.

I responded by reminding him that he, too, hadn't asked a thing about me either. I told him I'd had an HIV scare (kind of), I quit my job, got my first paid writing one. He was both concerned and happy for me, so we talked all that out, and then I asked him about William, properly.

'Well . . . he fucking slept with Steve. Remember, that

builder fetish guy we once met on the common? Turns out, he slept with him, repeatedly. And I found a video! A fucking video! I can't . . .'

'Fuck. A video.' I feared, for a moment, that I'd also slept with Steve on a Grindr rager. 'Is Steve that builder who isn't actually a builder but dresses like one, really convincingly, for gay nights? A kind of ginger, brown, grey tricolore beard?'

Ace confirmed it was indeed Steve with whom I'd slept that had torn him and William apart. I was planning not to mention to Ace, and then, burrito in hand, it effervesced from my mouth because I'm always on the hunt for my next shocking story.

'Are you fucking kidding me? Now two of the men I love have slept with Ste—' Ace stopped himself.

'Two of the men you *love*?'

Clock ticked, break over, back to rehearsal we went. But he loves me, apparently. Which I think I knew. He also gendered me as male, but I just wanted to savour this moment of validation instead of hitting him hard with a 'get my pronouns right' retort. He usually gets it right anyway, he calls me 'his person'.

My first piece of journalism was published and I shared it on Facebook, proudly. Three people commented on it, on the site, all of them calling me some form of freak or pervert. That was gorgeous.

Emailed Jen more pitches, and now she wants me to write one about dominance and submissiveness in homosexual relationships and whether that pertains to gendered stereotypes that uphold normativity. Frankly, I think that most gays are now synonymous with normativity, but I didn't tell Jen, obviously. I invoiced £120 for my first article and calculated that in order to survive I must write three to four of these articles a week. The problem is I only have, like, six things to say, and I've already said one of them.

Time for some new experiences.

17th April / le 17 avril

I finished my dom-sub piece, and was deeply proud of myself for finally being able to quote Cheryl Cole in something the public might read.[6]

The next piece I've been working on is about exploring masculinities in the gay community. I think, after only two published articles, I've worked out my beat (as they cringingly call it in journalism), which is 'homopolitico'[7]. To me, it seems unremarkable: every fucking person I know is a hardcore homopolitico, with radical sexual, social and party politics. But in the world of traditional journalism there's actually a dearth of any such sort of inclusivity or diversity, and that's just among the gays, let alone any other, lesser-represented voices.

There's also this godforsaken theory that only women and other oppressed people can, and should, engage in personal journalism because the reporting, the fact dishing, should be left to straight white dudes. It's infuriating, but

6 It was a lyric from her masterwork 'Parachute', by the way; a truly stunning moment in the pop canon.
7 Made the word up, but sounds gorj, right?

actually it makes writing way more exciting for us. I'm here to take up space and tell you what it's like to *live* these experiences, rather than report on them like some armchair anthropologist. The ways stories are told and accepted as 'good' and 'proper' and 'to a standard' are dictated by the most privileged and, thus, dull. There's a complicated question about selling your trauma to pay your rent but, since I can't afford therapy, perhaps that'll be helpful anyway. The whole point of writing about personal experience is that some people, somewhere, might connect with it.

Anyway, for this piece about masculinity I've spent five days anthropologically exploring the gay male community. The premise is that this is a sort of survey, an ethnographic study, of gays in London right now. Here, I present my findings:

1. **Grindr/Scruff/Recon/the apps**: The apps have arguably killed opportunity in the gay community. Now, you can switch on, click click, boom: and you've got three bears spraying their loads all over your back while you think about what takeaway to get on the way home. Indian. Our sex has become a virtual transaction, often no more than a transfer of data, and Grindr has developed a currency based on muscular torso pics, racism, and femme-phobia. A usual Grindr chat goes:

Top or bott?

Bott, but sometimes vers

Wanna fuck? U accom?

> *Sure, sure, any pics?*

Torso pic: sometimes hot, mostly boring
Face pic: often them on holiday somewhere, cropped
very tight, a bit burnt
Dick pic one: taken from above while sat on the toilet,
imagine them pooing
Dick pic two: flash: too high, pubes: oddly shiny, boxers:
undesirable, stiff cotton
Dick pic three: good pic, hot pic. Sometimes this one will
be with weird precum visible, which is literally never a
turn on; sometimes it will be them bareback in some
Twink, which makes me both worry about STIs and
also makes me jealous: 'Who the fuck is she?'
Rare, oddly angled, hole pic: so rarely got right, often
taken in a smeared mirror that makes their butt hole
look, frankly, sub par. Sometimes, however, a dirty
hole pic is the hottest thing in the world.

> *Come over. So hot. Play safe only*
> **Send location**

Three hours later, after mediocre sex: Block.

2. **XXL:** Interestingly this is specifically a bear sex club, so
   is built entirely on deifying the hyper-male form –
   muscular bears or big-bellied rugby men only. On entry,
   on a Friday night, I wear trainer heels and a fringed

dress and, naturally, I'm standing out from the crowd. Some of these burly men love it, looking me up and down in the way only gays and the women of *Dynasty* do just before a physical fight; others are visibly disgusted by my feminising presence at this should-be masc mecca. A bouncer, front of the queue: 'You can't come in here wearing that, boss; it's menswear only.' I'm deeply shocked. Luckily Glamrou, my assistant ethnographer for the night, quickly steps in: 'Oh please. Gender is literally a lie. XXL, more like XX-transmisogyny. I'm gonna Tweet about this!' The bouncer's eyes shift side to side: 'Right. Fine. I love it, but if my boss sees I'll get in trouble.' He lets us in, and grabs both our arms as we enter: 'By the way, I get off at one a.m., and would love to see both of you from a bird's-eye view, if you get me?' Glamrou and I giggle like little school-theys, which causes more polarised looks from those around us. Inside, the place is alight with testosterone, and toplessness, which we despise. I also dislike the fact that there are no women or femmes here, except me and Glam. Glamrou and I dance, sweat, drink tinnies of sweet, gross Red Stripe. I talk to three huge, burly men with their bendy dicks hanging out, and I'm heartened at how undeniably camp they are even if they are wearing a costume of excessive muscle. Eventually, I take two of them into the dark room, and I suck their dicks till both of them cum all over my face, my neck. I lose Glamrou and find them later in McDonald's. Have a Chicken Legend with cool mayo and feel really stunning.

3. **Chariots Sauna/general saunas:** There's a strange
   code that everyone in gay sex saunas seems to
   understand, though there's certainly no rule book. If
   you like someone you don't look at them, you definitely
   don't speak to them, you simply walk past them and
   prod them as if checking the ripeness of a tomato. If
   they like you back they'll likely follow you to a corridor/
   jacuzzi/sex booth. I enter Chariots in Vauxhall, on
   Saturday night, alone. Heart pumps hard as I walk
   through the café-bar where they serve tuna melt
   paninis twenty-four hours a day – delicious, but
   perhaps the only thing less arousing than estate agents
   on a Christmas pub crawl. I take a moment to
   appreciate the myriad ways gays have found to have
   sex, and smile at the reclining, naked older men who
   use this as a literal community centre, many of whom
   have probably got wives at home. Head through
   corridors and shower, eyeing up guys. Some have
   evidently taken excessive amounts of drugs, and feel
   momentarily worried for them, then I chastise myself
   for being judgmental. Next, walk down a corridor
   edged by sex booths. Catch glimpses of assorted men
   inside: bottom twinks moaning for men to come and
   fill them up like parodies of busty blonde women
   they've seen on porn; five people in one in a kind of
   renaissance-style tableau. Feel very fat as I realise
   all five have twitching abs and tight little buns.
   Accidentally walk into pitch-black orgy room, step on
   a used, spermy condom and feel someone try to finger
   my butt hole. Unsure, not feeling it, bum clamming up,

leave orgy room in search of a jacuzzi. There, get talking to an incredibly sweet old man called Patrick who ends up holding his nose as he goes under water to give me head. He takes me to the smoking area, lights my cigarette, and stands over me – dick at eye level, precum glistening (hot? I can't tell). We head down to a sex room, where he lubes me up and puts on a condom, and shoves it in me, his whole weight bearing down on me, and it's very, very hot and I love his camp whispers. As we go for it another guy comes in, equally old and chubby, and asks if he can put his dick in my mouth. I oblige, excitedly, and then they switch around. We all cum, I shower, I leave. I walk out into London, my hair wet, the sun bulging through the clouds, forcing dawn, and as I ride the tube I feel thankful for these sensitive men who made me feel very sexually attractive in a scene full of muscle and masculinity.

4. **Heaven/Soho:** We used to frequent these places all the time – shots, shots, shots, dancing, surrounded less by sex and more by camp queens getting their kicks to the likes of Kylie and a mass balloon drop at the climax of the night. Here, we used to go to dance and never to score. It was under the roofs of the various G-A-Y franchises that my friends and I all found our gateway drug into:

5. **The east London gay scene:** Much cooler, far more politically engaged if you search for the right kind of night. Denim sits on this scene, in its own little way. It encompasses everything from queer femme-girl-only

Edgware Library
Tel: 020 8359 2626
Email: edgware.library@barnet.gov.uk

Customer ID: **********0263

Items that you have checked out

Title: Diary of a drag queen
ID: 30131057314202
Due: 19 February 2022

Total items: 1
Account balance: £0.00
29/01/2022 12:52
Checked out: 4
Overdue: 0
Hold requests: 0
Ready for collection: 0

Items that you already have on loan

Title: Murder isn't easy : the forensics of
       Agatha Christie
ID: 30131057723840
Due: 19 February 2022

Title: Summer of love
ID: 30131056669838
Due: 19 February 2022

Title: The wardrobe mistress
ID: 30131056346965
Due: 19 February 2022

nights to parties like Batty Mama, BBZ and Pxssy Palace, which, rightly, lift up and celebrate queer bodies of colour. Those nights are truly beautiful, and offer a varied conception of gender to the point where, for one night, people can freely move without worry and violence.

There are other nights that we all know are basically designed to make money off straight people gawping at drag queens and pushing queer women out the way, but one doesn't want to be too shady because I have a lot of friends who partake in those spaces to make cash – even I do sometimes. One thing I will say about those nights is that, no matter where they are, they literally reek of farts: straight men coked off their faces, farting their way through queer space as if it were theirs. The only people who should be able to fart in those spaces are the queers and the little twinky bums who have to get it out of their system before Daddy checks the pipes at the end of the night.

6. **Other:** The moneyed and cultural capital-obsessed homos of middle-class London. Think galleries, think 'soft-launches', think fashion gays, think bookstores that serve craft coffees, think panel talks about 'gay mental health'.[8] I think these are the worst kind of gays, after the misogynist, muscle-obsessed ones. These are the kind of gays that find my loud, queer mouth displeasing and inappropriate, and my class background unsightly.

---

8 Yes, I'm aware I did one a few days ago, but I needed the money.

> Unlike the muscle gays who are obsessed with the aesthetics of masculinity, the cultural capital-obsessed gays are cosy in their campness or queer sensibilities, but are loathe to actually seek out and fight for rights for queers who differ from them. They hand-wring about gentrification while funding a new gallery space, they think marriage was the be-all and end-all for the gay rights movement and they don't follow a single trans person on Twitter. Regarding masculinity, they essentially aren't comfortable losing out on all its privileges just because they take it up the poo pipe. Not my scene.

So what of gayness and masculinity? What's the conclusion? The conclusion, I think, is that masculinity is very hard and, if society shows us anything, failing at it can be even harder. Failure is abused and mocked, and while the gay male scene might offer the most diverse portrayal of masculinity in the West, it's still full of men who've internalised this violence against them because of said failure and then, in turn, replicate this violence against men who've failed more than them: the mascs hate anyone more femme than them, the femmes hate anyone more fat than them, the fats hate anyone more disabled than them, the whites hate anyone with browner skin than them. All of them hate women. And so we are divided and conquered. Of course, gay men can also be some of the most beautiful, wonderful, caring creatures bouncing around the atmosphere, but they can also be just as violent as the men who took their power. You know if this is you, and you know if this is not. We've all done it, we all do it, I'm doing it now.

19th April / le 19 avril

Tonight we have a Denim gig at that queer wrestling place.

I'm already late getting ready because I spent the day trying to make a dress out of some old fabric I found in a cupboard full of shit that was left in Wally before I got here – a kind of wipe-clean plastic tablecloth printed with dark brown and red fruits on a white background. Turns out, in dress form, I looked the spitting image of a used tampon, which could be a cool look, but it won't work with my neon-pink thigh-high boots, and anyway, I'd sewn it so hastily that my silhouette was like a badly stuffed boxing glove. I also spent half an hour making out with Hatty because it's fun and we love telling each other that the other is a really good kisser.

I'm feeling oddly nervous about tonight's gig. Not the gig bit – once I'm in geish[9] I always feel ready for anything stage-wise – more the dancing after, when the club bit turns dirtier, and everyone starts finding their Saturday squeeze. I detest these spaces; I always feel like the last one picked in PE class. I especially dislike being picked last at PE when I'm in the line-up with Ace.

Of late we've been in much more contact. He slept over at Wally last night, in my bed, which is just a series of old sofa cushions placed side by side, after we went out for Turkish food on Watney Market and drank so much bring-your-own-beer that he couldn't face the journey home. And

9 Drag colloquialism for make-up. Just googled spelling and realised it comes from the word 'geisha'. Now I'm thinking that probably the word isn't mine to use.

there we returned so quickly to old us: laughing, smoking (he's started again since he binned William, thank God), him not checking his phone every twenty minutes to see if William's got back to him, engaging each other in deep conversations. I'm less cutting, more considerate, less 'cold-for-no-reason'. He and Hatty also found each other ferociously funny, and by the early hours we'd polished off a full bottle of cheap tequila and had dressed in the most iconic clothes we could find, blasting out Lady Gaga's best song ever – 'Fashion!' – while filling saucepans full of freezing cold water and pouring them on each other, à la Jennifer Beals in *Flashdance*, soaking the carpet in the process. There's something so freeing about fucking up your surroundings. It was a sensational, borderless night where we all moved over each other fluidly, with the ease of three sisters who maybe also wanted to have sex?

After we had collapsed in bed, still soaking wet, Ace looked at me and told me he loved me but didn't know how that translated into reality. I welled up, and asked if that meant he was too embarrassed to think of us together in public.

To which he stayed silent. To which I got the message. To which I turned over. To which he kissed the back of my head.

Tonight the indefinable will become the acidulous. I, the less visually desirable of the pair, will be celebrated for my drag look, my voice. But, after the show, I'll be chatted to, but never up. If I had a sequin for every time someone's come over in the past to me to ask about my hot friend (Ace), I would have about thirty-eight sequins. Tonight will be no different.

There's no feeling in the world like it. To be looked over by someone who knows you and by someone who doesn't at the same time, then to watch him kiss another all night as if it were the most glorious kiss both had ever had, as you wait, hoping that, actually, he will see you tonight. You put yourself into the new guy's position, and imagine the feeling of the mouth and stomach fireworks they're both experiencing as they drink their cocktail of kissing, booze and a dab of something serotonin-freeing. The human experience is so obscenely lonely when you think that every single person is never feeling the exact same thing.

But there's them, the Saturday night squeeze who had the courage to actually make a move on Ace, and then there will be me, later this evening: twiddling my thumbs, dancing with strangers who look over my shoulder to see if there's anyone hotter than me to end the night with, while Ace and whoever this man is are against a wall, unstoppable, eating each other. There's no feeling in the world like that in which you're kept interested by meagre suggestions of love here and love there, and then cast aside the moment someone with pulsating abs steps in front of you in the club. It's that song by Robyn, 'Dancing on my Own'[10] multiplied by the confirmation that you are, in every way you'd suspected as a teenager, undesirable.

Anyway, must get into make-up and have a bottle of wine to take the edge off.

---

10 I know this is a reference from *Girls* but it's, frankly, ubiquitous. Plus I have a tattoo of Robyn's logo on my leg because I thought it was arty (I miss being nineteen).

22nd April / le 22 avril

When I was a teenager I used to write all my experiences with homophobic abuse, at school, with friends, at home, in a little notebook and keep it inside my pillowcase. I used to think that if I wrote them down I could stop the words or the stones or the saliva turgid with hocked-up phlegm from bedding down inside me, instead leaving all those encounters there, in a closed book, nearby but out of sight.[11]

When I left home for university I toyed with taking it with me, but I decided against it. The night before I left I took the notebook into the shower with me, opening and soaking each page, watching the ink run down the drain, choosing to finally excoriate these endless tales of pain from my possession, knowing that leaving Lancaster and going to Cambridge I would finally be among people who understood and accepted me in ways I'd never known before. A classist assumption, I soon realised, phobia of all kinds penetrating class boundaries and chasing me wherever I've ever been like a recurring dream.

I have a lot of friends who say they have never experienced such violent homophobia as me. I don't understand why; we are equally as queer and as camp. I wonder if it's my bigness that intimidates men, and how at odds that is with how unmissably feminine I am. Their masculinity unable to compute the contrast.

But I stopped keeping a diary of homophobic abuse, as I

---

11 I also had a book for pictures of men's torsos I'd torn from magazines, but I kept that under my bed.

learned to understand the world more, to recognise the systems of oppression that lead other oppressed people to take their rage out on someone like me, like us. Instead I built a better circuit board to compute these varied, but fairly constant, incidents.

However, this computer is malfunctioning, and I can't understand what happened to me three nights ago. I really am unsure how to write this down. But I feel like I need to, to write it here, as an account, so I can deploy these feelings of shame and purge the violent energy from my body before it manifests into more bouts of unsafe sex or torrid self-hatred or getting a credit card and maxing it out at Balenciaga which, frankly, would be a disaster.

After Denim I waited for Ace to finish snogging someone. Together we got an Uber back to Wally as the streets never feel safe to inhabit after dark when one is in full drag. As we stepped, heels first, out of our car and towards the front door, some men appeared, vodka bottles in hand, yelling vicious homophobic slurs. Naturally, as we learned at high school, Ace and I stuck a middle finger up at them, and we shouted simple retorts of 'fuck off' and other reactionary, unintelligent defences. As we crossed to the middle of the busy road, a lone wolf from the group peeled off, smashed his vodka bottle on the floor, and ran quickly across the shard-covered tarmac, heading for Ace. At that moment, a bus came and, as I was in the middle of the road, while Ace was now by my front door, I instinctively held the lone wolf back from being hit by the bus, which would have led to his certain death.

And there, on a concrete island in the centre of the dual

carriageway, he stared me square in the eyes, and said 'thank you', in absolute earnest, for saving his life. Relieved, heart still shaking my oesophagus, I went to respond, at which point he, looking me square in the eye, recoiled a fist and punched me so hard in the face I heard my nose crack and my brain bounce around my skull like a jar of pickles being shaken. My sight disappeared and I was floored, my mouth filled by blood coursing from some unknown location on my face.

I have been many things and have had many things done to me, but never have I been punched square in the face. A full-on physical hate crime.

Imagine a scenario in which someone despises the very fact of your existence so vehemently, so fervently, that, even when you have genuinely saved their life, they feel you still deserve physical punishment for being. I can only envisage being on the receiving end of that exchange. I don't even think he deserves physical punishment for inflicting this on me.

I haven't left the house since I got back from the hospital. My door, the corridors, the pavements are covered with aubergine circles of dropped, now dried, blood. A full bloody handprint has now dried, cracked, and is peeling off the light-switch in the corridor which I reached for to get to safety. I can't connect any of that to me. I feel different now. Sadder now. More disappointed now.

I feel exhausted now. I'm going to sleep.

24th April / le 24 avril

I don't think it's possible to instantly tell how something like a violent attack will affect you as time goes on. I've been attacked so many times, in so many ways, and I find it self-indulgent to talk about it. Before, I couldn't fixate on the homophobia in my past, because overcoming it was the only option. I used to come home from homophobic school, off the homophobic bus, through the house door where I would act miserably so my parents would assume it was hormones not hatefulness that was making me silent. I would go into my bedroom and lock the door. The back of the door was covered with hundreds of images of Madonna and Celine Dion, framing a small mirror I'd bought from the market in Lancaster. I used to take off my clothes and wrap myself in a cheap faux fur blanket I'd bought from Matalan, like a dress, put in my crackly headphones, and press play on songs that would make me feel like a superstar.

I used to look into my own eyes, and I would say to myself, promise myself: 'You're a superstar. You are going to have an extraordinary life.' And it worked. It lifted me to a place where I was not just healed, but where I felt formidable.

The long-lasting effects of the homophobia in my past have made me more powerful. That is very sad, especially for that thirteen-year-old who had to do all of that work to just be a thirteen-year-old.

But that thirteen-year-old is stronger than me, over a decade on.

Since I was attacked five nights ago I can't go outside, especially at night. I feel like myself and my friends, my wonderful friends who have come to visit in all their queer, joyous droves, have been burdened with the rage of this man who got away into the night to enjoy his freedom, while we toil and angst over the constant threats to our safety.

I've been very jumpy and spatially aware: a car door slamming feels like an attacker, a loud voice or the hydraulics of a bus make me flinch like a terrified animal. I've worn only black clothes: giant black swathes of fabric, hoping I'll be less visible, wanting to be nothing more than a shadow. I even considered, for about thirty minutes, trying to change my walk, which has always drawn attention to me. But I felt like that was the definition of internalising their violence, and then they'd win, so I've kept mincing, my tiny internal protest requiring mammoth amounts of bravery.

Emotionally I've felt an equal, uncomfortable mix of defeat and fury. Fury that there is no structure in place telling me that my identity is acceptable no matter where I look. Fury that the only thing any policeman or authority figure assured me was that 'this happens all the time'. Well, fucking do something about it then.

Fury that people seem to take pleasure in reminding me that I'm 'a piece of shit faggot' (Northern line, 2015), that I should 'die of AIDS' (Tooting, 2015), or that I am worthless enough as a human to use as a punchbag, while these abusers get to walk away and relish in the safety afforded them as straight and white and male while I am left having to put in hours of emotional labour to remind myself that my gayness and my non-binaryness[12] are okay. I am left in pain and

---

12 A made-up word, but all words are made up so STFU.

unable to complete my daily tasks because my head throbs and my nose crunches and my personality crumbles at the hint of anything that could even signal attack. I was very strong and very intent on taking up space and now I don't know where that part of me is; it is knocked out of me, somewhere on the dual carriageway. Myself, my radical friends and my family have to spend their time and energy helping me overcome the actions of a selfish man, absorbing his rage and transforming it to our anxiety.

I feel fury that sometimes, when I'm alone and everyone is sleeping, I lie there recounting all of the instances of homo-, femme-, queer-phobia I have encountered, then I multiply that by every LGBTQIA+ person in the world, then all of my critical and emotional faculties bulge into a space in my brain that I hate, a space where for a moment I wonder if I've been wrong this whole time. That everything I've so proudly represented these years was a mistake. That I, in fact, was never a superstar in the first place. That if this many people around the world really think that what we are is so heinous, so vile, so grotesque that it inspires beatings and killings and imprisonments and disproportionate levels of homelessness, suicide, incarceration, sexual and domestic violence, that maybe I am wrong and they are right and everything about me is heinous, vile, grotesque. I cry into my pillow, which has a picture of Celine Dion on it, and don't know how to stop and feel so selfish and so disgusted at myself for even momentarily abandoning my queer siblings. Then I fall asleep and forget I ever felt that until I feel it again, another night, after another particularly bad encounter with violence.

I feel selfish when I compare myself to others who experience far more suffering than this. I feel embarrassed that I was punched in the face and can't go outside. I feel desolate that all the years I have spent building myself up against constant homophobia, able to take anything, have been undermined by one fist in the face. A hard fist. I feel a growing fear of men. I feel so loved by the women and queers in my life, and my wonderful, heartbreakingly kind brothers, James and Harry, and my sister, Danielle. I feel determined to both bury this, to wash it away like the words in my teenage notebook, but to also address it head on, unlike so many of my other feelings, which I push off the emotion cliff. I feel like I'll never be formidable. I feel like my heart has been broken and I don't have the energy to fix it.

27th April / le 27 avril

Some promises I've made to myself:

I'm not going to wear black; I'm not going to be scared to take up space; I'm not going to avoid make-up or drag any more; I'm not making sure there's no nail polish on my fingers any more, checking for tiny specks and frantically scratching them off when found; and I'm not going to put earrings on in the morning and then decide against it.

I'm going to work to find my femme energy, which I know is somewhere among all these brittle parts of myself, that feel like they've been stretched and peeled apart from each other and injected with fearfulness.

Yesterday, I thought of my mum, who used to tell me that she loved me but worried about me being attacked for looking a certain way or acting explicitly 'gay'. For a moment, I had a feeling that she was right and that I should have listened to her and given in, even though I knew the only way for me to survive was to set myself alight, make a spectacle of myself. I called her and told her what I was thinking. And she told me that she was wrong and that if I'd have listened to her I wouldn't be the person I am now and she would have felt eternally heartbroken for that.

'People like you are a beacon of beauty; you show so many of us just how beautiful the world can be. You have changed so many people's universes, don't ever forget it.'

We were both sobbing.

'Don't you dare change the way you are. You've worked so hard. Take them all down. Do it the way you always wanted to. Be loud. Do it for all of us who can't be or don't dare to be.'

I'm going to go out to get some food as Hatty is at work. I know I'm about to break all my promises and decide on an all-black health-goth kind of look, desperately camouflaging myself into the dusty streets of east London, but it's only been five days since I was boxed on my doorstep, so failing at them is absolutely fine.

May/mai

3rd May / le 3 mai

A note from my diary, this day last year:

> Last night I wore an actual nun's cassock and a dip-dyed
> wig to the gay club. Safe to say people weren't really
> into me in all my full-length black-sack glory, but I was
> feeling it so hard. Halfway through the night, all of us
> rejoining into a circle after various split offs and ram-
> pages through the different rooms of the club, Glamrou
> dared us all to play kiss-chicken – a game where you go
> in for the kiss and see who can hold for the longest.
>
> Glamrou was crap at it. Every time you got close
> enough they would flick their head away and laugh
> hysterically. Sometimes it's so liberating to behave like a
> teenager. In fact, not one pair made the kiss, all succumb-
> ing to the position of the chicken, except myself and Ace.
>
> After we'd come up for air we looked in each
> other's eyes, inhaled deeply and both, at the same time,
> exhaled a breathy 'Woah!', the world slowing around
> us, the sound of Loreen's 'Euphoria' muffling.
>
> I know my penchant for falling for friends and,
> worryingly, unlike the many frogs of gay dating gone
> by, this kiss felt like the kind that turned us both into
> each other's princess.

It's funny how some moments in our history dwindle into
insignificance, while some elongate and become long
stretched memories that exist in full technicolour, taking up
far more time than the seconds it took to do the deed.

Since I was attacked, Ace has all but moved in to Wally, there by my side most days and nights when he's not teaching young kids who've been kicked out of their schools to read and write. A literal saint. He's unquestioningly sacrificed his time to sit and watch shit videos with me, or read while I apply to various internships and jobs, or go to the shops to get me Nurofen or a tub of Häagen-Dazs Pralines and Cream. That's actually his favourite flavour, not mine – it makes me feel sick but I don't tell him that, and let him enjoy both the ice cream and the thought that he's doing the sweetest thing for me. Which he is.

Last night he was awake, reading, and I'd closed my eyes, nearing sleep. He brushed my hair from my brow and kissed my forehead and whispered, 'I really do love you.'[1] In written form it sounds painfully saccharine, but in the moment I decided to keep pretending I was asleep so as not to disturb his secret confession. So filmic. I'm Bridget, he's Darcy.

6th May / le 6 mai

The one good thing about my temporary agoraphobia is that I've had loads of time, when not consumed by dread, to apply for a ton of jobs. From internships[2] to social media

---

1 At this I got what I call a 'commitment erection', which is when you get an erection about emotional commitment. Just me?

2 Note that internships are the devil, a) exploiting free labour and b) allowing only privileged folk who can afford to work for free to do so.

positions,[3] from the PA to editors, to fashion cupboard assistants – I've been hurling my CV out left, right and centre. I even applied for a junior position at *Hello! Fashion*. Obsessed.

I've developed, also, a new obsessive skill: anxiously stalking editors and writers on Twitter and Instagram and submerging myself in their worlds in quite an unhealthy way. It's actually really embarrassing, and I'm unsure how I'll fare if I were ever to meet them – me knowing everything about their front-facing selves, them knowing literally nothing about me.

7th May / le 7 mai

When you're attacked you learn many things about the world, about its inequalities, its violences, its unfairnesses. You learn empathy. You learn to view the world through the lens of violence: what's given and what's received. But the most prophetic thing you learn, perhaps, is that, whether you like it or not, the world goes on.

I got a job!

Well, an internship, but it's paid and it's at a very high-profile fashion magazine. Let's call it *Chic*.[4]

Let it be known, in writing, that if I am to die and this diary be found: I have, right now, at this second, been offered a job at *Chic*.

Chic is the magazine my grandma used to buy for me

---

3 I don't know what's worse, though: an unpaid internship or a paid social media position?

4 lol, *Chic* ;)

every month, in which I'd fall deep into the pages: pages of Viktor & Rolf couture or Van Cleef & Arpels diamonds or Alaïa silhouettes or McQueen show reports or endless fantasises that took me far from where I was. It was one of the first things I ever saw that taught me that the world could be bigger than Lancaster. And every month, as it plopped through my letterbox, I got a glimpse of what I thought true luxury was. And, for someone who didn't realise they already had it in abundance back then – home, love, friends, smarts – it represented everything I would spend the next years of my life aiming for.

Funny how life can be so disparate: on the one hand I still morph into a trembling little deer at the thought of leaving the warehouse; on the other hand I've just been welcomed onto the first rung of a career I've wept over thousands of times. This is every fashion gay's dream. Now what to wear?

10th May / le 10 mai

Hey, I ran into your mum at Morrisons and she told me you're now the deputy editor of *Chic!*? Honestly amazing! Always knew you'd go far at school! If you ever have any openings I've always dreamed of working in fashion? And I'm so good at make-up now! xxx

Oh my God! Deputy editor at *Chic*? Are you kidding! So proud of you, queen; next time I'm in London you have to take me on a tour of the fashion rooms!! Maybe I could send you some ideas and stuff? Obviously no worries if not, just thought I'd offer! <3

Hi there, it's Linda – I used to teach you at Rock Solid
Sunday School! How are you doing? I added you
because I heard that you're now the deputy editor of
Chic magazine? Amazing news! Everyone here in
Lancaster always knew you'd go so far; you were born
to be famous!! Anyway, my daughter, you remember
Lara, is looking for work experience at the moment.
She's in Year 11 and I know she would just love to
work at *Chic*. How can she apply? Sorry if this is out
of the blue – but God gives to those who ask, I always
say. Let me know, L xx

Today I awoke to these three incredibly random messages,
from three incredibly random people. I called my mum,
wondering what on earth's gone on.

'Oh shit, yeah, it sort of got out of hand . . .' she explained.

It's really not like her to lie.

'I ran into Debbie – you know, that awful woman with
alopecia—'

'Mum, you don't need to mention her alopecia—'

'Anyway, she was being really boastful and awful about
her son who just got accepted onto an acting course in London and it just came out.'

'What did?'

'That you're now deputy editor of *Chic*. I didn't think
anyone would care, I was just trying to one up Debbie.'

She's the source of my unhealthily competitive side.

'Well, was it not enough to one up her with the fact I got
a beauty internship at *Chic*? I mean that's still a pretty big
deal.'

'Oh, I know, I know, and I don't want to diminish your achievement. But I just wanted to really stick the knife in, you know?'

'Well, what should I do now? Should I set them straight?'

'If you could just take one for my team this time, just tell them you're deputy editor, go on, for me? How embarrassing if everyone finds out I've been lying—'

'Mother, this is utterly terrible parenting. But yes, I'll do it for you.'

I've responded to all messages explaining that I am indeed deputy editor of *Chic* and that when I start my new role I'll do what I can about Lara's internship or Sunita's make-up skills. Here I am, a mere intern, but at home I'm the deputy editor. And I'm fine with it.

13th May / le 13 mai

In life there are some questions that are frankly too big, too monumental, to even consider tackling. I can usually conceptualise most things, work my way through them and around them. But the question of what to wear to your first day at a job at *Chic* is one of the few unanswerable questions. I would pray to God, but fashion's never been her strong suit.

The whole point of *Chic* is that it's culturally definitive in the fashion arena: it sets the trend,[5] doesn't follow, and while trends are reserved for the tiny, tiny few of us in the world who have bucketloads of money and time and taste

---

5 For rich white ladies.

(wealth and taste are so infrequently bedfellows), that is not me. It's also not the job of someone at *Chic* to be on trend; they must be ahead of it, surely? And, let's face it, while much of the produce of this British institution is somewhat staid, white-washed and anorexia-inspiring, within its walls it still houses some of the most influential people in the fashion world.

Over the week I'd laid out various options of various outfits, ranging from a giant leather bomber jacket embroidered with a very eighties paisley pattern to a jewel-toned fashion turban. I quickly scrapped the turban because cultural appropriation, and gave it back to my friend Violet who is very stylish, and we both agreed that, while it's Prada, the turban should be left to gather dust in the back of the wardrobe.

I'd settled on a long dress with a fringe at the bottom in black, Prada heels also donated to the cause by Violet, a trashy ruby necklace and a very oversized maroon bomber jacket. I wanted something that said both, 'I'm new here, but very cool' and 'Give me five years and I'll be editor-in-chief', which is why I added the rich white-woman jewels.

This morning, outfit ready, I stepped outside, in near full face – it's the beauty department, after all – clutching a Miu Miu patchwork tote that Violet also lent me, teetering in the Prada heels. I stopped, lit a fag, and felt momentarily terrified by my visibility.

I was basically in full drag on the morning commute, save for a wig and lashes. I took a moment and a deep breath, reminding myself that at the end of the terrifying journey was my first step to my future – and when I get to that future I can get cars everywhere, anyway. I galvanised myself: the outfit was more important than my safety. I've always been good at illogically ordering my priorities.

As we buzzed through the tunnel towards Bank on the DLR, I saw two men laughing at me, one of whom was taking my picture. It felt like my arse was going to fall out the bottom of my dress and I kept letting out little farts of fear.[6]

I tried to remind myself that this happens all the time, but couldn't quite hear it. 'Seriously, fuck off.' I hurled my rage down the train, direct like a laser beam.

'You talking to us, mate?' They were laughing. 'Why don't you fuck off, you fucking faggot?'

And then I did something I've never had the courage to do before. Addressing the sardine-like commuters on this packed train, I harnessed the potential power of the people:

'Hello, my fellow train riders. Sorry to disturb your journeys this morning, but I'd just like a show of hands as to who, in this scenario where these two men were taking pictures and laughing at me, thinks I should fuck off? Show of hands.'

At this only the two men, of about ninety, raised their hands.

'And who, of those of us who haven't voted yet, thinks indeed that these two men should, in fact, fuck off?'

The entire carriage, bar the two men, raised their hands straight to the sky, engaged fully in my voting system and saying things like, 'How dare you?' and 'If you don't like it, get off our fucking train.'

---

6 Made worse by the kind of clenching high heels force upon you.

Democracy, when done well, works.

Revolving doors. Reception. I was greeted by Gillian – *'not Jillian with a J sound, for God's sake, but Gillian like the gill of a fish'* – an Alexander McQueen scarf clinging to her incredibly posh, very long neck.

'Quick, it's morning briefing. Don't you speak, just listen.'

Everyone collected around a white table, every single decision-maker in the room as white as the table, and as posh as the calla lilies set at the centre.

'Bobbles: it's honestly all about bobbles. The nuovo hair-tie, the must-have luxe pony-puller, the bobble!'

The women around the table scribbled in their customised Smythson notebooks with the zeal of the twelve disciples listening to Jesus preaching the Sermon on the Mount.

I fought the urge to laugh, hard, at these once-inspired brains foaming at the mouth about bobbles. Literally bobbles.

'Do you mean like hair-ties? Would you not say they've always been in fashion?' I piped up.

All of the long-necked women craned toward me, eyes darting as if I'd just killed their children.

'And who are you?' the actual deputy editor queried.

'I'm the new beauty intern . . .' My genitals disappeared inside me like a snail into its shell.

'Well, girls, I think the new beauty intern should take the bobble story, don't you?' They all nodded their heads in support, as if they'd won at a game I didn't even know I was playing.

Joke's on them, as it turns out. It was a first-day byline – even if it was about bobbles.

17th May / le 17 mai

Okay, been thinking a lot about *Chic* and wondering how I might see past my infantile fantasy of what it meant to me as a teen queen. How do I now, a much more politically advanced me, tackle the racism and the sexism and the fattism that the magazine has upheld for near a century? 'Change it from the inside,' Hatty advised me.

In the room it is utter madness. Even after five days, I've noticed how people are blind to the inequalities that plague the industry, and the wider world. That's not everyone, of course, but so many of the older, white people who run the magazine are so cemented in their upper-middle-classness that the utterance of words like 'queer' or 'black' or 'equality' are met with a furrowed botoxed brow, deemed as *inappropriate* topics of conversation. I wish I could bring them all to Wally to meet Hatty and the Denims, and my other rad anarcho-queer friends, to show them real inappropriate conversation.

For instance, today, someone on the beauty desk told me that she thinks women of a certain age should have surgery, that it's a woman's 'responsibility' to age gracefully, 'and if that requires a knife, then so be it'. Despite Hatty's words ringing in my ears, I didn't dare speak back, and I definitely didn't want to raise the subject of misogyny or classism or ageism. Yes, surgery is great but by no means is it anyone's responsibility. It's not her fault; her name is, and I'm not kidding, Theodora – she had no chance.

There's one girl, Amnah, a fashion cupboard intern who is equally tearing her hair out. We're each other's only office allies – meeting up by the loos to have a moment of 'What in the fucking hell did she just say?' before going back to our menial tasks. Today those tasks were comprised of swiping different make-up samples across different smooth surfaces to see how they would smear, ready to be photographed like those beautiful glistening smudges of make-up or cut-up lipsticks you see on the glossy white pages of the magazine. It was pretty fucking satisfying, I shan't lie, decimating these expensive products into smudges and smears – the same impulse that makes you want to eat certain soaps or lip balms.

Anyway, there's a question the fashion industry really needs to ask itself, especially within the corridors of *Chic*: in order to work in this part of the industry why must we be required to compromise both morals and intellect?

Fashion and dress, at least for the communities I move in, have proven to be incredibly, irreversibly powerful tools of protest, of coding, communication – the hanky code, leather and latex wear, drag, gender non-conformity, that jacket worn by a member of ACT UP! in the eighties that read '*IF I DIE OF AIDS – FORGET BURIAL – JUST DROP MY BODY ON THE STEPS OF THE FDA*'. But here we flutter around with an air of superiority, as if we're solving world hunger when really the chance of an engaging conversation in this place is as likely as there being a woman of colour on the magazine's cover. The central feature in this month's issue is literally on types of butter.

Types. Of. Butter.

And this is what is important to women and basic baby-gays? I think absolutely not.

While I like the idea of changing things from the inside, the likelihood of that feels like it's disappearing quicker than my social life.

21st May / le 21 mai

Here it is: my magnum opus, my *Riverside Chaucer*, my *Complete Works of Shakespeare*, my Bible, my Beyoncé *Lemonade*. My indisputable peak.

It was 5 a.m. at the club last night when I first clocked the time and regretfully had to tear myself away from friends to make the long walk home, alone. About an hour and twenty minutes later I woke up, the bright May sun forcing the day upon me. I'd slept through my alarm, and I had thirty-six minutes to make it to morning briefing. My commute, if all goes well, is exactly twenty-four minutes door to door because the warehouse is in Zone 1, something I still can't quite believe.

Down to the wire, in the twelve minutes between waking up and when I must leave for work I must become army-general-like in my decision-making, even though I'm a pacifist. A decision had to be made:

1) A much-needed shower and time to pick the right outfit.
2) A much-needed hangover poo, a much-needed shower and no time to pick the right outfit.

As any good fashion queer knows: aesthetic is everything, so I, with absolute resolve, chose to bypass the poo.

How bad could it be?

I made it to work on time, the outfit was good – a trainer heel and red leather jacket – but while I sipped a coffee I felt the hangover poo edging toward the outside world, fuelled like a rocket by my first hit of caffeine.

The problem here, the real pressing problem here, is that you simply can't poo at *Chic*. Perhaps you can pop out a tiny pellet off the back of a discreet fart, while doing a sit-down wee, but the kind of mammoth, toxin-filled hangover poo I had brewing: not a chance.

I'm in an open-plan office. And it was a busy, hot day today. In the intense space between needing a constant IV feed of caffeine and there being no time to take a lunch break to find a place to poop I was stumped, the poo growing inside me, the pain from holding in my prairie dog worse than possibly imaginable.

But I kept on holding, tensing my pelvic floor muscles, an act I thought would eventually pay off beautifully in the favour of any future top lucky enough to score this queen.

At one point in the afternoon, I had genuinely reached a state of poo-induced euphoria. I was honestly floating on air, had pushed past any human limit and was into a space of true bodily resilience. I was James Franco in *127 Hours*, I was Linford Christie running the hundred metres. I was Jessica Ennis bringing it home for Great Britain. I was Jesus, a prophet. I was a mother lifting a car under which her child was stuck, finding strength not in her physicality but deep within her soul.

For a moment, I was God.

Then, around 4 p.m., I hit a low. A severe low. I slumped, my brow sweating, my fingertips oily, my ass muscles so exhausted from lactic acid overproduction that I no longer had agency over them.

I was about to go down in fashion legend as 'that queen who shat her dress at *Chic*'.

And then a light appeared, my editor:

'You look so unwell you're making me feel unwell. You can go early if you want; I think we're done for the day.'

I nearly broke down, but kept my composure.

Tube. Heat. Poo. Pain. So much pain. A vow never to drink again. Tube. Heat. Poo. Pain.

I arrived at Liverpool Street and broke into a run.

A Wasabi – no loo.

A Santander – obviously no loo, that's a bank.

A KFC – a loo! Halle-loo!

I'd found the Holy Grail and it was a single empty loo. I was finally free from the shackles of my poo oppression.

Flush.

The water started to rise, rise, rise and slowly, to my horror, it started to brim over the bowl and onto the floor of the tiny cubicle that opens right onto the restaurant. With it, to my utter chagrin, my hangover log dislodged from its position and was lifted out of the bowl and onto the water-flooded floor, still fully intact. One hardy poo.

The only course of action was to leave this poo there, on the floor of the loo; me. A terrible person – I did not think for a second about the poor person who would have to clean up the contents of my night out.

I had to escape.

I opened the door, ready to make a dash for the stairs, but before I could, the water flooded out ahead of me, through the doorway, carrying with it my giant poo, right into the packed restaurant. It travelled surprisingly far on the back of the water, like those stones in curling (the nichest sport) as they slow toward their destination.

Screams; cries; one man is so disgusted that he throws down the remnants of his chicken leg and walks out, stepping over my poo, leaving the beautifully crisp yet greasy secret recipe skin on the table. I think for a second that nothing would make me put down a piece of KFC chicken without eating all the skin, poo in the room or no poo in the room.

This was it. I could either run from my problem or face it head on. And so I went into autopilot mode, cleared my throat: 'My apologies! We've had a little accident, but it'll be sorted any second.'

I dived back into the loo and wrapped my hands in a whole toilet roll. I paced back gingerly, careful not trip on the flood, approached the poo, stared at it, desperate not to let it get the better of me. I bent down, knees clicking, the whole restaurant literally silent and aghast, watching as I took my poo into my own hands. Watching as I took control of my destiny.

I lifted the poo, still intact (!!), and carried it with me back to the loo, broke it in half, dropped it and flushed it, along with my trauma.

I was in such shock that I became tremendously dignified in the face of this utterly indescribable experience. I washed my hands, apologised to the good patrons of KFC Liverpool Street and left the restaurant into the world, nobody on the street aware of this life-changing occurrence that happened not a hundred feet away.

With such a story also comes the most wonderful personal litmus test: if they don't love me pooing in KFC then they don't deserve me.

And, more than that, I learned the irreplaceably valuable lesson that if I can survive that, I can survive anything. Everything I ever need is inside of me. I am changed, but I'll still never poo at *Chic*.

This has been my magnum opus, my *Riverside Chaucer*, my *Complete Works of Shakespeare*, my Bible, my Beyoncé *Lemonade*. I have reached my indisputable peak.

23rd May / le 23 mai

I think about my funeral all the time. Literally *all the time*. My friends know now, if I'm zoned out and looking a little on the emotional side, I'm probably thinking about my own send-off.

I think of how utterly devastating it would be. I don't want any of this *let's celebrate their life, let's all wear yellow and have a shot in their memory* shit. No, I want emotional devastation. I want 'Change' by the Sugababes, performed by every Sugababe ever. All seven/six(?) of them.

Today we were sat in a read-through of the next issue – which my boss oddly invited me to, even though she evidently likes me less than her husband, who she argues with over the phone on the hour every hour. He sounds like an uncompromising wanker who passes all his fragile masculinity on to her, which she then channels on to her team.

Anyway, I was in the read-through – flicking through page after page of young, white, upper-class playwrights and models and thinking about my funeral because it's far more interesting than anything in the pages – and at that moment the art director zoomed in on me: 'You, beauty boy, any thoughts?'

Utterly gobsmacked, and misgendered. I hadn't been asked to speak since day one, when Gillian – who was now glaring violently my way – banned me from using my voice.

'I think it's really pretty. But I think, if I'm not mistaken, almost every single person in the pages is white? Is that not a little irresponsible of us?'

And, there in that boardroom, I no longer had need to plan my funeral, for every editor just buried me alive in their heads. No memorial service. Not a Sugababe in sight.

And so I cleared my desk, swiping a lovely Tom Ford lipstick in the process and a La Mer lip balm. I have been gently dismissed from an internship at *Chic*. I have been relieved of my moral compromise. I'm aware of the privilege in being able to pick and choose the work you will and will not do, and there at *Chic* I'd definitely breached various political parameters I thought were set in stone for me when I entered the all-white white office on day one. I'm lucky to have the CV points, but I'm luckier to have been let go.

Turns out your twenties is perhaps about learning that

the things you wanted aren't really ever what you thought they might be.

26th May / le 26 mai

Since *RuPaul's Drag Race* got all the basics hyped about drag, the earning potential for queens has somewhat exponentially risen, thank God. The number of brands and companies desperate to align themselves with the LGBTQIA+ cause is staggering. As our presence and our market influence grows, each awful pinkwashing, patronising campaign becomes more transparent, brands happy to feature rainbows and glitter and anything that signifies queerness without engaging with the reality of things like, say, AIDS or trans issues or anal sex or people of colour. The world is willing to accept the clean side of gay life: namely white, beautiful, successful, healthy men. And if the straights love anything it's a drag queen: one who is fab, pink and glam – never filthy, political or intelligent. It makes them feel transgressive by proxy.

It's a hard line to prance, really, because with this shifting lens of 'tolerance' also comes the aforementioned pay cheque. I have a friend who danced all night, for £400, at a Morgan Stanley Christmas party. I have a bunch of friends who dressed as giant drag squares, crosses and circles and bopped up and down on a PlayStation float for the duration of London's apolitical Pride parade. Morgan Stanley. PlayStation. This is how a drag artist makes money, atop other means like bar work or graphic design or occasionally, for the super-smart, having a sugar daddy.

The thing about these jobs is that I don't know a single queen who can afford to turn them down. Better to pay rent and dance for Nando's and still be able to make your rad art.

That's why when a friend of mine called, offering me a job singing at the National Horticultural Society, hearing that I'd quit *Chic* (the story I told everyone, to make me look much more principled than I actually am), I accepted – for the princely fee of £350.

It was hell on earth. I assumed it would be a glamorous affair – 'how posh!' I thought when I Googled the society. I soon learned that that was merely the building in which the event was housed; the event turned out to be pokeryou. com's annual piss-up.

Imagine for a second, if you will, a room full of men who invented an online poker playing site on which you can choose to have your dealer wear a bra and knickers while doling out your cards. Imagine for a second, if you please, being a drag queen in that space after they've all finished dinner and moved on to after-after-dinner drinks.

It's safe to say that some of the words uttered were not words of praise for this queen singing their lungs out. I was an exotic fruit, a circus freak, an accessory ripe for the abusing – leaving with an arse so slapped by passers-by it hurt to sit down in the Uber.

So, with the £450 cash (I demanded an extra hundred – danger money), I decided the only thing to rid myself of these dreadful ass slaps and the visuals of these clammy men creaming over Russian roulette tables was to book a flight to Berlin. Lily is there for a month at the moment and so I choose to spend my money rather than save it – pushing the pounds made from the bleakest gig into some seriously queer joy.

28th May / le 28 mai

Berghain, Berlin. The eternal Mecca for queer clubbers from around the world. The ex-power station turned impossible-to-get-into club. Filled with all the expected druggy techno world stereotypes: Rick Owens queers in black drapery thinking they're God's gift to creativity but in fact they haven't actually done or made anything of note in the last five years but think a nose ring is queer activism; Berlin daddies with a European kind of intellectual masculinity, awfully dated nineties tribal tattoos, well-sculpted beards, and more leather harnesses and jock straps than T-shirts. They often love G – the gay party drug that doubles up as alloy cleaner. There's the thirsty twinks who finally, after five tries, make it through the door and up the stairs and into Panorama Bar, who somehow all have enough money to be wearing head-to-toe Vetements; arty girls who adore techno and love that shop Weekday, who sport an array of haircuts comprising of angular lines and are likely studying at the RCA and once modelled in a Doc Martens campaign. There's the old-school clubbers in their fifties who smell like sweaty tights but are really into the party and shout things like 'Berlin non-shhtoppppp!' as you pass them. There's the very, very rare straight dude who sticks out like a sore thumb and for once has no traction in the space; and then there's that one drug dealer in the second-floor loos who literally never leaves. There are many tribes within this tribe.

If you've never heard of Berghain it's because, obviously, you're a loser.

No, I'm kidding. But among queer folk it's a place of legend, which opens on a Thursday night and doesn't stop until Monday. Queers in Berlin call Sunday-morning Berghain 'church'. One time I saw a fully naked woman being carried out of there by three bouncers into a snowy Berlin dawn, screaming valiantly 'I was the Queen of Party!' in a thick German accent. And you know what – she was. It inspires such devotion in people that they literally move to Berlin for Berghain.[7] I knew this one quite niche girl from uni who disappeared into a Berghain stupor for her whole year abroad and returned shockingly skinny, hooked on gay party drugs, with an experimental psycho-geographic dissertation whose title was, no joke: 'Berghain Has My Soul'.

This shit is some strong shit.

The queue has never been a problem in my experience, although it's known as the hardest door in the world. The key is to stay chilled. I have a friend – the journalist one, Amelia – who once got in wearing a top and jeans from Brandy Melville: not the usual look of the Berghain set, but she's so chilled she just strolled through. Another friend of mine, Jacob – an incredibly beautiful, cool model and the perfect Berghain client – was rejected because he was so nervous. It was fine, though: the next night we arrived and walked him right in.

The key is to avoid any over-the-top gestures or evidence of nervousness, otherwise the famous bouncer, known for

---

7 All while claiming to be artists, of course.

his savagery, will sniff you out and, once he has, there's not a hope in hell of getting past the big steel doors and inside the rumbling beast. As you slowly trudge up the dirt path to this huge techno machine, the windows crackling under the pressure of the bass from some internationally renowned DJ, you watch as he turns people away in droves – their dreams of euphoria dashed, their nights ruined.

'Keep your cool,' Lily and I whispered to each other. Neither of us has ever been refused, but there's always a slim chance. We got to the door.

'How many?'

'*Zwei*,' I said in my terrible German accent.

'Go.' He gestured with his hands to scoot through the door. And we were in, where queertopia awaits.

Inside, it's a cavernous, gigantic, loud place that sits at the intersection of brutalism, dystopia, utopia and pretension. Take your eyes off your partner for a second and they'll be lost to a sea of ecstasy-jacketed dancers, clouded in the smoke from their thousands of cigarettes. There's the garden to relax in, the sofas by the loos, the two humongous, indescribably big dance rooms in which the floors bounce and at least one drag queen loses her wig. There's no feeling quite like how cool you feel when you're dancing all night inside the guts of Berghain. There are the sex rooms – decorated in that very Berlin vintage butcher shop kind of way – all meat hooks, concrete and plastic-flapped doors. Lily and I frequented them sporadically through the night, sucking the odd dick there, rimming the odd butthole here. She's into gay men at the moment, 'plus there's just so many more for the picking in Berlin, and they have a much more sophisticated view of gender here. All this for twelve euros? A bargain.'

While the door policy sounds awfully savage – I always feel so sad for the folks who spend months planning their trip down to Berghain, some flying from as far as Australia only to be rejected at the door – Lily reminded me that a ticket to utopia is not an easy one to get; it actually costs much more than €12 entry and a choker from Urban Outfitters. And she's right. 'You have to have earned this experience, and our lives have been spent earning the privilege. We deserve something.'

She's now sleeping on a mattress on the floor in our apartment for the weekend, and I'm sipping coffee, looking out the window as the sun sets over a slightly wobbly-looking Berlin – maybe that's just my hangover. Must get ready – another all-black outfit and a smudge of eyeliner, I imagine – we're going again tonight.

June/juin

1st June / le 1 juin

~~~~~~~~~~~~~~~~~~~~~~~

As we fly through the air from Berlin to London – Lily deciding to ditch her drug binge and come meet everyone in
London – I'm thinking about queerness.[1] I tried to ask Lily
what she thinks it means, but she just told me shut the fuck
up as she hadn't slept properly in over thirty-six hours.

I couldn't sleep. I fucking hate flying, and the plane is
currently rattling through the clouds, reassuring us nervous
folk that we aren't in control. Hence why I'm writing now,
thinking about queerness, trying to take my mind off what
feels like impending death.

Queerness is by definition indefinable. People who don't
understand it find that a really annoying thing to hear –
people who are desperately trying to work out how to be
queer so they can have as much fun as all the queers.

It used to be an insult. It's also a term used to describe a
huge swathe of academic thinking – queer theory – and a lot
of that is about subverting structures and questioning everything like time and gender and our roles in society and
binary modes and stuff. I was obsessed with the latter at
university,[2] and was a receiver of the former the whole time
at high school.

But, for most of us (well, me at least), queerness doesn't
live in lofty theory books or the vocal cords of bullies. It lives,
instead, in everything we do and say and feel. For me everything feels queer because my experience of it is queer.

~~~~~~~~~

1   Lol, when am I not?
2   No wonder I failed vet med: 'Hey, I can't diagnose your gerbil but
have you read Judith Butler?'

That feeling is especially recharged in a place like Berlin.

Now, there's nothing worse than a stereotypical Berlin obsessor, who you can often find in the corner of gay bars in Dalston wearing a mesh vest and sports shorts, devouring any and every chance to slip Berlin into the conversation: 'I love your socks. They remind me of my fuck-buddy in Berlin. Oh, you've never been? Berlin is like my spiritual home. I love its energy, the streets are so wide and the drugs are so pure and the history is so present and the men are so virile yet tender and everyone's an artist and I love how the brutalism of the East side reflects my inner brutalism and is the rectum a grave?'

All this crucially misses the crux of what does, in fact, make Berlin such a queer haven. And that crux is the fact that Berlin has a really strong relationship with fun. There's so much value and sanctity placed on the idea of partying, euphoria and nihilism.

So many of their spaces are predicated on exploring and accepting pleasure that – in comparison to somewhere like London or New York whose priority is success, money, capitalism – you are taken to places it's not possible to reach anywhere else.

And, when so much of being queer consists of things that are definitely not fun, it can't be emphasised enough just how liberating, powerful and radical having *real* fun can really be. It's better than any drug, better than any drink, almost better than cigarettes, and definitely better than an unspeakably dull job at *Chic*.

3rd June / le 3 juin

'It was genius. I looked to my side and there's Lily in the same orgy as me.'

Hatty and Ace laughed as I revelled in retelling mine and Lily's outrageous sex stories from Berlin over dinner tonight. We had gathered for impromptu family fajitas so Ace and Hatty could finally meet Lily.

'Honestly. It was so liberating: the boundaries between platonic and sexual love really fell away. Lily and I had never entertained the idea of group sex together before but it was actually very, very freeing,' I said.

'I've been saying for months that we should start a radical masturbation/pleasure group, once monthly, at Wally,' Hatty chimed in, her eyes glistening like they do every time she hears a new, exciting depiction of how far the limits of queerness can stretch. 'Would anyone else be into it?'

Everyone went a little quiet, and then Lily said, 'I mean we *just* met, and I do technically have a boyfriend. His rule is that anonymous group sex is fine, but with people I know it's not.'

'But a group wank? Like exploring pleasure?' Hatty pleaded, desperately wanting her idea to take off.

More silence. Personally, I was into the idea, but with Ace in the room there falls a somewhat awkward air whenever sex together, in any form, is brought up. There are moments when the option appears – like in kiss-chicken that time, or when we kissed on the last day in his parents' house – but most of the time even touching is out of the question. It's that thing where your legs meet under the table at a restaurant or your knees knock when you're in the cinema absolutely hating Wes Anderson's *The Grand Budapest Hotel*, and a surge of electricity and awkwardness zings through your body and you can do nothing but jolt away from each other. So, yes, the mention of sex is out of the question.

I decided, instead, to bulldoze the conversation by airing more extreme sex stories from my life of late. There was the Grindr guy who wanted to rim my unwashed butthole, so I let him but didn't really enjoy it myself. He did, though, which made me smile. 'Bless him, I think he actually wanted me to shit in his mouth but he didn't dare ask and I definitely wasn't going to offer; I'd had enchiladas for lunch.'

There was the guy who was obsessed with my balls and spent an actual hour sucking them and sort of pressing on my gooch trying to find my prostate but missing it. 'He did find it, though, when he fucked me. He just didn't know he had.'

Then there was the Irish guy who was unusually muscly – not usually my vibe, and not usually a body type I could get. It then became pretty clear that the reason he wasn't scoring most men, and had settled for chubby me, is because he had about as much charm as tonsillitis, and he spent the whole of our meet with his phone on loudspeaker trying to get through to Hackney council because his central heating was broken. 'And we both came in unison when the automated voice said, "You are number thirteen in the queue, your call is very important to us," and then he burst into heaving sobs and screamed at me to get out. I wanted to stay to see if he was okay, to coax some of his gay shame out into the open, but he was adamant that I left, immediately.'

And then there's this other guy, who I actually met in Berlin but lives in London. 'His name's Peter and he works as a librarian at UCL. We had really beautiful sex, actually, like really pleasure-focused sex. I'm really into him, I thi—'

'That's the time, fuck, it's eleven, I have to go,' Ace erupted, before leaving in a huge rush – dropping a tenner on the table for the dinner and drinks, then disappearing.

'Woah,' as the door clicked, 'he's clearly very hung up on you, queen,' Lily advised, from her objective position.

'What? No. He just had to get home for work tomorrow,' I replied.

They both looked at me, raising their eyebrows, as if to say 'grow up and do something about this'.

'Was it the sex stories?'

'No, it was the guy Pete. His face literally turned puce at the idea of you with someone else romantically,' Hatty urged. 'Go after him . . . now!'

I slipped on my shoes and ran, which I never do, out the door and toward the station. I saw Ace in the alleyway between Tesco and Efes Turkish restaurant, standing still, evidently upset. I had been insensitive. Sometimes I think I speak that way in front of him to hurt him. It takes two to tango, but sometimes I just step on his feet.

We faced each other silently, momentarily lost for words. Then Ace took a deep breath, as if he'd made a decision to open up. 'I know it's all my fault, I know that, and I know I backed off when you made yourself available,' Ace explained emotionally, 'but I just hate the idea of you developing feelings for another person than me. I feel like I've trashed all this.'

'Well, do you want this?'

'I don't . . .'

He paused.

'I don't know.'

He paused again.

'I don't know if we should just draw a line under this.'

And then we kissed. By a giant blue wheelie bin, which someone had comically graffitied the Prada logo onto, in an alleyway that smelled overwhelmingly of piss. And none of that mattered because we were kissing and not drawing a line under this.

I'd rather not know than draw a line. Purgatory is better than hell.

10th June / le 10 juin

Ace and I have these two genius friends who still use the term 'fag hag'. Literally everyone else I know has ditched the label for being offensive, degrading, misogynist and predicated only on a woman's relation to a gay man. It's bleak. But these two, Laurie and Chelsea, adore it, knowingly. They're like Patsy and Eddie – chain-smoking, glorious women who are actually killing their careers while also popping up in different locations every weekend on Instagram. So, naturally, when Ace and I were invited over for dinner we were incredibly excited.

I'm currently not working on any writing stuff, and I was in the throes of chasing £400-worth of invoices from last month, so the promise of a free meal is like manna from heaven. And so Ace and I took the train to Brixton. We've spent the week apart after I sent a very intense text message to him the day after we kissed by the bin. I thought it was super chill, but when I read it back that evening with Cecily and Ellie and Lily, they all shook their heads in disappointment. Apparently it read as though I was asking for a relationship because I'd said, 'Let's just see where this goes!'

I fucking hate texting.

Anyway, Ace and I were kind of awkwardly moving around each other on the walk to Laurie and Chelsea's place, but after three courses of oddly paired foods and a shit ton of wine we were a little more relaxed, now actually able to look each other in the eye.

After dinner, in vintage style, we decided to play this game we used to play at university all the time in order to legitimise our bogus decision-making – *Consult the iPod.* Essentially you ask a question you don't know the answer to – Will I ever find love? Am I going to be a successful journalist? etc – and press shuffle, the first song providing the answer to your unanswerable question.[3]

Laurie: 'Will John ever find me truly attractive again, after my shit and menses extravaganza?'[4]

iPod: 'Reflection' from *Mulan*. We all decided it must be

---

3 Others call this therapy but I'm too broke for that.
4 Earlier in the evening she'd been recounting a story where she shat on the floor and dropped her full mooncup on top of the shit and her boyfriend walked in. Incredible!

a message about loving yourself in order to be loved by someone else.

Me: 'Was I right to leave *Chic*?'

iPod: 'Sisters Are Doing It for Themselves' by Eurythmics. Frankly, a great answer.

Chelsea: 'Was I right to end it with the giant duke?'[5]

iPod: 'Living for the Weekend' by Hard-Fi. None of us like this song any more, on account of the fact we're no longer sixteen, so we shuffled again.

iPod: 'Blue Velvet' by Bobby Vinton. Shuffled again. (Number one rule of the game is that you shuffle until you get the answer you want.)

iPod: 'I've Got the Power' by Snap. Perfect.

Ace: 'There's a guy I like, it's complicated, and I don't know what to do.'

We all assumed he was talking about me, and the room tensed up as we waited for the iPod's choice:

iPod: 'Young and Beautiful' by Lana del Rey. Not sure what this means.

But it was evident Ace did. At this, he swiftly exited the room, while picking up his phone and uttering a firm: 'Right! Here goes.'

All of us, somewhat baffled he hadn't planted a wet one on me, listened silently as we heard Ace making a phone call in the next room. We heard him coming back, none of us quite sure where he'd been and who he was talking to. The door opened, and to make it look like we hadn't obviously

---

5 Chelsea had just broken up with an actual duke because his dick was just too big.

been talking about him, Chelsea, best foot forward, asked: 'Have you ever sucked a really smelly dick?'

But the conversation didn't flow. All of us were baffled, and we waited for Ace to explain his somewhat odd move.

'That was William. He's out dancing, over the road at Hootananny's. I'm gonna go meet him.'

A palpable feeling of shock, a real blow, engulfed the room.

He packed his bag; he left. Going off to claim his prize. I spent the next few hours weeping onto the remnants of dinner while weaving through my humiliation, as Chelsea shook watery espresso martinis and Laurie handed me cigarettes and lit them with her Zippo lighter, which has a picture of her own breasts printed on it.

11th June / le 11 juin

I got a commission today to write about being gay and holding hands in the street. It's great because it's cash in the bank, and it's kind of aligned with my interests. It's also frustrating, though, because I had pitched a piece about this community of late-teen fisting gays who live in San Francisco, but my editor thought it was 'too much'. While I'm not a nineteen-year-old fisting bottom, it's baffling to me that people would rather read an article about the politics of holding hands in public versus taking a fist in the ass.

But those words – 'too much' – sting, in any context. A lot of my life I've been treated certain ways – either fetishised or fetishised then rejected – because of being too much. Naturally, I'm feeling burned by Ace's sleight last night, so I started weeding out ways I've been *too much* over this incredibly strange, and somewhat exhilarating, time we've spent semi-courting each other. Was the text I sent after we kissed too much? Or is my big body too much? Is the way I speak or dress too much?

Thinking back over past rejections, this was kind of the theme of them all.

There was the time in Benidorm, back in 2010, when I went on holiday with my girlfriends from school to celebrate the end of our AS levels. From my diary at the time:

17 July 2010, Benidorm

I'm feeling fucking tragic after last night.

So, all eleven of the girls descended on the strip dressed to kill. Matt and I demanded we go to a gay bar because we were intent on finding some other gay guys somewhere on the face of the planet! And the men here are so hot, like so chavvy and muscular and have really sexy tattoos like the lion on the England flag and stuff. I just go weak at the knees for manly men!!

Anyway, when we got there the weirdest thing happened: as we were going in the door Matt grabbed hold of my hand, only for a second, and then squeezed it. We both looked into each other's eyes, both unsure what to make of it but deffo feeling something. Half totally wanting it, half knowing that if people at school found out it would be a mega problem.

Anyway, I'm not sure if it's a thing at this point, and then we started dancing together and Matt was wearing these shorts that made his dick look really

bulging and he kept like pointing it at me. We were so
drunk, and even tho we def know that we have weird
feelings for each other we never thought these were
sexy feelings. He asked me to go to the loo, and we sat
on a sicky-smelling leather sofa and I just decided to
fucking tell him that I was looking at his bulge. He
replied saying that he didn't think we would really work
as a pair and that he just can't see us together. It's so
embarrassing because I ran home crying even though
I didn't even know if I felt it in the first place. Anyway
now he's at the pool and he's reading my *Belle de Jour*
book and I'm too mortified to go down and join them.

A side note – I am absolutely obsessed with my old diaries.
They are the bleakest thing ever and I honestly open every
paragraph with the word 'anyway'. I especially can't believe
I would use words like 'chavvy' and put a heart under every
single exclamation mark and glorify manly men. When I
look back at myself all those years ago I don't really remember what it felt like to actually be that person.

I do remember feeling chronically single and achingly
desperate to find boys who, through their adoration, might
prove to me that all that self-loathing and inability to see
myself as worthy of romantic love was just your classic
pubescent hormone rollercoaster. I always assumed that all
those problems would disintegrate the moment I found a
relationship. By the time I was eighteen and off to university, I was the only member of my schoolgirl group – 'the
bezzaz' as we said then, in the north – who hadn't had a
significant relationship. They were all coupled up, having

sex, wondering about their futures together. I left high school already feeling like too much. But, as one does, I stepped into my outrageousness, my too muchness. And surprisingly this brought me some wonderful friends.

But when it came to dating, while the best things about me were the big things, the too-much things, I spent a while after Matt working out how to be smaller in a relationship. That's how I met Jake. God. Jake.

Here's how that went:

29 November 2011, Cambridge

I have been dating this man called Jake. Thus far the men in Cambridge have either been science nerds who can't really speak but just look at you with a kind of intensity that either means they want to kill you or rim you, or Tory douchebags. Jake is a medic, he's from Kent and he's camp and very sociable, and votes Labour. It's all win-win.

Until Tuesday things were going great. We had been on a bunch of dates and he'd even changed his profile picture to one of us together at a club. After our seventh date, on Monday, he came back to my room and we had anal sex for the first time. It was beautiful and really intimate and, as we fell asleep and he stroked my hair, he whispered, 'I think I'm falling for you.' I reciprocated, and naturally was on cloud nine. I felt like I'd found someone who actually wanted to be with me.

On Tuesday I texted him to see if he wanted dinner. No reply.

On Wednesday I texted him again to suggest a drink. No reply. He changed his profile picture back to one of himself looking drunk in a giraffe onesie. For some reason my critical faculties didn't kick in at this.

On Thursday I texted him a third time to ask if everything was okay. No reply. I was so distraught I had to leave a neurobiology supervision, and lied to my tutor that a made-up auntie had just passed away. I'm going to hell.

On Friday I texted him again, somewhat desperately. No reply. I was going crazy. Crying all the time, half-hoping he was dead then I didn't have to face up to the fact that a guy who would actively choose to publicise his ownership of a giraffe onesie had in fact rejected me.

But tonight, Sunday, I decided it was time to take matters into my own hands. It was pouring down outside and I was in my room pretending to revise, in reality obsessively going over every single detail of what had happened on Monday night. Once more, I texted him: 'Hey, I'm next door at Chelsea's, can I come over for a chat?' A lie.

A reply! What the fuck?

'Sure. In half an hour?'

I got dressed, backcombed my hair and applied some Benefit Hoola, and headed over in a cab.

'I'm sorry I didn't reply this week,' he said. 'I've just been thinking a lot about things and I don't think me and you are going to work out. You know, I'm a doctor – I'm clinical, I'm busy, I am looking for stability.

You're just so much to take on and I realised I couldn't see you and me outside of our bedrooms.'

Stunned. But oddly not surprised. Wishing he was actually dead. I got up to leave, when – 'But before you go, if you want to give me a blowjob or something, that would be nice. For old time's sake?'

'Are you fucking kidding me? Go fuck yourself.'

And so we're over. Another relationship in tatters because I'm too much for someone. I have always been enjoyed as an idea, but never as a reality.

I was already internalising this overwhelming feeling that I was too much, even though I thought I'd learned perfectly, after my mishap with Matt in high school, how to make myself small enough to be desirable. I always prioritised the other guy in the conversation, I always dressed on the less outrageous side when I was with someone, I always agreed with their taste in music even though I think the Beatles are wholeheartedly dull.[6]

It's not something I've left behind, really. I am always trying to reduce myself to accommodate the insecurities of other gay men. Ace was the first example of someone who I didn't make myself small around. Then there was Ethan.

19 January 2012, on a train from London to Cambridge

I had an interview with a celebrity stylist, to assist her on her next job. It went pretty well. I FaceTimed Ethan,

---

6   Don't @ me.

as he told me to call him once the interview was over, and he said he had someone to introduce me to.

That's funny, he didn't ask about my interview. He was in bed, early morning, and he was topless – looking incredibly sexy and smart at the same time, there in his flat in Kreuzberg, Berlin. He turns the front-facing camera to his side. 'This is Phillip, my new boyfriend!'

'Hallo! How are you? I've heard so much about you!' Phillip is the last person I want to hear from right now.

'I'm good! But my train's here, I have to go! Call you soon, sorry!'

I then spent the next two hours performing my sadness on the train back to Cambridge, weeping gently as I listened to 'Stay' by Rihanna, pretending to be in a movie of my life – that's a much easier way to cope with yet another round of rejection. This is what heartbreak feels like. Ethan, I think, is the one. Well, was the one. Whatever the one means.

And these rejections are the bigger ones. This list isn't exhaustive – it doesn't include text breakups, men who left during the first date, those who saw me and my false nails when I arrived at their door as organised on Grindr and said, 'This isn't really my thing, mate, sorry.'

And then, of course, there's Ace. A rejection that has been more a work in progress – a slow chipping away at a block of marble until it's now formed something really rather ugly and painful and full of confusion. I have repeatedly put my faith in the idea that someone's reciprocated love might be enough to excoriate all of the negative feelings I've internalised about myself, but every time I do I end up not only with more, but with the old ones confirmed – tattooed over my insides like the big butt of a cosmic joke.

There's no hope for Ace and me any more. We've both ensured in varying ways that there's no real chance a relationship could work. Each time he goes back to William or I reach for Grindr and an outrageous dinner-party retelling, it's as if we're taking out the other's heart and tenderising it with a steak mallet. We've decimated any chance of a relationship: if it's this painful when we're not together, imagine what it would be like if we were.

But, funnily, every time it hurts a little less. I can't tell if it's because we're both becoming increasingly immune to the other's thoughtlessness – like how we're all hyperdesensitised to pictures of human atrocity in the news – or because we're slowly remoulding what was once a feeling of endless potential into a huge vat of bile and resentment.

14th June / le 14 juin

Thousands of people gathered in Old Compton Street, Soho, last night to honour the forty-nine people who lost their lives on Sunday morning in an Orlando nightclub in the biggest mass shooting in US history.

I was there with Hatty, Glamrou and the rest of the Denims, Ellie, Cecily, Violet, Pak and William.

For this night we were all family. Any dynamics disappeared as we paid homage to the queers our community had lost on such brutal grounds.

At 7 p.m. the sound of a single whistle pierced the tension, and silence fell across the crowd, which spanned the entirety of the street, for a minute's silence. Wild cheers, applause, and streams of tears followed as a rainbow of balloons were released into the sky, one for each fatality. The sound of the gay men's chorus echoed off the houses with their rendition of 'Bridge Over Troubled Water'.

'I have never been a rainbow kind of lesbian,' Ellie said through tears, 'but right now I feel like part of that rainbow.' It is incredibly infrequent that so many people who fall under the umbrella of LGBTQIA+ have cause, and a space, to congregate. In a community that experiences so much continued oppression and can feel so fractured, last night's vigil felt like a moment of unity.

When spaces of sanctuary are attacked and invaded, it is up to our community to come out in force and recreate our own sanctuaries. On Monday night that is what London did, in a global act of solidarity with Orlando, specifically the Lantinx LGBTQIA+ community.

Once the vigil had finished, the streets remained full: people were voguing, lighting candles, and singing their odes to the lost lives. Spirits were shattered at the atrocity of the shootings, but raised by the remarkable sense of cohesion between us.

As queer people, our lives are a fight and a continual cycle of forgiveness against those who attack and oppress us. This moment was painful yet bittersweet: for once, we were allowed a space, to be at the centre of the conversation. It's tragic how it takes such violence to make people perhaps stop and think that life for LGBTQIA+ folk might not be all pink pounds and sequins. If London's vigil proved anything, it's that love, togetherness, strength in numbers, and forgiveness will help us heal after hate, as much as I hate to write such a fucking cliché. After our collective mourning is over, however, we must look forward and ask what changes have to be made globally to prevent attacks like Orlando from happening in the future. We need to mourn, but we also need action.

I was asked to write a news article about the vigil for an online media outlet, so I spent a while recording the feelings of people from the crowd. I wanted to write a few of them in here for safekeeping:

Akowsa: *'We had to be here tonight, for the queer people who lost their lives in Orlando, for their families, to show that we care about ending hatred. We need to do more things like this, to show that we are here and we won't go away'*

Alison: *'It's scary people are on edge, and it did cross my mind: is this the smartest thing to do? Do we want to congregate? But if not, when? We have to come together, because without that, there's nothing else.'*

Alice: *'As a queer woman, I don't feel separate here tonight. Maybe just for tonight, but all the borders which separate us in the LGBTQ community have fallen away, and any animosity has disintegrated, which is amazing.'*

Tyron: *'There's a sense from a lot of white queers that a lot of battles have been won, particularly for those from a middle-class background; and I think this has shaken a* lot of people out of that view. It's really important now for the LGBTQ community to self-analyse. We are making things difficult for each other. Something which has been glossed over in the press is that this was also targetting people of colour, trans men and women of colour, Hispanics, black people. And you know there's still a lot of bigotry against our fellow queers within our own movement; "no fats, no femmes, no Asians, no blacks" – we see that all the time.'

Sarah: 'In all honesty, I'm not sure why people are reluctant to name this an LGBTQ hate crime. I think people are reluctant to think that hate crimes still happen, but in reality more than a hundred LGBT people still experience a hate crime every week in the UK, and many more go unreported. Violent hate crimes are rising, and they happen every single day'

16th June / le 16 juin

A phone call with my dad. Went something like this:

'Are you okay after the news about Orlando?'

'I'm finding it all quite overwhelming, actually.'

'Sure, but remember that the world isn't out to get you guys all the time. This was someone who was very unwell.'

'I know it was someone who was very unwell. But – and this is very hard to communicate to you as someone who's heterosexual – this does confirm our worst fear as queers. There are people all over the world who actually want you dead, believe you should die, because of this thing inside you that you can't change. And every time someone says or does something phobic we are reminded that we are despised and hated. So while I agree the world isn't out to get us all the time, it feels like it's a pretty common dynamic. And that makes me feel so, so sad, in the pit of my stomach, and I can't stop crying and thinking about all the injustice done to people like us.'[7]

Silence. I could tell he was crying along with me, having understood something I've been trying to articulate for so long, at other times in the past when he's told me to look on the bright side or not worry about a potential Trump presidency or the murder of yet another trans woman of colour. That those things don't directly affect us. But they do. Anything that's an attack on an individual member of our community serves as a reminder of the violence that's out there, waiting to happen to others like us.

'Sure. You're right. I can't imagine how that feels. I love you. I am here, next to you.'

'Love you too.'

20th June / le 20 juin

Sometimes I wake up in the middle of the night and write down ideas that come to me on a piece of note paper. This morning I found one of these notes under my pillow which, almost illegibly, read:

Grandma, top anal tips

---

7 Poor Dad, he was just trying to help.

21st June / le 21 juin

I always stare at queer people when I see them – on trains, in coffee shops, on the street. It's hypocritical really because I always talk about how much stares can hurt, can single you out as something other. Being gawped at makes you feel clocked, and thus instantly freakish, or it makes you feel like the starer is poised, ready for attack.

But when I see a queer person I'm still so excited that we exist. I can't help it. I try not to, but I always find myself craning to see, half hoping they'll notice me so we can exchange a knowing, coded glance like queers of the sixties used to exchange conversation in the secret language of Polari, half hoping they won't notice so I can bask in all the glory of their visibility, overjoyed to be associated with them above anyone else.

Anyway, right now I'm waiting in a café before a Denim rehearsal because we've been booked for a fucking gig at Glastonbury and after we all died and were resurrected I started writing this, and I've just spotted someone staring at me. They look like a queer person, and it's so warming to smile back and take a moment to appreciate an understanding of another without even saying a word.

Okay, so I smiled back and he got up and left. Savage.

22nd June / le 22 juin

Every year, towards the end of June, all the queers I know start talking about Pride. I can't go this year because of

Glastonbury[8] and when I discovered the clash two days ago I actually felt absurdly relieved.

Now that sounds surprising – that I would feel relieved to miss Pride, which was originally set up as a day to protest for our right to exist[9] – but it's just become so centred on money. It's become a huge event where loads of people go to get wankered and wear glitter and say things like, 'God I love Pride, it's just like so fabulous!' Yes, we need allies – but we don't need them to claim Pride as their own.

It's also become pretty militarised and corporatised. The army marches, BAE marches, the Red Arrows are even flying over all in a bleak attempt to normalise war and war-mongering institutions, which both kill LGBTQIA+ folk in other territories and persecuted them here for decades. Last year at Pride I remember seeing an armed police officer, and a friend of mine who's considerably less bothered about shit and just wants to have fun, was like, 'Oh well! In a crowd of this many we need some security!'

But that's the point: it's not security. It reminds me of male violence, and is definitely painful and triggering to queer migrants who have come from places where war and gunfire is a lived reality.

On the minor side, it always makes me feel shit about my body. It feels like the one day a year that every muscle gay has trained for and they are there to let you know about

---

8 Ugh, even I'm jealous of me.
9 Back then it was called Christopher Street Liberation Day, and it started in 1970. It was, apparently, pretty rad – but it also had its problems centring on racism and trans exclusion. So not that rad after all.

it. Literally, what's with those vests that are just a flap of cotton? And I can't even imagine how it feels as a queer person of colour – all you see is white bodies.

As for me, I'm off to Glastonbury. Which is, of course, the radical anti-capitalist bastion perfect to replace Pride.[10] Better get packing.

30th June / le 30 juin

I'm sitting, covered in make-up and mud, speckled with faeces, outside the front door of Wally, waiting for Hatty to come home – after I left her having sex with two girls in a floating pod full of rubbish above a pond in the Healing Fields. I was going to wait there for her, but she wasn't even packed and I wanted to beat the early morning rush. So I'm sitting here diarising in the sun, surrounded by a wet tent and two suitcases, drinking a warm can of Aspall cider – 'the champagne of ciders' as my northern friend Chris always says – smoking and realising I hate cider.

I feel I must preface this next entry with the fact that I was in such a haze of escapist euphoria that I do not know exactly when or exactly where everything that follows happened, but I know that, at some point, it did.

We arrived on day one, the day before everything kicked off, on 23 June, and before we could take a sip of that first stunning summer pint, mass devastation swept Glastonbury's liberal fields, as it was announced we would be leaving the

---

10 Ugh, I'm such a walking contradiction.

European Union. Brexit had happened. We had all postal voted, and of course had been desperate to remain.

To say it put a dampener on the week would be an understatement, and coming back to London today you can feel the tension of such an unknowable future for so many thick in the air.

So there, among herds of heartbroken music fans, we decide that from our position in a field nothing could be done but for us all to collectively mourn, and collectively escape.

On night one we did what all the gays do – arrived at NYC Downlow early to beat the queues of straight folk desperate to eat up a slice of what every mainstream publication has dubbed the best club on earth. Of course it's a queer club – if there's one thing we know how to do best it's throw a party.

There, in our circle made up of the Denims, Hatty and Pak, we drank and danced and smoked. Some popped pills and floated around another dimension for the duration of the night. We all ate pitta breads that Hatty had stored in her trusty festival tote bag, to keep us going, and Hatty and I both got fingered by the same guy but in different holes. He had a handlebar moustache and was wearing a PVC butcher's apron, steel-capped boots and nothing else. It was the first time in six years Hatty had made sexual contact with someone of the opposite sex, so we found a quiet place by a bin between two clubs where the fantasy stopped and you could see the inner workings of Glastonbury, where we downloaded on what Hatty's developing sexual fluidity meant. Both absolutely wasted, we decided we were both really desperate for an orgasm and so we lay down side by side and had a wank, comically waiting for the other until we were ready to come. Which we both did in absolute unison. We embraced under the stars until the sun crept up and injected its pale filter into the sky and for a moment being in the world was as good as being in any fantasy.

The next day, we repeated the same thing – music, dancing, drinking. Afterwards, we dragged up in the back area of the Downlow, as Denim had been invited to perform a set on the stage. And we had a secret weapon up our chiffon sleeves to make our presence unforgettable.

After wading through mountains of drag detritus to get to our seats, we sat down among glorious queens like Scottee, Ginger Johnson and Rodent Decay. These queens are all very different, but all equally influential on the east London drag scene. They throw nights that explore everything from fat drag to sissy scumbags, and Ginger even writes a panto for Selfridges every year, which they all star in.

Nervous about our performance, and whether our amazing guest will turn up or not, Glamrou ended up drawing on comically humongous lips. After we held back the tears forced out by the laughter, so as not to ruin our make-up, we five sisters along with Scottee and Ginger crowded around their mirror and advised them on where to draw her lips. And there in the middle of the mass migration from London to the countryside we'd carried with us our wonderful queer bubble.

Five minutes until we go on and there's no sign of our guest star.

Two minutes, nothing.

Thirty seconds, and just as we were handed our mics, Florence Welch arrives in style in a golf cart wearing fringe everything from head to toe, perfect for a set with a bunch of drag queens.

And the rumour had spread: the Downlow now full to absolute capacity, and the crowd's drug-powered roar vibrated so loud the stage physically wobbled. I was so drunk at this point I had to cling to Aphrodite for support.

After our set, triumphant, press queued up to speak to us and take photos of these five misfit queens and a Glastonbury headliner.

Literally high on the atmosphere, Ace and I decided to take up the offer of this girl we'd met who turned out to be a Lady of a neighbouring manor, and split an ecstasy pill. I was terrified, and even though I know so many people who take them regularly I wondered if tonight would be the night I lived my hardest and died my fastest. But before I knew it, Ace had taken his half and was kissing my half into my mouth, pushing it down with his tongue.

We were both in full, somewhat bust-up, drag, and we wandered around feebly holding each other's hands, being swayed from location to location by an overwhelmingly huge crowd that didn't in any way overwhelm us, pulled with its movements like a fish swept by the current of the ocean.

We found the group, but stole away to behind the portaloos as these magic pills started to release their wonder on our bodies. I literally couldn't breathe. This half a little blue thing pushing you to that euphoric state just before orgasm, where every touch makes you feel like you might shatter, where you have to place a strategic breath between every word because even the bodily vibrations from talking release too much pleasure and serotonin to handle.

I said I needed the loo, pacing up the stairs of the com-
post toilets, trying to keep my balance, and as I went to close
the door Ace's hand stopped me from doing so. He had
brought in water, which we ended up drinking by kissing
and pouring it into our open, connected mouths like in *Fatal
Attraction* when they fuck on Alex Forrest's sink.

We kiss, unstoppably, somewhere between rage and literal ecstasy. Spurred on by this chemical, we step into our
feelings for the first time ever and decide to choose pleasure
over responsibility.

There, in a portaloo, we had our first sexual experience
together, and perhaps our last. Who knows? But it lasted
for about half an hour, which felt like a lifetime, which felt
like a nano-second, which felt like the most overwhelming amount of pressure and tension being released into the
atmosphere like spraying a can of deodorant into the air and
watching the particles gradually settle. The rest of the night
we spent dancing and touching and loving each other and
our friends, and anyone we encountered, in a way not possible when bound by the ties of reality.

It was completely expected and completely out of the
blue. But, surprisingly, as with anything that's meant to happen at some point, the next day there was no awkwardness or
immaturity or stunted communication. Ace and I spent the
weekend rolling through Glastonbury towards each other and
away from each other, finding ourselves in the strangest
places alone together. Like in the hardcore techno area sharing balloons with five straight guys who'd flown over from
Jamaica just for this patch of techno somewhere in the middle of a field some thousands of miles away from their starting

destination, as five fire breathers unfurled from silks above us like tacky butterflies from chrysalises; like watching Lily Allen's dad sing an acoustic set in a little tiny bar built into the side of a hill; like in the stone circle as smiling crackheads asked for money, which Ace and I didn't have.

He left a day early, he had to get to work. We didn't kiss goodbye or make any promises, but we left with a new level of comfort with each other. The litmus test of whether we could really *do* it passed with flying colours.

I danced with Hatty and Glamrou all through the night, before packing down and heading through various dimensions – a train, a bus, a tube, an Uber, a comedown – and back to here, on my stoop, in an entirely different world to the one which I left.

I've just checked my emails, to affirm I'm still attached to the real world, and I've seen two very exciting things: a job offer as a contributing editor for *LOVE* magazine, something I applied for on a total whim before I left, and a commission to write a hot-take on Brexit from a working-class perspective.

I'll deal with them tomorrow.

July/juillet

2nd July / le 2 juillet

Having sex in drag is popularly termed a 'kai-kai'. Derived from the term *to kiki (verb): when two queers chat, laugh, giggle and gossip*, the kai-kai takes that a step further and into fucking.

It's never something that's really been presented to me as an option. Since I got attacked, especially, I avoid going anywhere publicly in full drag for safety's sake, so it would mean fucking in the club toilet – and 99 per cent of gay club toilets are not my desired space for such activity. But the other night with Ace marked my first kai-kai, and it was in a toilet worse than that of a gay club. That's growth.

The actual experience of doing stuff in drag was not much different to that of doing stuff out of drag. All the parts work the same, and it's actually quite fun messing up your make-up for such a good cause. I was tucked, so there was the awkward part of peeling off gluey duct tape layered over genitals, as your adoring lover watches on patiently while you accidentally yank out the few patchy pubes you have left after years of this shit.

I have a friend, James, who actually only fucks in drag. 'Well, the men I like also like me better when I'm in full drag. We call them chasers – we dropped the "tranny" bit because that word's offensive.'

I invited James for dinner while she got into full face to go meet a client. I'd asked her over to catch up, but also to seek advice on the Ace situation that I am currently shockingly relaxed about. James isn't so good at talking about others, something I always forget until she's settled in for the night and we're discussing whether she needs to change dentist or not, so we never actually got to the topic of Ace and me.

'Some are clients, some are lovers, some both at once – they're the best ones. I enjoy sex work in drag, actually quite a lot, more than when I did it as a boy. It gives me permission to act in whichever way I please – you know what I mean, the *Queen!* – and also punters pay more. I've found the richer they are, the dirtier the stuff they want. Perhaps it's a chicken-and-egg situation – they can pay for anything they want, you know? I had one guy who wanted me to shit on his suit in his office somewhere in Canary Wharf and I did it, after I watched him wire me fifteen hundred pounds.'

Fifteen hundred quid? To take a dump in drag? It's so tempting.

5th July / le 5 juillet

I have texted Ace every day for the last three days in a row and haven't had a single response. I haven't yet called. I'm currently surprisingly calm about it but I'm giving myself one more day's grace period before that's no longer the case.

Have, naturally, turned to Grindr and have since met:

- Guy, 38, who sensually fed me a curry and then dipped his erect cock into raita before slowly walking toward me, pointing it at my mouth, while making an aeroplane sound – like the kind you make when you feed a baby; of course I received his Concorde, which was great after I plucked up the courage to ask him to stop making baby noises.

- Couple, 26 and 44, who wanted to Eiffel Tower me – which they did. An Eiffel Tower is when one participant fucks you in the bum and one in the mouth and they high-five/lean their hands in a diagonal position above the fuckee, thus taking the shape of the famous French monument.[1] After, I stayed a while with them, and we watched *Will and Grace* and ate poached pears and yoghurt and then they both gave me a tag-team blowjob while the Amy Winehouse documentary was on mute in the background. That bit was weird – watching this tragic story while I got a double bj.

- Guy, 35(ish), who only wanted to very gently suck my toes. Imagine a little lamb sucking at a mother's teat.[2]

- Guy, 29, very drunk, came to my house and asked me to treat him like a sex slave. I find the terminology there very problematic for me as white person so I said no to that. Instead I ended up making him a cup of tea and he wept while explaining to me he thinks he's developed a meth addiction and that he has a wife and a child at home but can't stop going onto the gay sex scene. I gave him some numbers of groups to call and services to access, because he said he wouldn't

---

1 *J'adore la France!*
2 Thank God I've sorted that athlete's foot.

even know where to look for something like that, and he gave me a hug before he left, and seemed very relieved to finally have someone to talk to.

- Guy, 40, Russian and very virile but not too masculine. This was the fuck I'd been looking for, and we did it in the street by my house, in the stairwell, the shower, Hatty's room, and on the kitchen floor where, half way through, I realised there was a thin slice of red onion stuck to my forehead.

6th July / le 6 juillet

I've been asked to write an article called 'how to be an LGBTQIA+ ally' and have been keeping a list of mine/my friends' thoughts.

1. Please, please don't make me work out your relationship to queerness for you. Likelihood is if you have to ask for my approval you probably don't deserve it.
2. Please don't tell me about the one time in high school you thought you had sexual urges toward your friend/ PE teacher of the same sex but never acted on it then or since.
3. Please don't try to outdo me on Madonna trivia. You might indeed know more but she is like 70 per cent of my identity and so it gets too emotional.
4. Queer people have very differing views on things; we are not a monolith, so each and every interaction with us might require you to expand your opinion.

5. Don't assume or question people's genders. They are what they told you they are.

6. Try to avoid telling queer folk what is and isn't queer/homo/trans/biphobia. You might see it, but we feel it.

7. Be cognisant of your own privilege.

8. Don't worry about getting things wrong, now or in the past; just admit it, accept it, apologise for it, and move on. We all get shit wrong.

9. That said, if you're going to ask questions about anal/how lesbians have sex/where the poo goes/what it means to be a top or a bottom/who is the girl and who is the boy in the relationship/whether a trans person has had surgery, please Google it. Remember we have spent years answering these very basic questions, to which we had to find the answers to ourselves. You can very much do the same.

10. Don't think that our only goal is acceptance and assimilation. We want much more than that.

11. Personally I'm happy for you to come to (some of) our spaces as long as you remember that for you it might be a party without the sexual pressure, for us it's an emergency room and one of the only places we can go to feel our oats, feel safe, and feel sexual. A good ally doesn't need to invade space.

12. Watching RuPaul doesn't make you queer.

13. Don't be afraid to step forward as an ally. There's nothing shameful in that – it's actually wonderful and you're super useful!

14. If you come out as an ally don't just say it – don't think rocking up to Pride or being chill about going to gay

bars is enough. Challenge your colleagues, platform LGBTQIA+ people, unlearn unhealthy phobias. Try to prioritise those who really need it in our community – not simply fab gay guys who lend you sunglasses.

15. Listen. That's the first thing to do. Learn. The second.

16. Be like my brother, Harry. He is the most wonderful ally. When I first came out there was no such thing, but he didn't bat an eyelid. He would be the first to my defence at high school and would laugh in a supportive way when I did anything outrageously camp or queeny. He was the first in my family to see me in drag, and even at his work – a bigwig, official solicitors – he sends around my articles and publicises my shows and says things like, 'My brother is an amazing drag queen.' It doesn't sound like much, but in a world where your worth is often predetermined on how well you run in the dick-swinging wolf pack, it takes a lot of bravery to fight someone else's corner. He reads, so much, more than I do, and will send me links saying: *I'm sure you've read this, but I wanted to send it in case you missed it!* Every time Harry gets drunk he leans in, wobbling on his feet, and gurgles into my ear something about how he couldn't be prouder of me. Sometimes I find it hard to say something back that doesn't just sound like I'm returning the compliment. But the truth is I couldn't be prouder of him. Harry's support has lifted me up too many times to count. That's not just tolerance, it's celebration for exactly who I am, who my friends are. That's the mark of a good ally. I love you, Harry.

7th July / le 7 juillet

No real reply from Ace other than:

> Sorry I haven't got back! Have been super busy!
> Promise I'm not ignoring, we will see each other next
> week at Denim? xxx

He's definitely ignoring. Will continue Grindr binge.

9th July / le 9 juillet

I was walking home when I noticed two other queers walking in the same direction. It was dark, the kind of orangey dark of horror movies that makes your heart naturally beat faster by association. It just so happens that my journey is down a twisty pathway then via a wide-open, very dark market street. The kind of twisty pathway and open market street that would be the perfect scene for a true crime-style attack.

But there, unlike most nights when I break into a light jog, hot on my toes ready to sprint beyond my bodily abilities at the sound of something as minor as a moth hitting a lamplight, were two other queers on the exact same journey.

We didn't speak. We just put our headphones on, blasted our music up, and walked home how those unafraid of violence are allowed to walk home: my heart slowing, my Kylie blasting, a feeling of relief akin to that when someone you know has a big piece of spinach in their teeth but you don't dare say anything, then they finally go to the bathroom and remove it and you can breathe again.

15th July / le 15 juillet

As a perpetually single queen, I've always loathed couples who share pictures of themselves kissing on social media, the caption always reading 'cuddles with this one', or 'date night with the boy'.

But recently I've succumbed to the lowest of the low, the pits of the human race, and I, too, have just posted a smugly captioned, semi-elusive picture of my (maybe) boyfriend on social media. I hate myself.

The funny thing is, my recent Grindr binge has, for the first time, speedily inclined towards an actual meaningful connection with someone.

We met on the 7th and have since spent every day over the last week together. During week one we did a ton of anal, and by yesterday we'd both been checked for STIs and have been doing it bareback since – something I consider sacred, and something you have to be incredibly careful with. I've slipped up here a few times, although rarely intentionally.

Anyway: he fucks me, I fuck him, we swallow each other's cum, and cum in each other's assholes. We even tried felching, which is where the cum recipient essentially farts out the cum into the cum-giver's mouth, the cum-giver swallowing their own cum now infused with the inside of the cum-receiver's colon. Sounds gross, totally, but there's something super intense and connective about sharing all parts of someone else's body – be that fluids, or toe-jam, or sweaty pits. It's completely freeing to be in someone else's physicality so deeply.

Shag numero uno – which was about a week ago – was amazing, but I kept my T-shirt on and left at 3 a.m. to take a cab back to east London (from south-west London, which is where Dom – which is his name – lives).

The second time, I took my top off and he came in my eye. Instantly guards were down, and he – as he's a doctor[3] – cared for my red, stingy eye. We laughed, chatted about coming out, he told me about the racism he's experienced on the gay scene, we postured over who Beyoncé's most recent album is really for, and he daubed at my eye with a wet tissue, both of us naked, penises flaccid, me sitting on the loo, him facing me on my knee, chatting through the night.

He went to work, and I stayed at his upon his invitation. That afternoon he texted me, 'I've just got us tickets for Beyoncé at the O2 tonight – can you come???' I cancelled on my friends Ellie and Cecily, choosing Beyoncé and all-night sex, knowing they would understand a queen's need for a much-deserved Bey and lay.

We went to see Beyoncé. It was three days in. He told me he wants to marry me, and the usual cynic in me would retort with my belief that gay marriage is actually a repressive, de-radicalising tool to make queer people think that we have 'equality' when it's actually just putting our sexualities in a context that heterosexual folk can understand. Instead

---

3 Finally, the big money.

I whispered, 'I want to marry you too.' Then we both cried as Queen Bey sang 'All Night'. Shortly after, he gave me an emotional wank-job, putting his big hands down my culottes, me climaxing in the middle of the crowd as Beyoncé belted out 'Freedom'. Freedom, indeed, it was.

This weekend Denim has a gig – not a big one, but a paid one at a new club night in north-east London. Oddly, I'm not so broke at the moment so don't need the money, and when Dom found £9 flights on Monarch Airways, he asked if I want to go to Budapest, and I – to the dismay of my fellow queens – didn't hesitate, sending over my passport details, unashamed about the hideous picture, for Dom to book the flights.

The queens are pissed. But they can do it without me.

The thing is, I've been in love three times already, and every single time it's been unreciprocated for one stupid, made-up reason or another. 'I don't want to jeopardise our friendship,' or, 'you're too amazing for me,' or, 'fuck off, fatty.'

There was Matt, there was Ethan, there's Ace.

There's Ace, who I'm probably still in love with, who still hasn't really been in contact since we left Glastonbury.

But this potential love with Dom, fast as it is, this fourth attempt at what might be the first long-term relationship I've ever had, will not be put on hold for a random gig and £80. Denim can wait; true love cannot.

Now it's Friday, of 'week two', at 5 a.m., and I'm writing this on my phone as Dom sleeps next to me on the coach to Luton. I fucking hate Luton.

But even the promise of Luton doesn't feel so bleak with Dom next to me. This is utterly maniacal, but I think I know that I already love him. It doesn't feel like lust, and it's totally unlike me to misread my own feelings[4] and over-attach at the early stages of any interest but, genuinely, I feel magic. A new kind of magic, which must basically be what it feels like to have someone actually, for the first time ever, like you back.

I'm not going to diarise this weekend, at least until I'm back, because – much like those trash people who post pics of their SO[5] on social media, I'm going to actually do what they are perpetually hashtagging and I'm going to #liveinthemoment.

I just took a crafty snap of half of Dom's asleep face. I posted it on Instagram, captioned 'Budapest with this one'.

If to be in love means to be human garbage, then love can come and collect me, crush me whole and dump me in a landfill. I'm done being recycled.

18th July / le 18 juillet

We'd got an apartment in District VII, in the Jewish Quarter. We spent the weekend back and forth between weird techno clubs and our bedroom, in this beautifully stark flat that housed nothing but a single bookshelf loaded with Hungarian books on labour theory, a mattress on the floor and a gentrification-esque lamp. Together we explored the depths of the gay sex scene across the city, from the tame to this underground club that runs a poo party once a month.[6]

---

4 Lol.

5 Significant Other: wanker phrase for boy/girlfriend/partner that removes any agency one might have in being significant in their own right. Same goes for 'other half' or 'better half'.

6 We didn't go to the poo party, sadly; that was next weekend.

We liked that one. It's much like Laboratory in Berlin, the sex club beneath Berghain. Once you arrive through flappy, fake-blood-covered plastic curtains, at the unfortunately named Coxx Club, the bouncers slide open a slat of steel in the door with an echoey clang. A glance up and down, surveying whether you're the right kind of clientele for this very specific establishment. Turns out we were – probably because we were wearing tiny little sunglasses at night – then the bolts ring open, and you're in.

Once inside, you're told to strip all your clothes off – 'you can keep the shoes' – before they're taken away and a number is written on your hand: the idea being that on entering the space you become base, anonymous, a piece of meat – a touch I thought was a bit on the nose.[7]

We took a self-guided tour; St Andrew's crosses spun to the left, tiny narrowing alcoves to the right, rooms purpose-built for fisting and more extreme sex acts peppered the perimeter. In one room there lay a man on a gurney, tailed by an orderly queue of other men patiently waiting to sound this slung kinkster.[8] Glory holes, prison rooms(?), a smoking area where everyone was sucking dicks, fag in hand.[9]

Dom and I decided to split up. He went off somewhere to explore, as did I. I always thought I'd be terrified of openness

---

7 Or very *Les Mis* 24601, which is way more my brand.
8 Sounding, by the way, is where you take a thin steel, or sometimes rubber, rod and slowly insert it into the urethra. It must be sterile, and my friend Jeremy – who loves it – told me that if you time it just right you can both orgasm and urinate at exactly the same time. Jeremy told me, with pride, that it's the most pleasurable sexual thing he's ever done, 'and honey, I'm in my fifties!'
9 Obviously this was my favourite.

within a relationship, but not only did it feel fine, it felt full of trust and understanding. I had no doubt that Dom liked me better than all these men, but this was about having different experiences.

I spent the night in Coxx doing a lot of kissing and touching of other men, consensually of course. At one point, a bald German guy with a head tattoo tried to put a finger in my bum without asking so, naturally, I grabbed it and pushed off. Just ask first.

Funny though, I wasn't really in the mood for anything to go up there. A side note here is that Dom is actually the first person I've ever topped. Until then I was your simple, run-of-the-mill bottom – constantly dodging burritos or avoiding one too many coffees in a row if even a sniffle of dick was on the horizon. Prunes were good on off days, but on 'on' days there was so much food monitoring that bottoming was bound never to last beyond my mid-twenties.

Later, as we left a neighbouring club, where we went for a prolonged, sweaty dance, I counted that I'd had sex thirteen times in this one night. Not every single time featured climax, but they all contained a sensation on the edge of that – drawing me closer and closer to one maximum climax at the end of the night, during which my ejaculate flew so high it cleared the wall of a bathroom stall.

As we walked home through that genius Budapest street, which houses all of the politician's super Hungarian-looking houses, we ate late night lángos and kissed from the outskirts all the way in. In bliss, we were kissing near the flat when Dom told me he had something to say. I knew what it was, I was feeling it too; I had been since the moment our flight took off. And there, in a Budapest dawn, my first mutual 'I love you' was about to be exchanged, a week in. Maybe I need therapy?

The air was febrile with potential, silent for a second and then: the bleepy, grotesque shrill ring of my iPhone, in my pocket. The moment was gone, but I kissed Dom and told him to hold that thought while I checked who it was.

Ace. Calling me at 4 a.m. from London. I tried to justify not answering, and Dom was begging me not to: 'but what if it's an emergency?'

I answered the phone.

'Hello, Ace, what's up? I'm in Budapest.'

'I'm lost.' He was wasted. 'But I just called to tell you,' he spluttered, and it sounded like he was falling onto a wall, 'that I ended it with William. You're the one.' And then he hung up.

Everything slowed down for a second, and I couldn't pinpoint my feelings for all the booze and the sex.

Dom asked what he was calling about. I paused, constructing a lie in my head, something about Ace losing his house keys.

'Where were we?' I looked up at Dom, the atmosphere totally swiped by this firework to the guts.

'I was just saying that . . . I think I'm falling in love with you.'

A pause.

'I think I'm falling in love with you too.'

And we rattled home to bed, high off each other and the way our armpits smelled and the way our body hair was curled with dried sweat, while our veins swelled with

MDMA and the beginnings of love. As I watched Dom fall asleep, I nipped to the loo, my mind darting between Dom and Ace, snakes and ladders. And in a 5 a.m. haze, I sent Ace the following, I couldn't resist:

I love you too. I'm sure we'll be too embarrassed to talk about this tomorrow. See you when I'm back. Get home safe xxx

20th July / le 20 juillet

Fucking hell the gays. Literally, you wait a lifetime for one to unblock you on Grindr and then two come along at once. But no – not for dating, or casual sex, or good conversation, or to put their card details on your Deliveroo – for actual love.

23rd July / le 23 juillet

People often wonder how you learned to be a drag queen. Personally, I think you're born with the impulse to be a performer, but as that hope dwindles the answer is to find a space that might celebrate your femininity. In terms of the actual practice of painting and dressing, that is a learning process, one which I owe all to my sister Dinah, or Jacob, and Ellie who put me in drag for the first time ever.

Jacob is a model who once had mumps so bad his face doubled in size. We went to university together, and after meeting at a particularly heterosexual gathering, we got to talking about how we were both dying to do drag – proper drag. After this we used honing our craft as a means by which to escape further hetty gatherings. We'd found our thing, our hobby, our baby.

We spent nights in his room drinking shit tons, doing no work, smoking a billion cigarettes, and pooling make-up kits – each of us attempting different techniques, Jacob endlessly more dextrous at this than me.

That's why a lot of drag performers become enraged at the sight of stag-do blokes who dress as sexy nurses and run around Krakow, or gays who think putting on bad drag one night a year is funny. Firstly, it's misogynist. Secondly, it undermines a craft that is about honour and history, into which we pour countless hours, carefully considering how to bring to life these characters that are often the key to our enlightenment.

24th July / le 24 juillet

Ace and I have been texting a lot, while Dom and I have been seeing each other a lot. I have my boyfriend URL and my other one IRL. One of them sends me funny memes and asks me how my day is going, while the other shares his food with me, a bed, bodily fluids, and sometimes some choice opinions. Like how he thinks identity politics is a waste of time, for example.

I love them both differently and am annoyed by them both simultaneously. Ace is non-committal – we plan to see each other and he always bails, but we have productive conversations about what needs to change in the world. Very Gen-Z. Dom never bails – he's there even when Ace cancels and makes me dinner without even asking. He listens to the boring bits about my day, but avoids any 'big' conversation, claiming he's too tired. This annoys me hugely – if we can't talk then all we can do is fuck and eat, which is what we've been doing for the last week. The descent into a bed-ridden relationship was actually comically fast: the moment he told me he loved me, it's like I was money in an ISA, sat there, secure, accruing weight instead of interest.

This is what, in maths, they call a conundrum.

While Ace and I haven't promised each other anything, I have promised myself to Dom. And so, because every time I'm texting 'someone' (it's always Ace) he tries to look at my phone, already oddly mistrusting me – which offends me greatly even though he has total cause to – I decide to broach the topic of an open relationship.

Open relationships, to me, have always seemed like a minefield of hurt.

Now, we all know 'the one' is a myth, like the moon landing or democracy. It implies that all relationships last happily ever after, when the truth is – most of the time, at least – they don't. No one ever said, 'It just works', 'We never argue' or 'We still have sex twenty-five times a week' without it coming back to bite them in the coochie when they, inevitably, part ways. Today, finding 'the one' – by which I mean a single, lifelong dedicated love – seems pretty unlikely. What if there's not one, but four ones, and what if they come along all at the same time? God, maybe I am Carrie B.

I feel somewhat manipulative coercing Dom in this way, like a Cersei Lannister type.[10] To clear this up: I'm not

---

10 Which is actually every goal, so I've decided I'm fine with it.

planning on sleeping with Ace, other people maybe, but not Ace. I just want to feel a little less guilty if mine and Ace's texting becomes a little flirtatious from time to time.

'Sure, we can always close the relationship if it doesn't work?'

'Sure. Love you. Now watch the telly!'

And, as simple as that, I go back to watching *Six Feet Under* in the crook of Dom's warm, hairy arm, while sending memes of Bree from *Desperate Housewives* to Ace.

25th July / le 25 juillet

A list of rules Dom and I agreed upon re: our open relationship:

- No sex with other people in either of our beds.
- No sex with exes/previous romantic conquests. (We never discussed texting . . .)
- Sex with condoms when sleeping with other people.
- No sex with the same person more than twice, unless there's a significant time gap.
- No telling about who/what/where/when unless asked.
- Do tell when it's happened, however.
- No cancelling on plans with each other to meet other guys.
- No choosing to go home with/get with other guys in clubs when together unless agreed upon in the moment.

I always felt like an open relationship wouldn't be the

right thing for me: I'm much more monogamy-centric, and I didn't think my history of extra-relationship rejection would prepare me well for intra-relationship rejection. But with Dom it feels easy. I don't know if that's because it's convenient for me, or if I don't really care about Dom, or if I trust him so much that this feels like the right step.

I always felt less queer because of my desire for monogamy. All the best, most radical queers I know practise polyamory, group love, and at minimum open relationships. When I tell these people I'm into monogamy it's often met with a momentary look of pity, of condescension.

It took me a while to realise that neither monogamy nor openness is correct. There's no way to be the most successfully queer. When I really pondered on it, I came to the conclusion that monogamy, in a scene that's harsh and unforgiving, where intimacy is scary and oft wrapped in barbed wire, might well be a radical act of care. The queers have rejected it so hard that it's actually become queer to be what was once deemed as not queer.

I spent years developing a queer justification for my monog-obsession. And so, at the sight of two men who want it, just like that, I take it all back.

26th July / le 26 juillet

I realise I've only been writing about men for a month, which, frankly, is beyond dull at this point. Both relationships are fine; nothing has changed. Dom got some bleach on some trousers I saved up for for ages and bought in New York and I still haven't forgiven him fully.

In other news – we have a new flatmate in Wally. Hatty and I met her at a club, where she was dancing from only the head up – rolling her head, her neck, flipping her hair, but static throughout the rest of the body. Hatty and I were hammered and we decided we wanted to dance like that, so we went over and asked if we could join in and I realised, after about five minutes of head-dancing, that she was my best friend from my early years of high school before she was moved to a private school by her Catholic parents because she'd come out as gay. Turns out she'd broken up with her girlfriend because she wanted to move to Bristol to take up pottery, 'such a dyke cliché,' as Leyah (her name) said insultingly. 'And now I'm looking for a place to live.'

Leyah isn't like the rest of our friends – she's kind, funny, queer, attractive and stylish in the way all my friends are – but she's less outwardly political and doesn't necessarily lead with her trauma. In conversation so many of us showcase our validity at being included in the things we talk about by recounting our traumas first: kind of like a ticket into the debate. But Leyah is relaxed; she listens and avoids revealing too much.

Anyway, I also started and then left a new job at *LOVE* magazine. I liked it, for the two weeks I was there, but it meant that I was unable to do any freelance work or paid drag jobs and when summed together I earned more in a month doing that than I would in three at *LOVE*. It's not that I earn good money freelancing and dragging, trust, it's that the pay at these magazines is obscene.

At home, my grandma is getting more and more unwell. I don't really know how to cope with that, and I don't ever really talk about it even though Hatty does this annoying thing where she says 'let it all out, baby' when I really don't want to. That's the only annoying thing Hatty does. But it was my grandma who bought me *Chic*, took me shopping, told me I could be anything I wanted to be in the world. Most gays have one great grandma. 'Once a doctor's wife, always a doctor's wife. It was my duty to the community,' she would say. She's starting to lose her words, and so before she does I pitched an article to an online platform about what she taught me about beauty, and I'm going to put it here so that it can be here forever. In honour of Kathleen.

What does beauty mean to you?

Beauty can be found in different ways, it can be found in looking at a person and thinking 'they are beautiful'. It's more complicated than just visuals. Beauty should move you. You're beautiful, my darling, remember that.

Do you think you're a beautiful person?

No, not at all, I don't think I look beautiful, but I think what's more important is that when people meet me, I try to be kind and nice, and to offer happiness, and I think that is beautiful.

If you were to pass on anything you've learnt to younger women, what would it be?

If someone came to me and said, 'Oh, I feel ugly,' I would say, 'Take another look at yourself.' You can't be ugly if you're a kind, giving, nice, warm person. Do some more thinking, work hard on how you feel about yourself – not your body and your face and your hair. That doesn't matter. Now my legs are in bandages, I am so glad I focused on being kind and having a happy life, and not on my appearance, because it doesn't really matter. If you enjoy that, that's okay, but it doesn't matter. I don't care about my legs, or how shapely they are. I remember being happy for other reasons. Looks fade; my mind and my heart have remained.

Here's to you, Grandma.

August/août

1st August / le 1 août

Over lunch today Ellie asked me what I really want from my life, and I said 'safety'. That's not very fun, is it? I used to want fame, and now I want safety? She said she wanted to be pounded meaninglessly, which I thought was far better.

4th-10th
(I had so much wine this might all be in the wrong order)

The human brain makes 35,000 decisions a day. Bafflingly, this means that somewhere within the tangle of my routine, I made the off-piste decision to actually take a nine-hour flight across the Atlantic to visit Fort Lauderdale: the place where spring break used to happen.

I was asked to go for work, for a travel feature (my first ever) for a niche magazine to whom I lied and said I'd done loads of travel writing.

The truth is, I was really looking to leave London for a bit, on my own. The situation with Ace was getting weirdly complicated, intensified by his turning up on the doorstep of Wally four nights ago, in the pouring rain, to ask if he could stay for a while. We spent all night awake talking in the same bed, not kissing or fucking, but definitely in some semblance of a pair who were way beyond the line of the platonic.

The situation with Dom is seemingly circling the drain, on the other hand, and the guilt I'm feeling about Ace is probably exacerbating the whole thing. He's become incredibly contrary and argumentative, and I've become incredibly noncommittal. Last week he came to a night Hatty and I threw – we decided to form a queer pop band by the way, called ACM – at the Royal College of Art. We killed it – the songs we've been working on for a while, on those nights on which we stayed up late and made up joke lyrics about positive consent and grotesque Barbie girls actually translating into possibly the most radically queer art we've ever made. Anyway, after our set – in which Hatty and I covered each other in Nutella and eggs during various points in the performance – the crowd were living for it, but Dom stormed home, leaving only a text on my phone, which read: *'When are you gonna grow up?'*

'If growing up means not being able to express my queerness – then never,' I replied.

I was hesitant about taking the trip, but I thought it would be the best for everybody. It's only six days anyway, and the grown-up thing is to run from my problems.

Day 1:
The flight – terrified of dying. When I do die, I want it to be glamorous. Perhaps in a gruesome onstage-leading-lady-style disaster, or by crashing my cheating ex-husband's yacht on the Côte d'Azur in a lavish rage. Not in TAP Air Portugal economy, fogged on three Zopiclone and a Jameson's.

Arrived. Suitably wan after all that in-flight agitation and self-medication, in the Sunshine State, the home of the homosexual, the place Edmund White in his 1980 gay travel guide described as the place to pick up a hustler. Rare is the moment where one is actually stunned by the beauty of American cities, but as the nefarious clutches of medical sleep wore off, I came to in a Marriott hotel room resting on the edge of the Atlantic. I grew up by the sea but the view of a boundless sapphire ocean blurred into creamy-blue sky was a new kind of sea view, one thankfully lacking the bobbing empty cans of Tennent's Super and floating used condoms I was more used to seeing.

Evening. Dinner by the hotel in its new restaurant because I'm a stunning glam VIP. I put on my best heels, a pencil skirt and a giant oversized hoodie and sat down to dinner alongside some rather remarkable guests. Kellie Maloney, former boxing promoter and since famed and unfairly shamed for coming out as trans; my friend, Shon Faye – the funniest person I know and a rightful Internet sensation, and Will, the editor-in-chief of the *Gay Times*. This was the first time I felt like I'd journalistically 'made it' because the wine was literally on Fort Lauderdale, so I didn't have to order house white!

Alexis, the President of the Southern Comfort Conference, joined us – and that's why we were all there, for the twenty-sixth annual conference visit, one of the largest gatherings of the trans community in the world. My entire stay in Fort Lauderdale was geared toward this event. The conference is one of the only ones of its kind in the States, and has become an incredibly popular destination for mainly older trans women from all across the world. There are nail salons, surgery workshops, 'how to dress' forums, dinners, karaoke, drinks, dancing, live music – all by and for the trans community.

Day 2:

In a winey stupor the night before, I requested a tour of one of only two AIDS museums in the world.[1] I was whisked around the museum by Ed, a handsome daddy type, and a self-confessed 'theatre queen' who used to live two floors below RuPaul back in New York – 'I was in the original cast of *A Chorus Line*,' he said, and there I died and went to gay heaven.

Broward County – where Fort Lauderdale is situated – has the highest prevalence of HIV-positive people in the entire US. Here is the right place to have a World AIDS Museum and its staff conducted extensive community out-reach and education in prevention, testing and treatment.

After this, we took a mini-tour bus with a driver who was like a butch version of Dolly Parton to the biggest archive of LGBTQIA+ memorabilia and literature in the States. Deep in the archives we rooted out games with names like Twinkies and Trolls (Snakes and Ladders but with much more dick), Gayopoly, Gay Dream Date, and Gay Trivial Pur-suit. Next, I'm handed the first-ever piece of published gay press in the United States, entitled *The Gay Blade*, distributed around Christopher Street in 1969, after the Stonewall Riots – detailing news stories about police raids and tips on how not to get busted for hustling. We unpacked the snake-print jacket worn by Carson Kressley on *Queer Eye*, which led me to rudely laugh over the tour guide's very serious analy-sis of the importance of the jacket. But it was just so comical:

---

1 Since AIDS has killed around 35 million people since 1981, it seems absolutely bogus that there are a pitiful two World AIDS Museums.

The Gay Blade next to early circulars detailing tips on how New York 'cross-dressers' should present themselves so as to not be arrested, next to this snake-print jacket, all venerated with same level of importance.

I arrived back to my hotel room, and am now sitting on a shady balcony chain-smoking Parliaments[2] and trying to deconstruct this day. An intensely gay day,[3] but not over-whelmingly so – which is strange for me seeing as I now have so much ammo in my arsenal for the Londinium gays who frequent the gentrified streets of Soho. What is the rea-son for this lacuna separating myself from my boy-loving brethren, despite our common lust for dick? Racism, femme-shaming, transphobia and misogyny currently feel endemic among my community.

But today also made me think that gays are actually hilarious. Only our archive could feature a top hat signed by Alan Cummings in gold glitter(!), next to thousands of pages of gay and queer political press, and view them both with equal importance.

We are also treated with equal importance here. I don't fear for my safety in Fort Lauderdale. What's more is that there is not only an acceptance of 'the gays, the drags, and the trans folk', but our presence feels more commonplace than the presence of the usual overbearing 'heteronorm'. At home we are low on the priority list, so all that's left is torso pics on Grindr and an excess of gay shame because we are being told both consciously and subliminally that our

2 The only straights I like. Pun intended.
3 When's it not, though, Henny?

identities are not valid. In Fort Lauderdale the tensions feel less pronounced than in London.

Day 3:

I was treated to dinner at the Hard Rock Hotel. It's monstrous, but you can smoke inside, so it's an instant jackpot. I was told that this very hotel is the same hotel in which Anna Nicole Smith passed away, and I was surprised when I suddenly welled up. Hers is a story of tragedy you would only find in that late noughties celeb-shaming press. It epitomises the demise of someone who was continually shamed for being brazen about who she really was: something that rings true for so many of us queers.

Day 4:

Bonaventure Resort and Spa, the day of the conference, most of it spent dashing between buildings dodging raindrops the size of rabbits. Everyone in the main bar was dressed to kill. After deciding to don a T-shirt and fashion-joggers I wished I was in something way less low-key. It was an incredibly glamorous social, populated with trans women and men who all sat and had dinner, drank wine, ate spinach with cold raspberry dressing, and prepared for karaoke (annoyingly I missed it). The attendees of the conference were mostly women over forty, and a lot of them seemed incredibly at peace with themselves and their lives back at home; they were just here to let their hair down.

The hotel in Fort Lauderdale was booked out entirely by members of the trans community, some seasoned attendees and some first-timers. To paraphrase Judith Butler: you come out of 'the closet' only to find yourself in another one – being trans constructs another closet that wider society boxes you into, a closet that is often hellishly more dangerous than the one in which you previously existed.

It struck me that this was the first and only time in my entire life I have seen trans people prioritised; the need to say 'I'm trans' fell away, that second closet disappeared, and people were free to remove politics from the discussion and instead talk about shopping, gambling, Justin Trudeau, their children.

For those who are safe to move in space freely, it's impossible to imagine how overwhelming a gathering like the Southern Comfort conference is for someone who is not. When every interaction as a trans person is a potential site of danger, violence, misgendering or transphobia, virtual and temporary physical spaces are all that are on offer.

I spoke with women from all over the United States, from Venezuela, Australia, the UK. Waiting for another Chardonnay, I got chatting to Diane, who had red eyes from crying. When I asked her if she was okay, she told me that today she had lived her lifelong dream, and that she was a little overwhelmed. 'I went to all the designer stores with a new girlfriend I made, and I bought myself an expensive purse! I never go out like this,' she explained. Diane presents as male back in Washington DC and Southern Comfort is the one time of the year she stops being a doctor, a father and a husband, and flies away to her real life, here in Fort Lauderdale.

Nicole, who was telling me about winning $900 on the slots earlier, eventually shares that she lost everything in her life when she revealed her desire to transition: job, children, partner, family, everything. She wasn't sad any more, though; in the same breath, she explained that she was happier and freer than ever before, and that if she had to shed a skin to be herself, then the skin perhaps wasn't worth having in the first place.

Fort Lauderdale is genuinely the first place I have ever been where queers, and those who belong to the LGBTQIA+ community, are actually celebrated and welcomed.

Day 5:
Flight home. On the Zopiclone. About to pass out but need to write diary before I do. The getaway wasn't just needed; it was, in some ways, totally perspective-altering.

I've decided that I'm done obsessing over the two men in my life. I've frittered away countless, untraceable years obsessing over men and maleness.

I've decided it's time to end it with Dom, and look beyond my dependency on Ace. My identity is so important to me, much more important than it being absorbed into paranoia at the behest of two men, all men.

11th August / le 11 août

Spent £230 – all the money left in my overdraft, bar £16.54 for the tube home and a Deliveroo – on some Gucci sunglasses. They're pretty hideous, but after Fort Lauderdale I was in the mood to re-embrace my more gaudy side, which has faded since I got beaten up and stopped having a job at a fashion magazine to go to.

Dom turned up at the airport, waiting with a sign that read 'The Queen'. It was touching. But while I was away I got a Facebook message from a friend of mine telling me they think they saw him at a gay sex club with his ex, Pete. I had ignored the message. I'd been waiting for something to exonerate me of my guilt for my interactions with Ace and it gave me a reason to chuck Dom and rediscover life outside of a double bed in south London.

So as soon as I saw Dom waiting for me I decided to ignore him. Quite harsh, but I needed a Costa[4] before I was going to pull the plug on our relationship. It didn't last long, as he spotted me in my hard-to-miss Guccis and started shrieking my name across the Arrivals forecourt, so he joined me in getting a coffee.

'Okay, it's true, I spent the whole weekend with Pete, but before you choose to leave me can I just explain why?' he said, before I even had chance to talk.

'I've been thinking a lot recently about how much I love you, about how committed to you I am. And while you were away I got scared that you weren't feeling the same for me, that you were becoming distant. So, when Pete messaged me to go down to Fire with him on Saturday I was planning to go to just let off some steam with some random guys. But I got more and more drunk and took more MDMA and everything started to blur and I started to feel overwhelmed without you there, so I turned to Pete for comfort. But when I woke up on Sunday in his bed, I could only think of you and how much I want to be with

---

4 Hate Costa. Favourite is Nero, then Starbucks, then Costa.

you in all your femme, queer glory. And so I wanted to ask you . . .'

And before I'd even had a sip of my frappe he was down on one pissing knee.

In Costa, in Heathrow.

At 7 a.m.

'If you would do me the great honour—'

Every dick I've sucked flashed before my eyes.

He reached into his back pocket.

Everybody was looking.

'—of being my husband.'

The whole of Costa's breakfast clientele were smiling, as if I was going to say yes.

Dom was still on one knee with a ring in his hand, a fixed, quivering smile held because I was taking my sweet time.

And there in Costa, via my stupid mouth, which was evidently unconnected to my brain, I said yes.

I am not fine with gay marriage. I am definitely not fine with this marriage.

And, today, that's how I went from being cheated on to being engaged.

19th August / le 19 août

Yesterday was my birthday and all my friends were busy.

I haven't yet 'found the time' to tell a soul about my engagement to Dom, except Ellie and Violet, both of whom I asked to be my maid of honour, not wanting to tell them I was in utter physical shock and, really, wanted to break it off with my accidental fiancé. Frankly, I don't think Dom was up for getting wed either; I just don't think he was fully ready to end our month-and-a-bit-long tryst.

Not one of my friends has taken to this man I'm supposed to be marrying. He's said some pretty shitty things to them – like the time he told my friend Rina, who's Japanese, that she would be good at making sushi, or the time he told a rape joke at a party and then shouted at me in front of everyone because I said that rape is never ever funny. And while my friends diagnosed our ill-fit for each other early, I protested so much at the beginning of the relationship that it was 'so amazing' and that we were just 'kindred spirits', that admitting I want to run for the hills would give them the grounds upon which to say I told you so.

Am I that desperate for love that I would stay with a person who does all of this to my friends? Am I that terrified of rejection that I would actually say yes to his guerrilla proposal?

Looking back on this whirlwind month-long relationship I'm actually severely baffled at myself.

This will make a hilarious story, when it's all over. That always calms me down.

But, save for anything better to do, I end up having a birthday dinner with no one other than Dom. He took me to a fancy restaurant in Soho and then on to see an all-gay dance troupe. He chose a birthday perfect for him, not me – an all-gay dance troupe? Really?

To add insult to injury, I hate my birthday and the attention it brings with it.

I'm a drag queen who hates attention. An oxymoron, I

know. To clarify, I don't hate well-deserved attention from large groups of people – *j'adore* the sound of a Denim audience, yelping, fainting and screaming when I hit that high note.

No, I'm good with that kind of attention; let's call it 'natural attention'. The kind I really can't stand is undeserved attention.

I don't hate it for the obvious reason of hating growing older, which is many people's reasoning for going into hibernation at the same time of year each year. Ageing doesn't scare me; I think there's something exciting about slowly bulldozing through the age boxes on official forms because the best people I know are older people: my radical grandma, Vera Duckworth (RIP), Tina Turner, Madonna, Celine Dion, Gandalf the Great, Cher. There's something liberating about accepting that your days as a stinky, broke adolescent are over, and instead gliding shamelessly towards the days where you own walls full of really smart-looking books that you've never read. I just hate the specific type of attention your birthday brings with it.

But for me, this kind of unwanted attention, which you feel like you've asked for, is something I'm used to in the bleakest of ways. That's right, folks, it all comes back to homophobia. For my whole life I've been the recipient of a lot of attention for literally just trying to present as myself. From how I dress, to how I speak, to the way I walk, to the way I think, to the people I hit on: everything about me, for as long as I can remember, has attracted unwarranted and direct violence.[5]

---

5 This is literally the most pointless problem anyone's ever had. Am I a snowflake?

And, yes, although all of the homophobia I've experienced is less important than my wonderful, supportive friends and family rallying around to celebrate my coming into being, I have come to relate that kind of undeserved attention irrevocably to the years of unwanted, undeserved attention I have received for being gay and femme.

To add insult to this stupid injury, birthdays always bring with them a huge amount of guilt. Growing up we didn't have much money, so every time a birthday rolled around it always brought with it this horrible feeling that your parents had spent a fortune on you, even though they couldn't afford to, even though you wanted them to. This guilt continues today because, as a drag queen, I often demand that my friends show me attention and adoration during my shows, so it feels excessive to ask for it on another day for doing nothing.

Anyway, back to last night. Dom, sweetly, had, in fact, planned a surprise party. Perhaps the only thing worse than an all-gay dance troupe.

Every one of my friends, my whole family, and some totally random people I've never even seen in my life.

Naturally, I burst into tears. It was so sweet. It was also a living, breathing nightmare.

My sweet, wonderful parents had come all the way from Lancaster, my brothers and my sister organised childcare and built me a photo album of all of us when we were young.

The Denims had all pooled their minimal cash to buy me a wig – flame red, set in a 1920s style.

Ellie, Hatty, Leyah, Violet and Cecily bought me a bottle of wine from the bar.

Pak gave me a book of Avedon photography. He knows I love coffee-table books because they signify a kind of cultural and economic capital I could never justify both now and when I was growing up.

Ace's family gave me more drink.

Then. Dom made a toast. I knew exactly what was about to happen.

'And speaking of changing worlds, I want to announce some news we have been sitting on: we've been waiting for just the right moment to reveal that we are engaged! I asked, it was a total surprise, and they said yes! And, yes, I'm the happiest person in the world! I'm so glad we can all share this moment together. To the love of my life! Cheers!'

I took brief comfort in the fact that this moment, like my KFC mishap or the time I got fucked on broken glass and had to nip to A+E straight after climax. Will eventually be added to that glorious collection of stories that detail just how unstable all of our early twenties were, to be rolled out when we're all desperate for a bit of nostalgia as we approach a life more settled.

The crowd were naturally baffled. Glamrou left, Pak laughed, Ace locked himself in a loo and cried, and then left. My parents were half happy, half unable to speak.

And then, as we walked through the streets of Soho, after saying goodbye to countless friends who didn't really know how to look me in the eye, Dom started to complain about the negative ways my friends had reacted to our news. And in that moment I couldn't listen any more, and I snapped, cruelly.

'I can't do this any more. I can't. My friends are the most

important thing to me, and they've all proved repeatedly that they're not these things you say about them. I don't want to marry you. I don't want to be with you.'

And he said nothing. He looked, for an instant, like the man I'd met and adored a month and half ago and swept through the sex dungeons and melancholic streets of Budapest with and I wondered if I'd made a grave mistake.

Then he walked away, and I was left with my one birthday wish having come true: to be left alone.

Turns out that's not so fun either.

22nd August / le 22 août

Breaking up with Dom has blown my calendar wide open. Instead of throwing myself into emotionally exhausting back and forths about where we went wrong, I've thrown myself into work.

And because of this up in productivity, it's going well. Denim has scored a residency at this niche café-bistro-bar-whatever called Brasserie Zédel, where rich people come to gawk at you while eating French onion soup. It's absurd; we're like queens for hire, and a lot of these posh people don't have the spine to be openly homophobic and so instead they offer words of encouragement to prove to the rest of the room that they are fine with the gays: 'Aren't you splendid!' they say through gritted teeth. The money is outrageously good though.

The *Guardian* finally accepted my fiftieth pitch – I'll be tracking down and interviewing every Sugababe ever, thus meaning I've hit my journalistic zenith and will never work on anything more important again. That's a lie, actually, because last week I interviewed the Cheeky Girls, who likened the UK music charts to Romania under Ceauşescu's communist dictatorship.

Hatty and I have been working in all our spare time to perfect our music, too, because we've been asked to play at a showcase for Columbia Records. And I've been asked to cover fashion month for one of my favourite magazines – which means I'll be going to Paris for the first time, as well as Milan, London and, quite terrifyingly, back to New York. I still have no money to buy new clothes so I'm going to have to go on a borrowing binge before I leave in early September.

Turns out, when you take your eye off obsession with men and thrust all your energy onto creating positive visions of queerness, the world gets a whole lot bigger.

26th August / le 26 août

A definitive list of things that are queer:
- Never going to the doctor even though you definitely need to this time
- Eating stuff off the floor and saying, 'It's queer, shut up!'
- Justifying terrible behaviour – cheating, stealing, lying on your CV – by deciding that you're queering the system
- Having someone live in your lounge because it makes rent £16 cheaper a month
- Using a political occurrence to post an image of yourself looking very, very good: think thirst trap full beat atop a caption that says 'my face when you vote Leave'
- Calling famous women 'mom'

- Avidly reading the *Guardian* but also thinking the *Guardian* is transphobic trash
- Long, drawn-out breakups
- Nude imagery veiled as radical art practice
- Accidentally sending texts about the person to the person
- Either being incredibly broke and making your whole artistic practice about it, or being incredibly rich, pretending you're incredibly broke, and making your whole artistic practice about it
- Buzz cuts
- Camo wear and construction glasses
- Those chains that lock with a padlock so people think you're into dark shit
- Thinking images of thin, white twinks shot by Tim Walker/Mert and Marcus will end homophobia
- Sex at the gym
- Baking
- Houseplants
- Justifying a drug addiction as radical self-care
- Justifying Ubers as radical self-care
- Oversharing on social media
- Having a very specific interest that everyone else has, i.e. astrology, baking, houseplant care, making your own skincare, comics, old anatomy images, tattoos, short fringes
- Obsessively following celebrities who have questionable sexualities and having very analytical discussions about whether or not they are homos
- Veganism, but eating meat when you're smashed

- Defining as communist but also loving dropping shit tons of cash on new stuff
- Swimming in public swimming pools
- Quitting smoking
- Going out for breakfast
- Variant hair colours and a septum piercing
- Socks and sandals
- Posting that meme on your social media that says 'not gay as in happy, queer as in fuck you'
- Realising a year on that that was actually too sincere so making a new one up where you read queer culture, like: 'not gay as in happy, queer as in have a huge collection of houseplants I call "my children"
- City breaks

A definitive list of things that aren't queer:

- All Bar One
- The Northern line
- Sincerity
- Rachel Dolezal
- Not knowing every lyric to the song 'Dip It Low' by Christina Milian
- V Festival
- Foldable bikes/electric scooters
- Fidget spinners (except that time Amanda Lepore spun one on her left breast)
- Images of thin, white twinks shot by Tim Walker/Mert and Marcus

- Cat memes on your main account (if you have a trap account then this is full of animal memes)
- Movie franchises
- Night-time food markets in Shoreditch called things like 'Ditch' that serve mini burgers and gyoza
- E M Forster books / Alan Hollinghurst books – they're gay not queer
- Top knots (was queer, stolen by men)
- Twee shit like Cath Kidston. Yankee candles became so mainstream it's actually now very queer to have one
- Deep-fried cheeses (baked cheeses or fondues are very queer)
- Banking/accounting/big money jobs
- Calling garments that are usually associated with 'women' a different name so they become passable 'menswear' – i.e. leggings become meggings, jump-suits become rompers

A definitive list of things in between:

- Wrestling
- *The Kardashians*
- *Charlie's Angels,* the movie franchise
- Miley Cyrus
- Poetry
- Long-haul flights
- Exercise
- People who take coke
- Acrylic nails (depends on the style and pattern)
- *EastEnders*

- Jeans
- *Celebrity Big Brother / Love Island*
- Glitter (this was ours but it's been co-opted by white people at festivals and festival-themed weddings so it's anyone's game at this point)
- Craft beers
- Gardening

31st August / le 31 août

It's fucking grotesquely hot in London. Like the kind of hot that makes you sweat through your backpack and worry whether your laptop's going to break from water damage kind of hot.

It's frustrating because when I look around on the tube it always feels like I'm the only one dragging a used napkin across my forehead, bits of tissue sticking along the way, to rid myself of the beads of sweat that have pricked through my now obsolete make-up. Hatty, as she sits there sweatless in a floaty nightie, tells me it's because I wear too many layers. And I always reply saying I feel too self-conscious to expose my fat body in any way.

But she's right: looking around the tubes and the streets and the buses, everyone's in teeny-tiny tops and I'm soaking through all four layers I'm using to cloak how much space my big, wobbling body is taking up.

My body is probably the most time-consuming obsession I have.

It's the thing I always go back to: when my mind is free of other anxieties or obsessions I always land right back to base, to my body, and my constant obsession with covering it. If I'm on a deadline, on a stage or on a dick I don't consider my body, or my hatred for it.

It disappoints me, constantly, that I preach body positivity, fat activism, all the buzz words that populate our feeds and then get sucked into nothingness by brands wanting to profiteer from another unflattering, terribly made Curve collection, while internally I only ever punish my body that works so hard for me.

So each year as the summer rolls around and 90 per cent of the population reveal their gym-toned arms and wardrobe of teeny tiny clothes, I start to torment myself over what my body looks like, taking on unhealthy modes of consumption, wearing a jacket in thirty-degree heat so I won't have to expose the piled-up rolls that populate my torso.

I recently met a friend, through Twitter would you believe, who's a vehement fat activist. She's very fat and very rad and very much practises what she preaches. And while it's evidently a lifelong process, I've been trying to shift my view of this body that I have deemed wrecked for so long, into one of gratefulness, adoration, power.

But it's hard to stay constantly in power over your fat body, and in love with all of it. 'Fat' has been deleted from public discussion. The word, the people, and any positive associations with fatness simply do not exist. The only time we see, or will talk about, fat in public is to state a negative. First, there's the classist kind of fat shaming: on those dreadful morning talk shows where the male presenter will shout a fat person down for spending their benefits on fried chicken. Then there's the patronising kind of fat shaming from random TV doctors: 'Are you not worried about your health? Look at all the terrible food you eat.' There's the coercive kind of fat shaming: all that 'summer body'/'can you keep up with a Kardashian?'/'lose those extra pounds or you'll die alone' crap. There are magazine covers, and sales techniques, that punctuate our lives everywhere we go, telling us 'if you're fat, you're gross'.

All my life people have pussy-footed around the fact that I'm just a bit fat. It's true, I know, the jig is up: I am fat. Often the confession of my awareness of my fatness is rescinded with a retort that goes something like:

'No . . . you're not fat, you're beautiful.'

'You just have a massive ribcage, you're built stocky . . . it's not fat!'

I would be lying if I said I didn't have a massive ribcage, sure, but that doesn't explain my double – sometimes triple – chin, and my party pack in place of a six-pack. These statements allow me to be either fat or beautiful – but not both, which I am.

Despite the fact that late-stage capitalism is designed to ditch the weak, to dump the chubs in the trash alongside people of colour, poor people, queer people, trans people, disabled people, immigrants and women, it is possible to be fat and happy and, as aforementioned, beautiful.

So today, on the Central line, I took off all my layers and stripped myself down to my T-shirt. It was terrifying, and I felt like people were looking at my jiggling boobs and my back rolls, snickering like the kids at school. But I did it.

It's my new mission. This time, as I lie here single, I will not think of the men I can't get or the diet I need in order to get them. Instead, tonight, I'm thinking of how I want to order a Deliveroo for dinner, how I know that will make me happy, and how that is surely better for my health and well-being, and my overall attractiveness, than chucking up another McDonald's in the same bush in your back garden three times a week like when you were a teenager prescribed weight-loss club by your doctor.

My body isn't seasonal, nor is anyone's. It's my vessel through which to experience pleasure: of eating, of sex, of smelling, of doing a really amazing shit. So this time when I start to obsess, I've decided it's high time to obsess over the pleasure I can experience in my body, not the painful ways in which I want to, and have tried and failed to, change it in order to take up less room in the world.

A KFC it is.

September/
septembre

2nd September / le 2 septembre

What does one pack for a month's worth of fashion weeks? In New York it'll be the tail end of summer, back in London it'll be my favourite type of parky September weather, in Milan it'll be classically sultry and all I'll eat is flattened crumbed meats, and in Paris the world will have tipped into autumn and a PVC rain jacket will protect the under-layer of an outfit from the torrents, but see it soaked through with sweat. Sweat isn't very front row.

I'm finding this whole thing pretty absurd – hiking up a humongous carbon footprint to go and watch clothes and then write about them is something that's hard to get your head around when the political, social and environmental climes are as tumultuous as they are right now. But I've always believed in the power of escapism through fashion, plus I need the cash. I always need the cash.

Plus it's really glam.

Plus I'm on the front row at Raf Simons. And Dior, lol. Hope I'm not too sweaty.

4th September / le 4 septembre

Before I left for New York, Glamrou asked if Ace and I wanted to go out clubbing last night for a rare night away from Denim-related stuff. I was packed; all my tickets, money, passport were in order and I'd ditched the Sugababes *Guardian*, article because all six of them responded with various degrees of rejections. What a blow. Now I'm one step further from my ultimate aim: a career in ghostwriting books for northern Z-list celebrities. Jenny Ellison, give me a call.

We started the night as all classy girls do – two-for-one cocktails, which we call 'cocks' because we're all homosexuals, at this bar with Barbies on the roof, which was where I had my traumatic birthday. We're trying to reclaim those spaces back from their association with that savage night. We then swung by the Med Café for a quick coffee and a glass of wine at the same time, and of course Ellie and her dad were there – they're always there, they call it 'the front garden' – smoking and giving us free drinks. We laughed for a little too long, while Bob (Ellie's dad) serenaded us with stories he'd collected from his decades working as a theatre director, which we'd all heard before but were happy to hear again.

Glamrou checked the time, and it was now nearing 1 a.m., so our only option was to hit XXL – the big bear sex club in Blackfriars. We had a shot of tequila, and jumped into a black cab, which we never do but we were already quite smashed and thus had no qualms about chucking a tenner away on what could be a simple tube journey. Out, into the queue, and Ace, Glamrou and I were already sizing up the clientele. It's the first time I'd ever been to a sex club with Ace, and while the idea of going queer clubbing with him before was one which inspired huge anxiety and pre-rejection feelings of rejection, last night I was feeling, frankly, nothing of the sort.

Of course I felt very much emotionally in love with him, but the usually unhealthy crippling jealousy was nowhere in sight. I don't want to plunder this too much, for fear of undoing it, however I think the key lies in my failed attempt at monogamy with Dom, and also a newfound belief in myself that I'm more loveable than a guy he'll find in a sex dungeon at 2 a.m. on a Saturday night, whose face he can't see. If Dom taught me one thing it's that someone could actually be in love with actual me, romantically, and not just the idea of me, and I'm grateful to him for that.

Pak joined us in the queue, with his flatmate Isaac and Isaac's new boyfriend. Things are still somewhat tense between Pak and Isaac, but the new boyfriend – a big, lovely bear – is actually very sweet. It's hard not to feel a little movie-of-the-week warm when someone finds gay love. Anyway, back to the sex club.

We got to the door, and it was the same guy as the last time Glamrou and I were here. We laughed that we weren't sure if I did end up sucking his dick that night, but his wink at my heels and his air of sex was confirmation enough. 'See you later, boys,' he said, tapping Glamrou's ass as we walked in.

'Ugh – boys – that's ruined,' Glamrou glumly remarked as we paid our entry fee and the lights switched from street orange to seedy red. 'I hate it when people just assume you're a boy.'

'Well, this is a male-only sex club,' Isaac's boyfriend piped up. At that, we all jerked our necks around in unison, offended by his gendering of space but aware he was totally right, thereafter questioning our patronage.

We lost Isaac and his boyfriend fairly quickly, and for the following two hours Glamrou, Ace, Pak and I pushed and pulled together, each time in different pairs exploring different parts of the dance floor, the bar, the loos. After too many Red Stripes and countless rubs from topless, sweaty bears whose collective odour takes me back to my childhood garage, in which there was a damp problem, we made a group decision to have a look in the dark rooms.

As we all approached the back of the club, and walked through the Green Room, we became an unstoppable *Sex and the City*-style force, like that bit in the movie when the four of them are walking down the street side by side.

I'm Samantha: slowly unbuttoning my fly, sliding off my top (which I never do unless I'm at a bear club, specifically in the sex room), pushing my fingers through my fringe to make sure the curls have extra bounce. I say something too filthy for words, and disappear into the dark.

Pak is Charlotte: prudish, shy, but desperate to find a husband. We've suggested that a dark room isn't as effective as other places in which Pak might be able to, say, speak to someone, but instead of listening, Pak points to his ring finger and says, excitedly, 'See you at the wedding!' before he steps into a sea of anonymous semen.

Glamrou is Carrie: sexy, coy, a writer and a former smoker. Before we part ways, they make their T-shirt into a sort of fashion crop top, and mutter a sentence perfect for any Carrie B cutaway. 'If sex with strangers is more intoxicating than a dinner date and a DVD, why are we so obsessed with finding true love?'

Ace is Miranda: clever and practical. 'Has everybody had enough water?' Bless him. I love him.

Every dark room is the same. Not architecturally, or in terms of the clientele, but every single memory I have of being in a dark room may as well be the same one. It's quiet – quiet enough to hear an orchestra of groans and moans and whispers and, if you're lucky and listen hard enough, the pattering of a really vigorous hand job. You can also always hear the faint throb of Kylie or house music. It's initially a daunting prospect: upon entry, a sea of shadowed bodies in various states of undress and pleasure greets you; some people on their knees, some in a circle looking down at one hard-working blowjobber sucking eight to ten dicks, some sitting on dicks, some fucking the person sitting on their dick. Until you're inside it, it all appears as one big, beating mass of flesh: pulsating with an intimidating, arousing mix of shame and sex and pleasure and power.

Once you're in it, it's like being absorbed into a sponge or being on a water slide: you lose all idea of space and time and dimension, and spend hours being carried around the room, from dick to dick, without even realising it. It's not uncommon to suck nigh on thirty dicks and not say a single hello. Sometimes, on the other hand, you connect with one person so intensely that you spend the whole night together, talking, kissing, maybe having sex, and feeling like you're going to run away together, like someone finally 'gets you'. In hindsight all of those guys were just very heavily on drugs. But it was nice while it lasted.

Last night was the former – no talking, just anonymous pleasure, circling round the room barely catching glimpses of the other queens, a few of whom had left.

And, as the night drew to a close, I took one more gentle tour around the room, landing on this guy whose face I couldn't make out, who just pushed me down to the ground, incredibly hot. It was only after about three minutes and an increasingly audible groan that I looked up as the light caught Ace's face. I stood up, slowly, and revealed myself and we spent the whole journey home both in hysterics but also deconstructing the cosmic meaning of what this chance encounter had meant.

When we got back to Wally, we finished what we started earlier, eventually falling asleep next to each other, naked. As I arose this morning to head to Heathrow, where I write from a Burger King, there was a note on my pillow left by Ace, which said the same thing I had written on a note when I left him for New York a year ago now:

> When you wake up, when you go to sleep, and every hour in between, I'll be thinking of you.

A nice note on which to leave, I think. I've learned, however, to leave expectations to a minimum. So I do just that and focus on the task at hand: fashion.

8th September / le 8 septembre

My guide to fashion week parties:

- You're on the list. Even if you're not on the list, you're on the list. At no point should it ever be revealed that you were never on the list.
- To confirm you're on the list you work at only the most important magazine/fashion house/P R firm in the whole of fashion.

- If you wear sunglasses and get your tone right and turn up looking frantic but in control, like busy is your forever mood, and act as though it's the person holding the list who's responsible for your not being on it, your chance of entry will increase four-fold, at least.
- Either dress way way up or way way down. No in between, no 'nice'. It's either a head-to-toe archive Miu Miu fluffy four-piece suit sent to you by Miuccia herself (stolen from the fashion cupboard at work) or banged-up trainers, a white T-shirt and grey sweat pants. Anything in between and you won't look suitably over it, or suitably under it.
- Once you're in, use the coat check. Rich people and fashion people are the only two types of people who won't chuck their coat and handbag on the floor and the initial entry is all about looking both rich and fashion.
- Then, once you're in and have a complimentary glass of champagne, take your pick between the four sub-moods of a fashion party and stick to it:

  1. Fucked. This is 90 per cent of attendees; too much coke too much chatting but you'll fit right in and maybe Marc Jacobs' boyfriend will follow you on Instagram once you've made a point of telling him you follow him.
  2. Bored. This is a hard one to get right, but will guarantee you ten points in cool rating. You must not: smile, remove your sunglasses, talk to more

than three people all of whom you know very, very well, take any photos or mention to anyone you went to this party even if someone asks you.

3. Fucked and bored. This will eventually be 90 per cent of the attendees. Conversation has gone dry, your boozy, friendly countenance has dissolved and your shoes are hurting. There's no more to be squeezed from the lemon that is this party, but Gigi just arrived and you want to wait to see if you can maybe befriend her for the Insta followers.

4. Yourself. A hard one to pull off; try it at your peril. One time when I was myself at a fashion party I ended up weeping on Rita Ora, telling her she'd saved my life. It's not even true. I then tried the same with Halle Berry and was forcibly ejected from said party.

• Never, ever, look the following people in the eye: Naomi Campbell, the door girl who knows you blagged your way in the moment she let you past, any of the big models except Poppy Delevingne because she's not quite made it and needs a friend from time to time, the famous female rapper you just met in the toilet, and the two girls you know but, if you do, will only talk to you about iPhone cases and what the *Vogue* party was like last night, and the Calvin Klein party was like the night before that. They will talk to you for three hours, and every time you think the conversation has dried up they will bring up a random mutual social media friend who you absolutely despise because they're a proud Tory but you can't say anything because one of these girls' dads is a director at Condé Nast. They will likely corner you by an outdoor fire or a speaker and you will either be too hot to concentrate or it will be too loud to hear them.

- Try to get into one official photograph taken by the guy with the swept-back grey curly bob who takes every photo. While posting about your party presence on social media has become unsavoury in the fashion party world, there's nothing wrong with showing up unwittingly on Getty images looking great then posting on Facebook, 'omg lol last night'.

- Do not, under any circumstances, stay until the end. You'll look desperate. Get out of there, preferably with a few friends, and act as though you're heading somewhere glamorous and not straight home to order a Pizza Hut and stream episodes of *Real Housewives of Cheshire*, which you're rewatching for the fifth time.[1]

10th September / le 10 septembre

I was nervous to come back to New York. Not that it had ever done anything to me, other than been a harsh mistress, an unconquerable thirteen-by-two-mile island that saw me sext for my boss and shit.

When I moved here last year it was the first time I'd ever

---

1 Hands up who misses Magali?

been: I wandered around for the first week, waited outside the *Vogue* offices to catch a glimpse of Anna Wintour, spent $16 on a cocktail at the Bowery just so I could say I had, all while fantastical Carrie Bradshaw monologues, quote for quote, raced through my head.

But it turned out I wasn't Carrie Bradshaw. Nor was I Samantha, and I definitely was never going to be a Miranda or a Charlotte. When I arrived into JFK this time, I was nervous. I had shed all my cultural touch points, my lenses through which to see the city, them having not quite fit the last time: I wasn't Patti Smith, nor was I Andy Sachs. I wasn't Lady Bunny or RuPaul or any of the queens who invented Wigstock and performed at the Pyramid Club. I wasn't Marsha P. Johnson or Stormé DeLarverie, nor was I Amanda Lepore, Joey Arias or Penny Arcade.[2]

For me, the idea of New York had only ever been a full fantasy – lived through obsession with these figures and the way they had lived New York.

As my taxi made its way towards the centre of Manhattan, I stopped and got out on my old street and decided to walk[3] from the Lower East to where I was staying in midtown (what a blow).

Perhaps because I was back here on my own terms, or perhaps because I wasn't longing for somewhere else, I stopped being nervous and just felt like I was seeing New York. And you know what? It's pretty grey.

---

2 If you're unsure of these names, it's time you used Google properly!

3 Which is unlike me. I hate walking.

11th September / le 11 septembre

Got fully fucked up with Lily and Cora last night, and we all ended up making out. We were bought shooters by some random banker dude who was obviously into the spectacle, and eventually he pulled me over to him, handed me another shooter and told me he wanted to pound my queen hole in the bathroom.

I was thinking of Ace, but we're not exclusive and frankly I needed to get some in if we were going to go the whole hog and go monog.[4]

He was fancy – well, he was wearing a custom Armani suit, which is code for money no style – and as we slammed the bathroom door he got his cock out and started calling me 'bitch', which I told him to stop: 'It's misogynist, you idiot.' I gagged as his precum snail-trailed on my glittery beard.

On my knees, he was moaning and sort of heaving with delight. Or so I thought.

Or. So. I. Thought.

Until a heave turned to a gip – which I still assumed was an (albeit weird) moan of pleasure. Until a gip turned into a bigger heave, his dick still in my mouth, and a heave turned into a full stomach of rich food, red wine and probably three grams of coke chucked up all over my head from the bird's-eye position.

Imagine that feeling of disappointment when a bird shits on your good hair. Then multiply that by a thousand times the volume and make it human sick and make it a

---

4 -amous.

club where a bunch of your editors are, the same one where Solange kicked Jay-Z in the lift. That's how my night ended – bathed in the worst of the six bodily fluids in the epicentre of fashion week's afterparties.

13th September / le 13 septembre

This morning, post a dance at one of Susanne Bartsch's parties in order to resurface onto the nightlife scene to try to reclaim my vomit-inducing vomit humiliation as iconic, Cora, Lily and I wandered off to buy apple doughnuts from Dean and DeLuca and sit in the park and catch up properly, before I had to go to shows.

As I sat there, I was reminded how lucky I am to have made friends like these in a city where everyone feels lonely. I was reminded of certain prevailing memories from my first time here, but they only served as a comparative mechanism to demonstrate how much one's life can change in, what, eight months?

I also managed to skim through my diary. I tried to mark out a specific point where the tide changed, where I became a person looking back on a series of diary entries feeling like both the same person who wrote them, but not remembering what I actually felt like writing them.

I landed on the entry from the day I quit my job, and then checked my phone to see a follow on Instagram from none other than my old boss Eve. I spent a moment considering whether this was actually fate, but then I blocked her (without even stalking her), which to me feels like huge growth.

Somewhere in there I talk about a man I slept with who asked me to run to something, not from it, which at the time I took down as total privileged frippery. I still think it's totally privileged – so many people I know, and so many I don't, are unable to choose what to run from or to – but it also strikes true, as I recall at that time feeling like something was chasing me, that feeling now a vestige of one, not an actual one.

Tacky as it is, but I reckon I was running from, or maybe being chased by, a paralysing fear of myself. When I was here before I felt like I'd paid my dues on working through all the ways in which I'd failed by society's standards, and so I figured everything from thereon would go swimmingly. I hadn't considered that I would constantly have to assess my choices and why I was making them. This realisation was perhaps why I scarpered to another continent the moment I could.

I don't think there's a singular, definitive answer to looking at yourself and liking yourself, but I think I'm starting to realise that therein lies the answer. There's no definitive stop, no point where you've worked on yourself totally to then arrive at a place where you're happy with yourself: the choices you've made, the way you treat others, the way you allow others to treat you, the things you do for money and the way you uphold systems that both hurt you and benefit you.

I always used to say to myself that it was important to work hard to be the person you eventually want to be, and you'll eventually become them. I used to think this would happen overnight: like eventually you save enough money to then tip from overdrawn to drawn.[5] But I can't see that actually happening – at the end of all the work there's no final eventuality other than an acceptance that my queerness, my fatness, my drag, my class, all my identities, my relationships, my love life are all messy, rolling, fluid. There's no turning point into stability, there's no end to the learning, and there's no one conception of yourself that you'll one day land on and be happy with. The person I'm working towards doesn't exist, because they're always changing.

15th September / le 15 septembre

Back in London and so many of the runway shows are referencing drag. Some are doing it well, some are doing it flimsily. I ran into an editor friend of mine and we spent a lunch discussing the appropriation of drag culture by the mainstream.

'We're all assigned a gender role, so is gender not anyone's to mess up? Is drag itself already an appropriation of femininity or masculinity? And what about drag lexicon?'

She was asking me a bunch of smart questions, and I was just sucking the dressing off salad leaves because I hate salad but that's all there was left at the fashion week café.

Yes, drag is appropriation. We've taken a lot from working-class black women, for example. A lot of the words I once bandied about, thinking I was getting the whole being a drag queen thing right by screaming 'slay' and

---

5 Is that a thing? I've been in my overdraft since I opened a bank account.

'shaaaade' and 'oooh girl' and 'you better work, bitch' and 'henny', I later realised weren't my words to use freely, even as a drag queen.

Of course I didn't say that, I just stared blankly and said, 'This would make a really interesting feature?', hoping to get paid.

'Doesn't drag get a free pass, though, because it exists in a neighbouring realm of oppression?' – her next question. Again, I said I didn't think so, but I was nervous and was thinking of the pay cheque.

What I really think is no, it doesn't get a free pass. It does get things wrong and that's okay. Drag thrives on the incorporation of aspects of different cultures – but I think where you fall on the race, class, gender, sexuality, ability hierarchy within society has to matter when deciding what cultures you can draw from. Can drag offensively appropriate? Yes. Can drag also undermine and put right that kind of appropriation? Absolutely. The best queens will do the latter.

We talked some more, and I stumbled over answers, trying to be as impressive yet chilled as I could.

'Why is there such a fuss about drag?' – her closing question.

I spluttered out some shit to do with power in failure.[6] But why is there such a fuss about drag? I've never really thought about it other than just saying, 'RuPaul, obviously.' Is it the sequins? The wigs? The make-up?

As I packed my suitcase for a Denim gig we have tomorrow, laying the sequins over the chiffon, packing the wigs

---

6 I really need to read another book.

and the heels, I wondered why on earth I had landed on living this way.

Of course, the sensory elements of drag are absolutely something to make a fuss about. But drag isn't simply the buying and wearing of these fabulous, subversive, glittering markers. It's not about what these markers are; it's about what donning them means. Drag comes from a place of absolute need.

Drag forces you to question the world as it's been presented to you. It asks you to step into a world of radical history, broken-down gender systems, and acerbically critical wit. Drag represents a world of possibility: a world where someone can create a whole new person and, if lucky, a whole new family of their own. Drag allows you to be anything you want to be.

That's why people who come to drag often devote their lives to it. To a precarious pay cheque, a rota of late nights and pricey costumes; to damaged skin and cracked nail beds; to bouts of scary homophobia and blistered feet. Because, beyond all that, drag allows you to become the kind of superstar you never thought you were allowed to be. It allows you transcend this terrifying plane. Drag is radical. Drag gives you new perspectives, allowing you to pull back the curtain and glimpse a world where you're free of all the restrictions that cause you pain. It's a healing aid, it's a therapy. It's an antidote to all the terror outside.

And while drag is probably the most fun you can have with your clothes on, the fuss is about more than just fun. It's about love – for yourself, for your siblings. It's about giving back to people, and saving a bit for yourself. It's about being the most glorious person in the room, while pulling everyone up to your level. It's about proving that, while you might be an outcast, you're quicker, cooler, funnier than the people on the inside. It's about proving that being a misfit is the best place to be. It's about showing there's hope, and that happiness and power aren't the stronghold of those in power. We have it, so much of it, in abundance. And we actually deserve it.

I decided to email my editor most of these ramblings, and she replied:

'Yeah cool can pay u £45 for 1000 words?'

Gorj! So glad years of my life spent thinking is worth £45! At least my Ubers for tomorrow night are covered.

17th September / le 17 septembre

Speaking of drag, last night we had a Denim gig – a thirtieth birthday for Glamrou's housemate who's a really attractive twink. Can you be a thirty-year-old twink? A contradiction in terms, surely, but he pulls it off.

I realised only when I got to central London for the day of shows that I'd forgotten the suitcase I packed, so I ran over to the costume shop where my northern friend Chris works – So High Soho, an institution – and together we constructed a look that was half Shakespeare half 'Sissy That Walk'. Think an oversized, foppish shirt, a wavy red wig, and some thigh-high boots.

Had lunch with Ace. We both discussed how it burned when we went for a wee and blood came out too, so we booked in to have a speedy STI test before the gig tonight.

Gig went fine. Ace flirted with an annoying cool guy from Berlin who makes short films about contemporary dance or some wanky shit, so I went to leave – a looming flight to Milan – but Ace asked me to wait: 'Two mins! I just need to say goodbye.'

Forty minutes and thirteen cigarettes later, I was furious – a mug once again, stood there looking like a Shakespearean jester, ready to draw a line under it. As I turned toward the corner to find a better Uber spot, I heard Ace shouting me.

'Stop! I have something to tell you. Well, ask you. I don't know.'

We both switched on our phones, which had been off for the duration of the gig.

'I want to be with you. Not just like the way we are. But I want to be with with you. Together. I love you. I just told Glamrou, downstairs, that's why I was taking so long and they told me I have to say it now or I'll regret it forever. Why just be best friends with the person everyone wants to be best friends with when I can be *the* person, your person, and you can be my person. You're already my person. Stop me, say something, oh my Go—'

Both of our phones picked up a bunch of texts.

Both of us received a message from the sexual health clinic. Both of us have gonorrhoea. Team.

'Wow, the most romantic moment ever ruined by the most unromantically named STI ever,' Ace sighed.

We got in the cab. Went home. I asked for some time to think, while I'm away in Milan at least. He obliged.

The usual me would have immediately said yes. But I'm

trying this new thing where I think about the things I need, just briefly, before I jump straight into a relationship. While the fantasy of jumping into a relationship with a best friend sounds just dreamy, de facto there's much more to consider.

I need to sleep. And get my clap treated.

19th September / le 19 septembre

Do I want to be this man's best friend or partner? If we go for it there's no going back. No matter the amount of frou-frou well-intentioned promises we make each other about 'working hard to maintain our friendship if we were ever to break up' or 'having an open and honest communication channel re: our feelings', there's absolutely not a single speck of hope that once you have moved through a relationship together, and then a breakup, things can ever go back to the way they once were, when you were simply best friends in the magical, hurricane-like place where you're on the brink of falling in love.

If we don't go for it there's also no going back. Firstly, there's no way to access the way we were when this all began. That incarnation of us, that simpler, more naïve version of us, is over – dead in the water. We've changed, both individually and with each other: we've inflicted scars and hurts that weren't there when the seeds of this thing were planted so greenly. Besides, all friendships change – especially the intensely unsustainable ones you desperately don't want to. There's no way those huge, wonderful thunderstorms that some new friends bring into your life can last forever. So while we talk about 'risk' about 'losing what we have', it'll never be the same for ever anyway. It might grow into something better or healthier, but it won't be what we have now. Beyond that, the what ifs would always slightly encumber our ability to be real best friends – seeing each other with other people, always wondering if he was the one that got away, as cheesy and delusional as that sounds.

I thought this would be easy. I dreamed of this moment in times when I felt particularly lonely or melancholic, and now I have fewer answers than I had before all of this started. I worry, for a moment, that I've done that awful thing where all I really wanted was the amateur dramatics of the chase, the rush of the turmoil, and now the outcome is positive it doesn't get my rocks off the way emotional torture does.

But now, sitting here, when I think about Ace I feel full, happy, warm and understood.[7]

And that's the only answer I need.

Of course I'll wait a few days to tell him – let him sweat – plus I have a Philipp Plein show to go hate on.

Ciao!

24th September / le 24 septembre

So I slept with someone else. A fashion person with whom I'd bonded over the preceding international weeks as we were both equally out of our depths. He's hotter than my usual one-nighter scores often are, and he wears loads of

---

7 And I have an erection.

Louis Vuitton because he once had sex with a very famous designer.

I realised that this was the first time in years I'd met someone organically and had sex with them not via a dating or hookup app, except Ace, and I enjoyed the process very much. The slow build, the flirt, the eye rolls across the runway at Dolce & Gabbana as they sent yet another bunch of irrelevant influencers down the runway.

I don't think I'll see him again, though, because he did that really annoying thing where someone forces your head repeatedly onto their dick. Usually I'm into this, so I couldn't put my finger on why I wasn't. But I wasn't.

I realised, too, that this was the first time I couldn't make particularly bad sex work for me. It just was bad and there was no fixing it. What was weirder is that he thought it was great.

At uni my saying used to be: 'You *can* polish a sexual turd' – which meant that even in unsatisfying sexual situations it was guaranteed there was always a story in there, and most often a happy ending. But this wasn't even funny or outrageous, and the happy ending came after he came and he spent the next, what, twenty minutes lying there tired, giving me a hand job as I slowly went soft at the sight of his evident apathy. In the end I thought about my rugby coach[8] from high school, which always does the trick.

Perhaps my inability to turn this sexual frown upside down was linked to the fact I feel already committed to Ace. But, before this whole relationship thing kicks off, I'd

---

8 Lol, me, rugby.

already told myself that having one final blow was going to be much needed. And while there was indeed a final blow, it wasn't really a blow at all; he just kind of gummed it like a baby with no teeth gums a banana.[9]

Perhaps I'm getting boring.

26th September / le 26 septembre

Agenda for today: 5 p.m. The Versace show. The final show on my Milan schedule, and one I've been dying to go to for as long as I've been able to wipe my own bum (a skill which came surprisingly late, because I used to love it when my grandma would wipe my bum and praise me by saying 'clean as a new pin!').

Problem is, there's a Wally party happening in London tonight. Everyone we know is going – including a bunch of the boys Ace has been dating on rotation from within our wider friendship group. The queer scene, while vast, is also amazingly incestuous.

As the day has crept by, and I've eaten yet another portion of crumbed meat, I've begun to spiral into worry: if I'm not at the Wally party tonight, I'll miss my chance with Ace for ever. He'll choose one of the guys there over me. They all have muscular torsos.

I have to make a choice: the Versace show of my dreams or a relationship with Ace. For the romantics among us it sounds like a no-brainer, but for me it isn't. From my

---

9 I should mention that I had a jab in the ass for my gonorrhea the morning of my flight to Milan.

new-fangled 'what do *you* need?' angle I would be a fool to ditch my Versace show for true love. Fashion is my first true love. After food. And Celine Dion.

I'm going to fly back.

OK, so I didn't fly back immediately. I went to the show for all of four catwalk models before I stood up (to tuts and head shakes of fashion folk who were on their phones anyway) and left to catch a flight to London.

27th September / le 27 septembre

A car.

A flight.

A wine.

A train. Another wine on the train.

A foot tapped in anxiety nigh on a million times.

A cigarette.

A tube.

A walk.

Torrential rain.

A key, a door, a flight of stairs: a massive party.

Wet. Dripping wet.

Ace.

I saw him in a see-thru shirt dancing with the lights behind him – beams shining through his outfit, a cut-out of a glorious body of a person I really do love.

There were none of his other boys to be seen. I dropped my bag, walked across the warehouse, and stepped right in front of him.

'Yes please, can we do this?'

'You're home!'

'Is your offer still valid?'

'It is!'

And then we kissed in front of every one of our friends.

We were there together, in the same place, wanting the same thing, for the first time.

We both laughed as we started to use tongues, unable to control ourselves, as we heard every one of our friends who has lived through the confusion of our situation cheer and clap in celebration. Savannah, Ace's sister, was shouting, 'It was inevitable!' repeatedly at the top of her lungs, and 'Euphoria' by Loreen played out over the amp Hatty had stolen from our local rehearsal room.

It was the most romantic three hours of my life. And the little queen inside me, who has been so bound in nets of rejection for so many years, was temporarily set free – and she sang all night.

October/
octobre

3rd October / le 3 octobre

For the first time I feel like I don't have to diarise every detail of my interactions with Ace to prove they're real, to take them from a jumble in my head to a tangible, organised thing on the page.

Because instead of being on the page it's jumped out of my mind, where I'd assumed it was partially made up like so much of my love life past, and into reality. Into kissing without spiralling out or needing to be high, into talking without an awkward feeling of there being so much unsaid, into touching without flinching after that electric zing – instead feeling it, leaning into it.

I had to go to Paris,[1] and Ace then surprised me the day after by coming too. I'm not so fussed about writing about what Paris looks like in love because everyone knows. And why waste time writing about Paris in love, when I could be in Paris in love?

I literally am Carrie. 'An American Girl in Paris Part Une'. 'A Northern Queen in Paris Part Deux'.

4th October / le 4 octobre

Been asked to write a non-binary how-to, which I'm unsure about, frankly, because there's no real how-to this.

Thus far, these are my notes:

- They/them/their is the most common pronoun used among non-binary people. However, there are also

---

1 When did I get so glam? Ugh, capitalism is so attractive, goddamn it.

countless other words and pronouns used. I know someone who uses Miranda instead of he/she/they/ze and it's amazing. Don't question someone's definition, just accept it and try to get it right.

- Non-binary folk are often seen in relation to binary cis gender, but we exist outside that in our own right, not in relation to. Try to reposition your view of us; it's way less hard than other things straights do like going to the gym or years of unhappy marriage.
- Don't conflate or compare gender and medical transition. There are endless ways to transition.
- Gender is often contextual; it changes for everyone. My gender changes a thousand times over the course of a day. There are endless genders, and I have been, like, six while writing this.
- We're learning too, experimenting with our presentation until we learn what's right for us.
- Non-binary genders aren't a millennial fad. We have existed for centuries.
- Gender is a Western and colonial construct. Think of the hijras of India, the two-spirits of Indigenous Americans, the waria of Indonesia, the māhū of Hawaii, the muxes of Juchitán, Mexico. We didn't invent non-binaryism.
- We all present ourselves differently but that doesn't make our identity any less valid.
- We aren't just words or online ideas – we are human and very, very real.
- We're actually really fun, just like you. Please don't tiptoe around us. Unless, of course, you're a

transphobe: then tiptoe. Tiptoe like you've never tiptoed before.

Trying to add something in about nail varnish, but it's just not clicking.

5th October / le 5 octobre

There's no sex quite like new-relationship sex. I'm fully aware and expectant that new-relationship sex will most probably dwindle into three-times-a-week sex after a month, once a week after a year, and once(ish) a month, with slightly more regular pre-bed hand jobs, thereafter until you break up or die.

But new relationship sex is much like a recipe. Not that I'd know because I can't cook. But I reckon it's much like a recipe:

New-Relationship Sex
Ingredients
1 year of yearning looks, to grease the tin
11 months of casual flirting disguised as best friendship, at near boiling temperature
10 years of romantic rejection, finely chopped
1 guarantee that new relationship person is into you/won't reject you mid sex (the worst), for the topping
1 new body to explore, whipped until smooth
100 per cent actually wanting to pleasure your partner, rather than just get your own rocks off with a guy on Grindr, to season

80(ish) sexual partners with whom you've learned some pretty impressive tricks, to finish

A pinch of desperation that you want to show your new partner your best bits, to help the relationship rise successfully

A dash of whipped cream, because it's hot

Method

Take all ingredients and the mash them together into a stiff aromatic mix where pleasure is the optimal consistency of the final concoction. Bake/fry/spit-roast mixture in interesting settings: club toilets, the back of a taxi, a bush, under the table at a fancy restaurant, a bush again, sometimes in bed but more likely on the floor next to it, in the kitchen, the bathroom, the hallway, the hallway, the hallway, in your flatmate's bed when she's out, in a dog park in the morning, on a tube late at night, and one time in the deep end of a kids' swimming pool after-hours.

6th October / le 6 octobre

It's every gay kid's dream to be a pop star. That is statistically 100 per cent fact. No matter how far you move away from that childhood dream – some gays are now allowed to play sports and be builders and stuff – every gay kid dreams of pop stardom.

It's something that I still secretly want: to be as culturally agitative as Madonna, as mainstream yet transgressive as Gaga, as wildly talented and politically empowering as Beyoncé, as important a lifeline to people as Liza or Judy. For me it's always female pop stars.

Well, today, Denim got the news that we had been signed – by an agent who wants to put us on stages everywhere. I'd always secretly wondered why I wasn't famous yet, but turns out it was just a matter of time (and six years' hard work, late nights, bad gigs and no money). We all calmed each other down, not wanting to get our hopes up, but it's always been my belief that if you lie to yourself about stuff enough, it'll just come to you.

So, diary, let it be known that on this day – 6 October – I became famous.

7th October / le 7 octobre

Three people. Three people are all it takes to make the perfect drag audience. I learned this, officially, this weekend, when Denim hosted a gig at this shambolic festival in Southampton, at the end of which I stripped in a trite ode to body positivity to a grand total of three people.

In a giant tent, I'd say capacity 350, three people watched me strip. And it was the most joyful moment, full of failure and transcendence and queerness where we, the four of us, had found a place free from external pressures and just were. Afterwards we all embraced and one of the women watching wept, and then stripped for us too.

9th October / le 9 octobre

We all experience our first death at different times. I've been lucky enough to dodge death my whole life, save for the occasional pet. But when it comes, it arrives from the side, often with no warning, and decimates the small things in your world, the routines or emotions that usually dictate the hum of life now rendered useless, inappropriate and trite in comparison.

This afternoon I was grumbling around the house, upset with Leyah for eating my grated Cheddar. I had been about to make the only meal I can cook for myself – pasta parcels, pesto and cheese – but the Cheddar was gone from the fridge. That's the best bit. As I stood there, vowing to seek retribution by stealing the most treasured thing on Leyah's shelf,[2] my phone rang.

'Are you sitting down?' It was Beth, one of my best friends from high school.

'I can be. Should I sit down? Are you pregnant?' I said, totally overexcited.

'No. I didn't want to call you out of the blue but you're so far away and I didn't want you to see on Facebook.'

'You're engaged! Oh my God, I knew it! Although I thought he would be asking you when you went to—'

'It's not that either, let me finish.'

I hear her intake breath, like the sound someone makes when they're trying to pull themselves out of heaving sobs. When you went through teenagerdom with someone, you come to know their version of this sound very well.

'Wait, are you crying? What's up?' I sit down.

'I can't believe I'm saying this, but . . . Ben . . . It's Ben. Ben's just been in accident and he was found dead on arrival.'

'Ben who?' I knew exactly which Ben, but I was clinging

---

2 A can of pale ale and a sesame seed bagel.

for one second more onto the idea that it might be another Ben, a more distant Ben.

It wasn't, though. It was our Ben. One of our best friends from high school Ben. He had been driving characteristically fast down a country lane near where we grew up, and had crashed into a tractor. Had died on impact.

'I'm coming home. Should I come home? I'm coming home,' I say coldly, not sure how else to respond.

10th October / le 10 octobre

It was only when I was pulling through stations nearing Lancaster on the train that I realised I hadn't visited my home town in over a year and a half. I speak to my mum every day on the phone, and my dad three times a week, my siblings too. I WhatsApp with all my friends from school on a group called 'Slags (No Lauren)' – a name made when one of our girls, Lauren, beat up two of our girls on a night out and it was decided we should make a group without her. We've never changed the name back, but we've all lost touch with Lauren, except when there's a red alert and we happen to see her on a night out. Then the evening is spent skilfully dodging her. There's also the terminal misogynist issue of the word 'slags'. But it's a funny word, we were all pure slags at high school, and my friend Beth named the group, so I feel like I have permission to rejoice in its reclamation.[3]

---

3 It must be noted here that there are a lot of words communities reclaim that are not yours to use if you don't belong to that community. Faggot is one, the n word is most definitely one.

Anyway, slags, I used to go home all the time, back when I was at university, and the years following that. But over the last year and a bit, I've developed a more complicated relationship with where I'm from and I've been putting off the work it might take to go back there.

It's a relationship I've rarely thought about, wanting to avoid facing the guilt I feel for actively distancing myself from where I come from, in every respect. I didn't know about my class until I was grown up – because when you're in it you don't see it. It's not something I had to deal with until I moved to university, where class difference played out everywhere.

My relationship with Lancaster stretches across a complicated nexus of strings that I've stretched to near breaking the more I desperately tried to assimilate into my new life in London, a life which I thought had more meaning.

At Cambridge I met a group of people who expanded my world view so shockingly, so irrevocably, that I constantly felt, simply, grateful to be allowed to go along for the ride. I was desperate to fit in with my new radical group of friends: confident, cool, political, and with endless amounts of knowledge and critical thought I didn't even know existed in the world. I just thought criticism meant, like, criticising someone's outfit because did you see what Charlotte wore to her wedding? Seriously pure tack, who wears a short dress to their wedding?? Omg and him with a tribal tattoo???

Of course my friends from Cambridge knew all about criticism – they went to Eton, St Paul's, Ampleforth, Westminster, Harrow, St Blah of Blah where daddy and daddy's daddy went. It's not fair to upbraid these friends for where they were sent to school but it is fair to talk about the vast differences these types of education proffered.

In truth, I've benefited from their education hugely. I've invested the way I talk about my queerness or my work with the way they were taught to talk and think about this stuff: with confidence, entitlement, knowledge and a vigour that allows them to take up space.

But with my upbringing it didn't work the other way. Until recently, I thought that where I'm from, and the culture that resides there, has nothing to offer: I can't explain gender theory with my rough state school education; I can't offer advice on post-structuralism when I've only known what it means for a few years and still don't know whether I actually understand it.

And I think about my friends, and my family. My girlfriends who say things like: 'Yeah, feminism and stuff, but some women are just fucking dicks.'

And: 'Okay, explain this to me: why do we need gay Pride when you're, like, out and stuff? We don't get straight Pride!'

And: 'I'm not voting. I'm just not into voting.'

These statements go entirely against my world view now. Often, when challenged and offered other viewpoints, my friends will be the first – quicker than any of my friends in London – to admit they 'didn't think of that!' Sometimes, when we clash hard, they'll call me a snob and I'll call them offensive, but we'll quickly be laughing and agreeing that we were perhaps both wrong.

But then I really think about my friends: the friends that stood up to playground bullies, my ten best girlfriends who collectively beat up a guy in my year because he'd pinned me against a wall and was repeatedly kicking a football into my face, over and over. I think about how so much of our youth was filled with getting fingered in parks, stealing booze from Amy's mum's booze cabinet and getting so pissed we all snogged and cried, always prioritising laughter over whether we might be perceived as smart enough, cool enough, well read enough. We didn't ever read – I can't think of a single close friend of mine who had a bookshelf growing up. And while I might later have been publicly humiliated for having never read Oscar Wilde – 'But you're gay?!?' – I can guarantee my best friends can tell a story with as much life, vigour, humour, knowingness as Wilde ever could.

It would be naïve to claim that class difference doesn't matter. But, as I think about the class I've tried to distance myself from, I consider how much of me it has produced and how grateful I am for what it's given me. While public perceptions might be that the working classes are stupid yobs, my experience couldn't be further from that. Here, in Lancaster, I was shown the ropes on how to live a fuller life better than any book or lecture or artwork might teach me. I was taught the importance of hard work, of accepting others around you as long as they're 'sound', of having a fucking brilliant time. I was taught the importance of family and about committing to your friends. I was taught how to tell a story and laugh about the impossibly hard things in life. I was taught so much that is valuable to who I am now.

As I pull into Lancaster, Beth is waiting for me in the car

park with Matt, Hannah and Sara and I get a text which reads:

> In car park! We can't wait to see you, baby. Meeting Becky and the baba at the Sun for a bottle of rosé – I think we all need a cry. xxxxx

12th October / le 12 octobre

Being at home is a strange thing for someone who's currently trying to prove to their family they've forged a successful adult identity. By this I don't mean that dreadful verb 'adulting' when used in relation to things like doing washing. I find that millennial trend a particularly bleak one, one which will make baby people of us all.

But no matter how good you've become at being away from home, in your own context, making your own money, forging your own routine, the minute you step over the threshold, into Mum and Dad land, you become the baby again – your siblings ribbing you because you're the spoiled one, the one who always gets their own way, the one who always 'goes on about politics'; your mum practically forcing you to the ground so that she can cut your nails, squeeze your blackheads and feed you vitamin tablets.

My dad is the exception to this rule: he and I have always had a very specific and sensitive bond. We would, and still do, have long conversations about things like the stars and family and mental health and what the provisos for success are in a rapidly changing world or just how Rachel Dolezal could've gone that far on her quest into post-racialism. My dad is a very special man, and he's also very, wonderfully, strange – I credit him totally with my love of a good shit story, and my often irrationally romantic side. While the world plunders what it means to be a man, my dad taught me very early on – as he lay on the floor next to my bed and made up stories about boys who were mermaids – that being a man wasn't half as fulfilling as being yourself.

My sister is one of the most memorable people I know, even though she's the furthest from a show-off you could find. She says the most inopportune or hilarious things as if she's looking for trouble. She taught me the power of the outrageous story in effectively breaking ice.

My brother, Harry, is a show-off. Just like me. Together we get into huge fights as my mum yelps, 'I can't cope,' at a louder and louder pitch, which only drives us further. He's also a wonderful person who is constantly trying to understand others around him.

My other brother, James, taught me how to party. Not like a soft-core drinks thing, like a blazingly wankered four-nighter at a festival. He's famously 'chilled', although since he had a baby he's become more serious (until they're in bed wherein he brings out mental stories of what he and his friends got up to all those times I was too young to go out and party).

And then there's me. While I don't want to sound full of ego or self-obsession here, I often think that our collective openness comes from the fact that there's a queer person in the family, a person who cracked open the normative dynamic and asked for more of us all. I write this having been told this by them. While we're just like other families in my home town, a get-together will so often consist of a conversation that flits from drag queens to childcare, dresses my mum asked our lightly homophobic next-door neighbour to make for me to stories from another stag do my brothers went on. When I visit friends' houses their parents say things to me, with a knowing wink as if they've really got the measure of us gays, like: 'Oh, there's a new gay couple living two roads over!' or 'Oh, your mum says you have a partner – she's so amazing about it all!'

But my family doesn't say things like that, not any more. We went from fighting to discussing fisting in a decade. And while that kind of candour, and the humour and love with which we all now approach it, journeyed via some dark pits and scary cul-de-sacs, we all emerged from the other side with an understanding that there's more to be gained by speaking about our differences than there is by trying to go through life smiling on the outside but wilting within. As I looked around the dinner table, I couldn't think of any other biological family I'd rather have, and they've proved time and time again that what they need isn't a façade or distance: it's honesty, and a chance to prove that they're *always* willing to learn.

13th October / le 13 octobre

I have been attacked for who I am my entire life. Going home there's a little map in my head of all these encounters: as I drove past my old school I remember the ache of a stream of Bibles being launched at me by two boys who were telling me to die; as I drove past my old bus stop I recall the sting I felt after five men on the bus straddled me, pinning me down, squeezing lemon juice into my eyes as they shouted 'faggot'. As I approach home I remember the darts in my lungs after sprinting there from a nearby petrol station, fleeing from three men who threatened repeatedly to kill me, over and over, in the most violent of ways, because I was wearing pink flip-flops. I remember feeling heartbroken the way a fourteen-year-old should never feel, as I threw my favourite pink flip-flops away that same night. As I wept, I promised myself that from then on, forever, I would wear whatever made me happy.

Foremost, I find these memories upsetting – for the little, confused boy I was then who never knew everything was going to be all right. I find it more upsetting that I still don't know if it is now. I also find these memories sickly rewarding, that I'm thankful they happened to me because they armed me with a quicker wit and a more advanced danger detector than most people I've ever met.

But today I went into town to buy a shirt for Ben's funeral. At university I was, for want of not trying to sound like a big-headed asshole, kind of known for the way I dressed. It wasn't always good – there was a phase when I wore teeny-tiny dresses held back by body harnesses to my veterinary anatomy practicals, where I'd use my acrylic nails to slice muscles of deceased animals for laughs. But that was my thing: for as long as I can remember, I used dress as a means of provocation, as a means to show, if not scream to, the world that I exist.

I was thinking back to the way I was at university when I was in Topshop in Lancaster, holding a blue and white striped women's shirt with floppy cuffs. Old me would have snapped this shirt up, along with a ton of other things that I would wear once and then exile to the back of my ethically questionable overflowing wardrobe. But holding this shirt, I was having a block about buying it, and it dawned on me right there in Topshop that I'd been having a six-month block, a block since I was beaten up outside Wally by that rogue asshole who never got his comeuppance. I realised that over the last six months my wardrobe had become monotonal: all-black everything, oversized if not drowning, and zero accessories. I'd even let my hair grow back to its usual mousy brown shade, instead of bleached blonde, blue, pink. I realised I could pinpoint the day I had stopped dressing how I wanted to dress, and it was six months ago, the day after the attack.

It seems blindingly obvious now, but there by the shirts in Topshop I let out a load of tears: tears that were representative of not only years of deep fear for my physical safety, but also of sadness for the fact that this punch to the right side of my face banged into me what the less violent of the daily attacks on my person were trying to for all those years. That I should be invisible, silent, unchallenging, ashamed, covered up. I felt momentarily guilty that I wasn't crying about Ben, but the funeral's tomorrow so I'll do that then.

I got to thinking more – about how myself and my friends have all battled and battled with people who just want to keep us safe: caring friends and family who ask us sweetly 'not to wear that'. To which we defensively tell them that we are fine, and we can wear what we want, and the dicks who have a problem with us can shut up. But they don't always. And when they don't it's frightening, and it hurts, and it leaves lasting scars that surface in absurd ways.

What's more, it makes you believe that there actually might be something wrong with your behaviour, with you, and with the way you present. No matter how hard you've tried and how many years you've fought to just wear a fucking heeled shoe, you internalise, you mutate out of yourself and into the 'acceptable you', and you don't really even notice.

After about four minutes at the shirt rail in Topshop, a sales assistant came over and offered me a tissue. I said 'no, thanks' and, while wiping away the tears: 'but I will take this shirt.'

The irony of this being literally a blue shirt is not lost on me: I am a million miles away from where I was. But in that choice I decided to make a further choice to chip away at that internalised self-loathing and fear, and rebuild both the confidence and the wardrobe that will get me noticed once more. People often say 'they'll spot you for the wrong reasons', but there are no wrong reasons, just wrong, homophobic people.

14th October / le 14 octobre

Today was Ben's funeral, and it was a peculiar day for us all. I loved Ben, the way you love the person you're most distant to in a close circle of friends, the one you wouldn't necessarily want to spend a day alone with, but value most highly in the well-oiled dynamic of an inseparable friendship group.

The way different members of the group, the Slags (No Lauren), went through the day positively correlated with how close each of us were to this wonderful friend of ours, the guy who had at one time or another, despite being a man of few words, said something more profound to each of us than all of us collectively did in our constant, brilliant, buzz of manic conversation.

When I was outed at school, Ben was the first to find me, to check on me. For a heterosexual boy of thirteen I still can't fathom how he worked out what to do. But he found me, being hounded by bullies from years above and below, and took me behind the drama block, put half a Lambert & Butler Blue in my mouth, lit it, and said, 'Look' – his feet shuffling, shoulders raised – 'I don't want you to think that I'm gay and stuff but I just want to tell you that . . . I love you and I'm very proud of you. In a place like this it takes way more courage to be you than it does to be me, mate. I've got your back' – eyes shifting – 'now pass that fag.'

I remember hoping so desperately he would kiss me – that would've been rom-com worthy – but I don't think I ever received a more beautiful reaction to any of my coming outs.

But today I didn't cry. I didn't post a long eulogy on Facebook – I hate that performative grieving so many people do on social media; already I've seen nigh on a hundred posts on Ben's wall from people who honestly had no clue who he was. I didn't even feel that sad.

Grief is millions of things; it's millions of people. My grandma said to me after the funeral that grief is like a tiny little pebble you carry around with you wherever you go. 'It might start like a boulder or a bullet, but eventually it turns to a tiny, beautiful pebble that takes pride of place on your inner mantelpiece. You carry it everywhere, never forgetting but eventually moving on. You must treasure the pebble, because while it's there for a greatly sad reason, it's better to have had a reason to put it there.'

I kind of understood what she meant by the last sentence, but as I tucked my grandma into bed because she can no longer get there herself, I took a little pebble and placed it there for Ben, and a little one for my grandma too who had changed beyond recognition from a bird of paradise to a real person who was ageing so quickly, and a little for parts of myself that I'd lost along the way too.

While some friends had wept and wailed at the funeral, I found it hard to believe that I would never see Ben again. For me, that's my grief, my little pebble: a life lived forever in slight disbelief, wondering when he'll poke around the corner, asking me a slightly nonsensical ontological question I'm not quite in the mood to answer, telling me drunk on Jack Daniels that he'll buy me this one, but the drinks are on me when I'm famous.

20th October / le 20 octobre

Until you've been out on a night out in a northern town, have you ever really been out out? When you grow up outside a cultural metropolis, where there's one dodgy cinema and a bowling alley that stinks of piss, the Night Out becomes religion, the centre of the week about which everything is planned. It's like a debutantes' ball – everyone's opportunity to debut their newest, shortest New Look purchase and to showcase the progress their Dove gradual tanner had made over the week.

A usual northern night out is full of unspoken rules and regulations:

1. Flat shoes? Are you fucking kidding me?
2. If you're bought a shot you fucking drink it.
3. 'Why the fuck you going home early?' – *never* go home early.
4. Pre-drink minimum a bottle of wine or 0.75 litres of vodka.
5. Arrive at Lancaster's only cocktail bar for strictly one cocktail. After that Emma gets mad because a cocktail is a fiver and she's famously tight.
6. Proceed to Wetherspoon's or Walkabout (closed down now) and purchase bottle of wine to consume for self.
7. Have a fight with Beth/Hannah because one of us is being 'peaky' about something totally illogical.
8. Fall down stairs in Vodka Revs – the ultimate shame in the ultimate destination.
9. Cry in loo because 'you just love each other so much' and make up from fight.
10. Dance for a bit, demanding the DJ to play song after song and getting visibly pissed off when he declines.
11. Drink more, dance more, and watch as Beth keeps revealing her tits because she wore a particularly chesty playsuit.
12. Take off heels and walk down to takeaway barefoot screaming about how much your feet hurt. 'It feels like daggers are goin' in me feet!'

13. Get takeaway.
14. Eat takeaway while covering yourself in mayonnaise and garlic sauce, ruining an outfit you'd spent all week planning. Matt used to eat mayonnaise with his fingers.
15. Sit in takeaway for at least an hour saying 'Hiya hun!' to girls from school and then rolling your eyes at them the moment they turn away.
16. Fall asleep in taxi/cry in taxi about how much you love each other.
17. Don't take make-up off.
18. Text girls to say 'love you gals best night ever!'
19. Repeat. Every single Saturday.

There's also a classic set of people you'll see, on a northern night out:

The girls: Generally glam, loads of make-up, one or maybe two gay men in tow. One from the group will be limping from her heels, one will be so smashed she's kicked out of the club and will absolutely lose it with the bouncer, one will always get with the same pervy guy from two years above you in school and another one will be jealous. They'll all fall out and make up minimum four times over one night.

The boys: I hate how gendered this is, but it's unlikely you'll find a group of non-binary folk on a night out in Lancaster. Anyway, the boys: the boys are fragile boys dressed in blown up body suits – muscular, tattooed, shaded and faded hair, and they will all be wearing either Lyle and Scott, Stone

Island or Vivienne Westwood if they've got a particularly good job in Manchester. These ones tend to have quite shiny faces. They'll all drink in a circle and bop instead of dance. They too will get in fights but they will be physical. I will at some point say something a little too over the top, and one of them will call me a 'fucking faggot' every time he sees me thereafter. I will tell him I fucked his dad.

The old lady lushes: My favourite. They're all called Beverley or Linda or Kath and they'll wear sheeny plum-coloured lipsticks called things like 'Iced Chardonnay' or 'Cheeky Champagne'. They'll have lots of old gold jewellery and will be guaranteed to be the ones laughing the most, their hair so lacquered you could crack a tooth on it.

The students: A much-disliked group among the townspeople, and you might encounter them on a weeknight. Once, I was challenged to a dance-off in Toast by a student from the uni, and the whole club – thus the whole of Lancaster – watched, enthralled. I was killing it, until I went for a high kick, fell over backwards, split my pants from waist to asshole and lay there as my exposed genitals were presented for all to see. My friend Beth laughed so much she was sick in the club.

Your auntie and uncle: Related or not, they're fucking everywhere.

One of your friend's mums: She's wasted, and your friend has to leave early, hugely pissed off, to take her home.

Things you might see: A baby in a pram in the club, a person wearing flip-flops, someone trying to beat up a bouncer, boys lurking outside the club in cars playing music very loud, a really flirty teacher, someone in a Day-Glo ra-ra skirt who's just put an ecstasy pill up her bum.

You'll never see a drag queen (there are places, but these tend to be in the bigger cities like Manchester, Newcastle or Birmingham where there's a burgeoning drag scene). There are lots of drag queens in Blackpool, and they're the amazingly iconic, rock-hard diamond ladies – the real old-school queens, the wonderful ones who are probably quite bitter having lived a life of brutal homophobia. They're amazing performers, and they definitely shave their arms. They're called things like Mercedes Bends and Miss Liza Garland.

Other things you'll never see: A busy gay bar, flat hair, subtle make-up, someone paying over £2 to get into a club.

These nights are strict in their routine. They are a tried-and-tested method that guarantees maximum fun, in minimum time, on a minimum spend. They never change, but why should they? Because on a Saturday night in Lancaster the people who spend their weeks working to the bone – as nurses, on farms, as teachers for kids with severe behavioural issues, as carers for their elderly parents, as builders and hairdressers and nail technicians and cleaners – have a place where they are like celebrities. We know everyone, we look amazing and we feel, for one night a week, absolutely, unstoppably joyful.

24th October / le 24 octobre

Tonight I was talking to my dad. We were walking our dog along the beach, dodging puddles and squelchy marshes that have eroded so hugely since my last visit home, and he recalled a certain type of nail varnish I used to wear, back in the days when my mum used to hate it.

It was when nail-art was all the rage, when companies like Rimmel and Barry M brought out a new formula each week: matte, shiny matte, crispy seaweed.

'This one was a crackle one,' he said, eyes aglow. 'It was black, and you used to paint it over coloured polish and it would crack, like scorched earth, and reveal the colour underneath. It was beautiful, I loved it, and I was so jealous, because it was so detailed and I've always loved detail.'

Blithely I told him he should wear it, that I'd dig it out for him. And then he told me that he never could: the world had come to expect him to look a certain way, and it would cause a stir among the people of our home town if he started wearing nail varnish. 'They'd think I was a freak,' he worried, before going on to list all of the things he wishes he could adorn himself with but can't because he's a man and that's not okay.

'But I wear purple shoelaces,' he concluded. 'I wear them to remind myself that I'm colourful, that I love colour and small things, and pretty things, and nobody will ever know. That'll have to be enough.'

And then, for all my complaining, for all the violence and all the difficulty, I thanked God that She'd made me queer, that I could wear whatever I wanted and didn't have to hide my true self between the rivets of my shoes.

I don't like many straight men, that's obvious, but for the first time ever I was stopped in my aggressive man-hating tracks and my heart broke for all the people like my dad who wished they could be a certain way, but can't because someone somewhere decided once that things should look like this. Yes, patriarchy affects men too, sure, and I've said this loads in conversation, but never have I felt it more than there on the beach with my dad. And there, at that moment, I had never been more glad to be different, to have been excised from that system by a process of gaylimination.

We came home and I painted his nails with the crackly stuff that I found in the back of my wardrobe. He loved it. And then we took it off. We'll probably never speak of it again.

26th October / le 26 octobre

I dropped my niece off at primary school wearing a superhero suit and she ran in, the little legendary butch she definitely is, not a care in the world – not yet having met the sting of people shaming her for liking more boyish things. I hope she never does.

30th October / le 30 octobre

I'm heading home to London today, having been at home for nearly a month. Denim has a Halloween gig in a bleak members' club in Mayfair, but it's good for the bank balance.

I feel the most upset I've felt leaving the place since I left for university. I don't know whether it's because Ben's passing made us all more fluid or volatile, or because I've become much more fluid and volatile in what I want, but as the train rolled off, I noticed the absence of the usual relief I felt when leaving Lancaster and going back to my queer life down in London.

I feel like the stretch between where I'm from and where I'm going has vanished, like the same person is simply travelling between the two places, not flitting between two lives. There is no escape, no running from, just travelling between.

For the first time I don't feel desperate to get out.

November/
novembre

2nd November / le 2 novembre

We've been kicked out of the warehouse because we are a 'fire hazard'. I didn't know until I returned because the Wallies didn't want to tell me as I was at the funeral.

Amazingly, they've found a house on the same street. I use the term house lightly. It's essentially a series of corridors in between two kebab shops (yes!) that has a basement prone to flooding and a terminal rat infestation.[1]

It's all we can afford short of moving to the Isle of Man, but our mantra is simple. We just say: 'it's queer' – 'rats are queer!', 'floods are queer!' – trying desperately to polish this property turd as most young people who live in London trying to 'make it' in the arts do. Unless you're one of those people whose dad secretly bought them a house, and then you just have the stress of having to pretend to be stressed about money and living costs and gentrification.

3rd November / le 3 novembre

People who say things like, 'I would genuinely rather have no money than ever work in that place again,' have never known what it's like to have no money.

6th November / le 6 novembre

Every cigarette I smoke makes me feel invincible. My friends, family, articles, the government, they all tell me to stop.

---

1   So nice to find a rental that allows pets.

They all show concern when I splutter mid way through a sentence, or when I can't quite muster the energy to climb the stairs at a particularly stairsy tube station. But they make me feel invincible. They make me think I'm not dead yet. And so I keep smoking – a lot – because sometimes I just desperately need to feel invincible.

7th November / le 7 novembre

I was scrolling through Facebook, idly, distracting myself from how little money there is left in my overdraft, when I saw something that genuinely took the words out of my mouth.[2]

There, on my feed, was Lara. Lara Cocks.

Lara Cocks, the new drag persona of Paddy: the ringleader of the homophobic bullies at school, now a fully fledged, all-singing, all-dancing, all-dick-sucking drag queen replete with lace fronts, padding and an actual Facebook page you could like. I was aghast, and so I dug more: going into the profile, right back to the start, which was two years ago, when Lara was birthed. This was the boy who would ash his cigarettes in my hair and make whole groups of lads chant 'puff puff takes it up the chuff'[3] when I entered the classroom or got on the bus. He always had a gay vibe, to be honest – his shirt constantly French tucked – but he was so terrifying that to even suggest a hint of faggery would see me battered worse than my butthole after a night at XXL.

---

2 This space symbolises my loss for words.
3 A catchy rhyme, I must admit.

Dumbfounded, I was going to ignore the page, but then I remembered that while he caused me some severe pain, it was probably because he was going through it too. So I liked the page.

And now I'm going to take my good karma and spend the day waiting on hold to Santander to request an overdraft extension. Gonna be gorgeous.

8th November / le 8 novembre

Turns out it's free to call Santander if you go in branch, so yesterday I made the trek to my nearest branch to make the call to get my overdraft extended. I thought about borrowing money from Ace and/or Hatty but they both extended their own overdrafts last week, which is where I got the idea, so probably a no-go zone, I imagine.

I thought about calling my mum but she's very broke at the minute. I thought about asking Pak but I owe him £500 because he lent me £200 for my flight from Reykjavik ages ago and also bought me a £300 Marques'Almeida puffer jacket that I wore once and then decided I hated.

So, there I was, inside a packed Liverpool Street Santander, on hold as lunchtime bankers ran in and out to check their huge assets hadn't been, I dunno – what's the worst that could happen to huge assets? – taxed at a fair rate?

Anyway, thirty-three minutes in, Kimberley from Liverpool answered: the thickest Scouse accent you've ever heard. Having grown up in the north, I love hearing another northerner, so we got chatting in that northern way only northern people do, in that way southern people hate.

I asked her how she was and she told me she was really sad because her family dog had just been run over by a lorry – which her stepdad was driving. Tragic.

She asked me how I was, and I told her I was really freaking out about money. I asked her about the overdraft and she said she desperately wanted to help but couldn't.

Thereafter, I suggested an exchange. 'What if I give you something people usually pay me for and you, instead of paying me, extend my overdraft?'

She was laughing, and asked what I meant, to which I responded: 'A rendition of Whitney's "I Will Always Love You", in dedication to your dog?'

She jumped at the chance, and said, 'Okay, maybe, only if you're good.'

And there, in full view of lunchtime Liverpool Street, two doors down from where my shit had shat on everyone's fried chicken dinner, I started slowly, as Whitney does, eventually charging into full song as I heard Kimberley breaking into a gentle weep on the end of the phone. I was trying to avoid the eye contact of everyone else, not wanting to wither away from embarrassment, but after I'd finished the song – fake sax solo, key change, big drum et al – at least fifteen people in the bank started clapping. And as I took a mini-bow, those sweet sweet words ran from Kimberley's mouth like honey from a bee, like cum from a peen: 'I've extended your overdraft for you – another seven hundred and fifty pounds.'

9th November / le 9 novembre

What's a relationship, really?

For my whole life I was fed an idea that it's movie-like, impossibly romantic, a cure-all for every insecurity.

But, as dating happened more frequently, I found myself changing in disingenuous ways just to match what I thought the person sitting opposite me at Las Iguanas sucking on a margherita would want.

But with Ace I'm trying to let all of me flow free. While I've very much wanted to be with him for a long time, in the eternal see-saw that was our courting period, I learned increasingly that when I look in the mirror and, for a second, consider my body and my person for myself alone, I realise how wonderful I am, how strong I am, how here, in the wreckage of my fat, hurt body, I know it deserves to be loved hard. I've never had trouble giving out love; I have so much to give. So I'm trying to put into practice a thing I only thought to be myth: to know I'm deserving of love in my fullness, in my flaws and insecurities. That I am deserving in my wobbliness and messiness – both physically and emotionally. To know that if this is undesirable to someone then that's a projection of their fears of effeminacy, their misogyny, their fattism, their insecurity, and not mine.

It's easier said than done – the slightest signal of Ace flirting with someone else at a party and I'm sent ricocheting back into my insecurity. Am I not masculine enough? How can a flabby, loud, northern drag queen ever compete against that muscular guy who's really succeeded at the whole 'being a man' thing?

But then, as I spiral into jealousy and self-loathing, I try to remove myself from the situation and ask whether being muscular and male over fat, femme, and full of love and sensitivity is actually who I want to be. And every time I settle on my wobbliness, my femme glory, knowing that I hold the key to so much more than being a man ever could, whether Ace wants it or not. And, thus far, Ace has wanted it too.

I always assumed being in a relationship would fix me. But it doesn't. Oftentimes it reflects your worst feelings about yourself back to you when the other person doesn't say exactly what you want to hear, or doesn't tell you they love you in exactly the way you need to hear it.

But recognising that a relationship is a bunch of failings and successes that snowball into a deeper knowledge of someone, a further understanding of who you both are together and separately, is what it's about. It's not about filling a hole or sacrificing swathes of yourself to fill theirs. It's about making a space where you just are. Ninety per cent of the time Ace and I are that. And the other 10 per cent – the fuck-up bits, the flirting with others bits, the not texting back for hours so you assume they're getting pounded by someone else bits – they create, paradoxically, a space to explore yourself and your worth. They give you a moment to reflect on yourself and remember that the grass is way pinker in your field.

13th November / le 13 novembre

Last night I had a horrendous nightmare that I was actually straight. I woke up in hot sweats, from a life where I had a wife and three children and was a wealthy vet who wore jerkins[4] and chinos and said things like 'the missus' and 'kids, shut up, I'm watching the golf'.

But then I opened my eyes, breathing heavy, and looked over next to me at Ace asleep naked. He has the most beautiful body, like it's carved from a chunk of soft stone you find on the beach near where I grew up. He has two little dimples above his bum and fluffy hair all over it. He has a sprouting of thick ginger hair on his chest – which he hates, but I adore – and a dip in his chest at the bottom of his ribcage, which ripples when he breathes in and out. His hair is red, thick like a mountain pony's mane, and his nose is ever so slightly bumped at the bridge and I thank God that She gave him at least one physical flaw so that I wasn't constantly in terror of his perfection. There's a scar on his leg from where his cat attacked him when he was young, and his mum, dad and sister always say that it was given to a neighbour, but I really think it was euthanised. I think about how weird it is that I'm thinking about cat euthanasia as I write about my boyfriend.

I replay the dream – the tidiest life, the loveliest family – and then I look around at the mess in our room: the ash trays full of cigarettes, the clothes jumbled all over the floor, the fine sheen of black dust that covers our room from Commercial Road's constant traffic jam. A Volvic bottle full of piss because I was home alone two days ago and was too scared to walk down the stairs to the loo because I'm always convinced I'm going to be attacked by an intruder when I'm home alone.

---

4 Such a stunning and underused word. xx

I go to kiss Ace on the forehead, and his breath smells like stale lungs, and I wonder if it's possible to love someone more than I love this person, to the point where even his smelly breath makes my heart beat faster. When I look at our life – mine, mine and Ace's, mine and all my friends' – so departed from what I once thought my life would look like, it makes me feel overwhelmed that I get to do it like this. If I started out in a place where that nightmare was my destination and this is where I am twenty-something years later, I consider for a second what life might look like in another twenty and I can no longer see a perfectly defined paint-by-numbers pathway. I used to be able to see everything – it was all written down in a book full of plans. And now everything is uncertain.

15th November / le 15 novembre

We were getting ready for a Denim gig last night, all sitting on the floor, squatting under blinky strip lights, in a loo that was overflowing with poo. In drag there's so many moments where you stop and wonder how all the choices you've ever made in your life led you to this moment as you're putting on layers and layers of make-up to go to your actual job while eyeing up a poo that is edging closer and closer.

I asked the girls what they think the most important thing a drag performer should know. The answers varied:

Glamrou said, 'It should be silly; we all need to have fun in an increasingly angry world.'

Aphrodite proposed that it should have something to say.

Elektra agreed with Glamrou.

Shirley said, fervently, 'That we honour our history.' And I agreed with her.

'Why?' I asked, but then everyone descended into gluing their eyebrows down because it's an urgent and detailed art which, if done wrong, could produce the hellish phenomenon known as Oatmeal Eyebrows.

As I painted on the rest of my face, squinting into a tiny compact mirror, doing it section by section, I thought, quietly, about all the queens and kings and gender artists who came before us, who put us here. For centuries it was religious or ritualistic: whether Aztecs or Egyptians, kabuki or shirabyoshi, or the misogynist men of the early English church system who *had* to take the female roles because women weren't allowed. Really dumb.[5]

It kind of went this way for ages, and then Shakespeare and all that really boring stuff. It was chill then, to be a man who dressed in women's clothing. Fast forward a while and you've got the revue shows of the thirties, around the time sexology deemed drag kings and queens to be of a third gender, around the time straight culture discarded it all. It became a thing of secret gay bars and underground private parties in the days where being gay was illegal.[6] But, as is the way with history, it's never made by the legislators or the people in power.[7] It's made by the people who resit, who are active and who have had enough – and, looking back on our history as

5 I know people are reluctant to write off swathes of history because their social context doesn't match ours but fuck it!

6 It should be noted that it's still illegal in seventy countries.

7 They just take credit for it.

LGBTQIA+ folk, it's drag queens, non-binary folk, trans women of colour, butches like Stormé DeLarverie.

Now it's big in pop culture but we're by no means safe because of it.

Later, after thirty minutes of listening to Kylie's new album, which we all decided we think is a three out of five stars, I said again that the most important thing about drag is knowing our history – because without it how will we take back our future?

20th November / le 20 novembre

A note from an old diary, nine years ago today:

I hate fanny. It's so scary and it makes me feel weird. That's why I told Beth she can't sleep naked! Eiw! I'm gay.

Sometimes I shock myself when I look back at the ways I used to be. I also relish looking back over my diaries to see how far I've come – to glimpse all the things I've, thankfully, unlearned. I also love that at the beginning of every entry I would start by writing 'Dear World!' – literally addressing the whole world, ready to go for whenever these remarkable works of non-fiction would be published in a smart move from a savvy publisher and I, with my witty childhood musings, would become a global superstar.

There's nothing more bleakly cliché than a gay man who flinches at any talk of vaginas. Hatty, Ellie, Cecily, Violet – all my female friends – have experienced this, and all of them tell me it feels deeply hurtful and only loads them with shame about having a vagina when it happens.

I complain when people shame me for the things I am or the things I've done, as do so many gays, so why has it become part of our cultural code to scream every time someone brings up vaginas?

21st November / le 21 novembre

I'm done with fashion – today I was asked to write an article called 'This Year's Ultimate Accessory: the Hair-Tuck' and it was literally, no shitting you, an article about how to tuck your hair behind your ears. It was 'URGENT!!', according to my editor, and as I sat there wincing as I wrote 650 words about Gigi Hadid and Jessica Alba,[8] trying to make the act of pulling your hair behind your ears a thing, I stopped for a moment, deleted the whole article, and with crystal clarity replied to my editor:

> John,
>
> I appreciate you have a content quota to fill, but this is by no means urgent and I can't seem to find the will within me to pull some crap out of my arse to talk about hair tucking. I'm sorry, it's just so painfully inconsequential. I will pitch you some features tomorrow.

---

8 I mean you're flogging a dead horse if you have to use Jessica Alba in a trend article: she's literally done nothing of relevance since she launched that baby food line years ago.

Now I'm terrified I've fucked the contact, but I felt like it was time to stop wasting my time for tiny amounts of cash and focus on something more important.

I'm going to watch reruns of *Desperate Housewives*. That's way more important. Such a shame Marc Cherry's a Republican.

22nd November / le 22 novembre

Yes, I fucked the contact. He replied saying that he was insulted that I couldn't get behind his editorial vision, which made me do a spit take of my coffee all over Leyah because to use the word vision for an article about hair-tucks is worse than saying being gay is a choice.

25th November / le 25 novembre

Something that always comes with the start of a new relationship is a moment when you consider that you might not have sex with anyone else again. Luckily for gays there's the whole open relationship thing which we oft revert to, but Ace and I are currently attempting monogamy because it's still very exciting to be exploring each other's bodies and we've both sucked enough dick to take a breather from others for a little while.

While our sex is wild in many ways, there's a difference in our sexual tastes. I'm very 'piss in my asshole and drink the contents' and, while he's adventurous, he's not so into the more extreme sides of sex: punching, pissing, degradation.

The thing about having such different sexual tastes is

that one will have to compromise to accommodate the other. Of course, the one who does the compromising should be the one who wouldn't be in breech of their consent if they were to make said compromise. Me asking Ace to punch me in the face would be great for me, but not for him – hence his consent breeched. Him asking me to suck his balls in a stairwell – we're both consenting, everyone's a winner and we teabag all the way home.

It's the first time I've ever considered this, to be honest, because before Ace my relationship with consent was very much based on, firstly, the fact I was looking for the wildest sexual anecdotes with which to shock my friends – this would often leave me exiting a sexual scenario wondering if I really had wanted to drink from the toilet like a 'mangey little mut', leaving a knot of discomfort in my stomach but with a great story to tell. The second factor was that I was never aware of what my limits were until I'd crossed them, so I'd think, 'Why not – he wants you to dress up like a Disney Princess and fuck you in his daughter's bed – cool!' Turns out it really wasn't, and thereafter I wouldn't ever be consenting to cosplay again. Not my thing. Ergo I only worked out what I wanted after I realised what I didn't.

There was a time, when I was at university, when I had my consent outright breeched. It wasn't a case of working it out on the job. No, this one was someone hearing me saying, 'No, I don't want that,' but powering ahead regardless.

I'd been dating this older guy from Cambridge college, in total secret, for about six months. We would see each other once, twice a week – for dinner, or cans of Fanta on his lawn, or to look over his vast array of rare butterflies, which were pinned inside dusty glass display cases across every one of his walls. It was a sweet relationship – he was angry, odd, and he'd get frustrated, but I found it endearing, and he really cherished me and celebrated things like my acrylic nails or my ever-changing hair colours, giving out tidbits of compliments like 'looks good', which would make me feel like a princess. God, I'm cheap.

Anyway, we had brilliant sex – uninhibited, vanilla in style, but with pleasure at its gooey core – which is why we probably worked for half a year. One night we'd gone out for dinner and I was feeling unwell afterwards, so I declined sex. He listened at first, but persisted in coaxing me into a blow or hand-job, his coercive language something I should have said no to, but in the moment I didn't see the harm in giving him a quick handy-j even if I was uninterested: at least one of us could get off. My lines on coercive language in a sexual, or any, scenario are now much tighter.

After about six minutes of lubey hand sliding, he climbed on top of me. Fine – we were kissing, it was his way of showing how much he was loving it. He started to pin me down, which I was somewhat into, assuming he was just enjoying my handy work. And then he fucked me. And I said no, both during and before. But he carried on, pushing deeper, holding me at my wrists, as I asked him to stop, kindly at first, then angrily, then worriedly, and the only thing he said was, 'Come on, you love this!'

It was in that second I realised that my line of consent had been crossed – this wasn't an experimental face-sitting balancing act or fetishwear session that just didn't quite do it for me; this was what I was so reluctant to name, for so many years after, as rape.

Eventually I got a wrist free and punched him over and over again in the shoulder. He pulled out and I pushed him off the top of me – the first time in my life I'd used my strength and been so thankful to have a big body. I leapt off the bed and screamed at him so loudly yet articulately it was like it was perfectly scripted. Then I threw an unopened can of Fanta at his face as he tried to approach me, missing him, and shattering the glass of his biggest butterfly case into smithereens, the wings of many of those precious butterflies chipped and crackled to pieces on impact. I walked home, weeping, in the burning sun, and all I could think about was the butterflies, and how damaged they'd been against their consent.

I've had a strange relationship with consent for as long as I can remember, a lot of it lying in what my sexual partner wants fulfilling, dictating the lines of my yeses and my noes. With Ace, consent is the beginning, middle, end of our sex – which some might think is boring or takes the sweating edges off the act, but I've never felt more considered or more safe, which has allowed me much more pleasure. For someone who has been seeking unsafe sex in various forms for a very long time, I'm coming to realise that perhaps to feel fully consenting – and not like a trapeze artist treading a wobbly line – is more sexually satisfying than any of the radical, dangerous sex I've ever had. Perhaps eventually it will blossom into both, but this time it will start with consent, instead of ending with a question.

27th November / le 27 novembre

A message from Lily:

So I have a friend who runs a record label in London and I want them to see *ACM*. How about I pay you a little yuletide visit? My family are in Guyana for Christmas (don't ask) and Jeremy is with family. A space for me at your table, perhaps? I might even get you something Balenciaga . . . Love you xxx

Me:

Are you fucking kidding me? Book that flight now, my queen! This will be the best Queermas ever! xxx

Lily:

Okay, amazing! Will let you know dates! By the way I said that Balenciaga thing as a ruse to get you to say yes – probably not gonna happen, I'm broke xxxx

29th November / le 29 novembre

So I was in the shop over the road from our new house, and I overheard a kid, tugging their mum's skirt, querying: 'Mummy, what's wrong with that boy? He's wearing a dress!'

It cut deep. It cut real deep. It cut even deeper when she replied, 'Oh honey, he's obviously just very unwell.'

All I wanted was pitta and taramasalata and instead I got diagnosed by a mother and a sweet babe.

I turned around, removed my Gucci sunglasses like a character from *Dynasty* and responded: 'I'm beautiful!'

December/
décembre

1st December / le 1 décembre

Denim are hosting a World AIDS Day party tonight.

A party sounds like a strange way to honour the virus that's killed 35 million people worldwide, that saw and still sees the persecution and stigmatisation of those who live with it, even though HIV and AIDS doesn't discriminate.[1]

But that's exactly the point: it is a party to honour those living powerfully, and those lost who with them took so much talent, beauty, and love. A party is the perfect way to do this.

That's because a party doesn't always have to be wild, or wasted, or joyful. A party isn't always about getting pissed, but it's always about the collectivity of people, sharing an experience of – yes – sex, joy, love. But also grief, pain, silence, quietness, all soundtracked by booming music which levels the playing field among everyone dancing. There you can fade in and out, together and apart.

Indeed, those who were lost to AIDS-related illnesses, and those who still suffer today, must be honoured with action – and there are people working to make the changes every day, from aid workers to councillors to hardcore activists who devote their lives to ending stigma, to finding a cure.

But on World AIDS Day it's a time to collect, look back, and celebrate. And so we keep dancing.

---

1 Just people, which is worse.

2nd December / le 2 décembre

'Well,' he says, 'I've never really,' he says, 'been to a drag show,' he says, as his hand slips down your back and onto your ass.

He's slurring his words, his breath so plump and hot with alcohol it instantly condenses on your nose, and he thinks you're his. He literally thinks you're his for the taking.

He's attractive, early thirties, long-term girlfriend, and he bought you a very friendly drink after the show, which you accepted as a kind gesture in return for what you gave him while you were on stage. And now, a few drinks later, friends gone home, he commanders you, tells you, over and over, about how he's never been to a drag show, as he clutches you and another beer.

You don't want him to touch you. It's a strange, dissociative feeling, which isn't one wholly of fear – though that's a part of it – but it's also of fury, of lack of surprise, of yet another night spent with someone unwanted, who thinks, because you're in drag, you are public property.

Touches come all the time: people grab you on the arm, touch your dress, feel your wig. They are fucking magpies to shiny things, and when in drag you're often both aesthetically and metaphorically shiny while also appearing as debased, because you're probably desperate for their approval, attention. Because why else would you be a drag queen?

As drag performers we're used to fielding certain types of behaviour: the drunk straight man who's curious, the hammered hen party for whom you become the most glittery accessory, the *Drag Race* obsessor who pins you against a wall and tells you which queen you're most like. Even the kindest of statements can become grating: 'we need a pic!' or 'can you do my make-up?' is like someone getting their account-ant friend to do their accounts for them, for free. Yes, drag is my way of life, an emancipation, but it's also a job.

They're all insidious. They're all a reminder that you're not necessarily human, that you're a totem for tragedy and triumph, for loneliness and love, for power and power-lessness.

I'm not saying the right response to a drag performer is to sit them down, make them a cup of tea, and ask them how they are. But it's to match their energy with yours. It's to respect their want for boundaries, even if, as a drag performer, they seem like the most boundless thing you've ever seen.

I'm not going to say the usual, tragic, 'drag queens are humans too'. But it's something like that.

5th December / le 5 décembre

A national newspaper asked me to write about class and going to Cambridge today, upon the news that there are more entrants from Eton per year than there are kids on free school meals. Vile.

I said yes, and wrote a piece about how isolating it felt to be from a different world – the underworld, as a lot of people saw it – recalling professors telling me to change my accent if I wanted to succeed, or being told there was no culture outside of Zone Two. I didn't even know what Zone Two was. One time I told someone I hadn't read *Harry Potter* and they didn't speak to me for the rest of our time at university. I told them we didn't have a bookshelf, but that just made it worse.

I spent three years at Cambridge trying to climb the mountain of class difference, trying to reach the peak where the social, cultural and financial elites live. I came from the bottom of the mountain, a place where I had never even known about class because the top was not in view.

It took me a long time to understand the key to being posh. Once you do away with your accent and your lack of confidence in your own voice, class difference comes down to the fact that posh people wear a lot of clothes with holes in them.

In my town you were not allowed holes in your clothes – you did everything to avoid looking poor. But rich people can pull off the aesthetics of looking poor because everyone knows – from their staff, to their colleagues, to their friends – that they're not. We all know the posh guy who just threw on this moth-eaten shit stain of a sweater while they were tending to the deer and writing their crap novel, before, in a jiffy, they'll dress for dinner.

I could never pull off the holes.

6th December / le 6 décembre

The worst kind of people:

1. People who ignore waiters/homeless people.
2. People who complain to railway companies over Twitter when their train's delayed.

3. People who talk about spirituality whilst dropping litter.[2]

4. Posh people who put on fake 'street' accents, or 'Streetoinians'.[3]

5. Men who preface every statement with 'Personally, I think . . .' before lampooning your opinion.

6. People who bring dogs into cafés and then let them do any fucking thing they want. These are the worst on this whole list.

7. Men.

8. The police.

9. Babies.

10. Obviously fascists, racists, transphobes, bigots et al but we all know this and I'm starting to sound like a broken record on that.

11. People who post angry statuses about that dog-eating festival in China but give no shits about human atrocities.

12. White people with dreadlocks.

13. Some gays.

14. Tories.

15. All gay Tories.

16. David Tennant.

17. Natalie Portman.[4]

---

2 I have witnessed this a whole two times: this is a whole category of person.
3 They're fucking everywhere.
4 Although she can def play me in the movie of my life.

9th December / le 9 décembre

Today I saw the man who attacked me on the Bakerloo line. He sat opposite me, we caught each other's eye and an instant shiver went through me, like when someone says, 'Oops someone walked over your grave,' or 'Oops that was a dick pic flying right through you.'

For all these months I couldn't remember his face, which I'm glad about, and in recollections of the event – which would rush to me, vivid as an acid trip, when I walked home alone at night or closed my eyes when I was shampooing – he was a hooded figure with a booming drawl.

But this man was absolutely him. I heard him speaking to a friend, and it was his voice, and when he glanced at me in the eye we connected in exactly the same way we connected just before his fist met my face. He knew it; I knew it.

I spent the first two stops anxiously considering moving down the packed carriage full of December shoppers, as I could feel his stares passing over me while he probably tried to work out exactly where he knew me from. Then, much like Harry Potter's scar when he's near Voldemort,[5] the scar on my nose started to crunch as it does sporadically from time to time, as if there's a chip of bone obstructing a small blood vessel.

So I decided to stay sitting where I was. I decided not to move an inch. I decided to sit and rub my scar and look him directly in the eye because I'd done enough moving to last

---

5   I've never read it, does this metaphor work?

us both a lifetime. The moment he clocked me staring he averted his eyes. But I kept on looking.

I grew ever more furious as the train whizzed through the tube tunnels, through decades-worth of dust and skin cells and breath from the lungs of Londoners and all its wide-reaching visitors. His included.

Most of my conversations, either the ones with myself or the ones with my queer siblings, are about analysing the world's structures to try to solve the mysteries of why we all behave in certain ways, why different people's situations and histories produce different types of behaviour in them. We spent months doing just that for my lovely attacker: trying to find rhyme or reason in his actions – 'He can't take his fragile masculinity so he lashed out at you,' or 'It was a cruel thing that man did, but we must locate the problems in the structures not in the actions in order to really prevent attacks like this happening again.'

And I buy it. I believe in it – that people's negative behaviour often stems from their own difficult backgrounds. The tag line for my favourite movie – *Burlesque*, a masterpiece starring Cher and Christina Aguilera[6] – is: 'It takes a legend to make a star.' That work of genius syntax can be transposed onto anything, and in the case of my attacker it would look something like: 'It takes a hard life, bad decisions, the plights of masculinity and a lack of exposure and education to make a queerphobic attacker.' Catchy.

These deconstructions of what makes people violent

---

6 I've seen it fifty-three times, really proud, someone call *Guinness Book of Records*.

towards people like me are integral in helping those on the receiving end of said violence maintain our faith in humanity.

But then, after a life spent locating these specific alleles on the genus that is social structure, trying to forgive our attackers, I'm sometimes pushed out of this mindset and into one which, simply, cannot understand these actions no matter the circumstance from which they arose.

And, as I sat there on this train staring at a man who transferred so much rage into my body that I still can't leave the house in full drag, that I feel like a trembling deer every time I hear a sharp noise, that caused me to mute and edit certain parts of my expression into obscurity, my brain can no longer compute these structures and all it feels is a lack of understanding brought on by clouds of scarlet rage.

In that moment I couldn't give one tiny shit that this man might have had a hard life. I don't have an iota of concern for his situation, the pain put in his body which he took out on mine. We too have received so much of that pain, and yet I can't name a single person in my community who has replicated such rage and passed it onto others the way our attackers do to us.

In that moment all my faith in humanity drained from my body and all I felt was an overwhelming desire to cause him some long-lasting hurt.

And then he got off, at Lambeth North, my eyes following his red Converse to the edge of the carriage as he stepped out into the world. And the rage drained, the desire to hurt someone disintegrated, and I clicked back into considering what caused his actions.

It's the right thing to do – both morally and politically. But it doesn't mean that sometimes you forget, even just for a moment, that it is. When there are people in the world who want you dead or hurt because of who you are, it's hard to always keep treading water, keep trying to find ways around their actions that somewhat absolve them. At some point, perhaps, people need to take fucking responsibility for their actions. I don't know.

But we've done it for centuries, and we continue to now. We've done the work, we know why we came into being in the all-sparkling ways we did. We see the power in rising higher. It's just such a shame that men like him can't do the same.

10th December / le 10 décembre

A call from my only friend from *Chic*, Amnah. She's iconic: I've never seen a better dresser, and I've never met someone with such an appreciation of style and aesthetic who desperately cares about the politics behind it.

She's a woman from Saudi, who came to London and found her people. She's a laugh a second – like a tornado screeching through the bar in which we decided to meet for a long, boozy lunch.

'I've got a project and I thought you might be the perfect person to do it with.'

'Sure, hit me!'

'You know how we always talk about the way fashion creates fantasy but excludes so many people from it?'

'Yes, and that if it's a fantasy why the fuck can't everyone be involved? Are fat people, black people, trans people, disabled people not allowed to fantasise?'

'Right, yes. Well, I got some cash to do something with this idea and I wanted to start a publication. I can pay you a decent hourly rate, and we can just make a fantasy where everyone's in it?'

'I'm in!'

As lunch stumbled into dinner, we drank three bottles of wine, three tequila slammers and ate a McDonald's. It was one of those afternoons where you feel like you've fallen in love with someone from the moment you sit.

'We're having a Queermas at my house, on the seventeenth. You wanna come?'

She nodded.

'Amazing! Bring wine, or any booze, one item of Christmas food and wear something show-stopping!'

11th December / le 11 décembre

I've been thinking a lot about 'where we are' as the LGBTQIA+ community. I was at a conference about queer grief and trauma when a friend of mine and I got into a heated debate: he was arguing that most of our problems are over, and I was saying that we've barely begun unpicking the wealth of shit that has been hurled at our community for the past forever.

There's that video series – *It Gets Better* – which he was citing as a good example, but I just don't see that. Maybe I'm a fucking cynic, and while this drip-feed of information and advice, which can thankfully be accessed at the click of a trackpad – much more easily than when I was a kid – is vital for the survival and education of so many distressed LGBTQIA+ people out there, is its message really true?

Yes, there are more movies, articles, political 'wins', and more gay, queer and trans people being granted a sliver of the media pie than ever before. But what does this all count for when, in reality, life for us is becoming increasingly punctuated by verbal, media-driven, and physical violence,[7] erasure of our communal spaces, and the swift dismantling of the meagre legislative support we have under a Tory government? I'm constantly so aware of being grateful for what we have, on the backs of those that fought for us, but sometimes I just feel furious.

Next year it'll be the fiftieth anniversary of the decriminalisation of homosexuality in the UK. And although we've made countless steps towards a better future for our community, there is still a dishearteningly long road ahead. So in order to tackle it, after a year of bad news upon bad news, in this new world of neo-fascist politics, we must seek to engage with the actual experience of LGBTQIA+ people: in order to ensure it actually does get better for ourselves, and for others, in order to make sure Orlando never happens again, in order to gain the rights we deserve.

I agreed to disagree with my friend on this one. We could agree on one thing, though: that our community is getting stronger . . . that our collective enemy in a world leaning

---

7 Homophobic hate crime has risen by 147 per cent since Brexit, according to *The Hate Crime Report*, published by Galop.

toward the right is sparking more political activism and unity than we've ever seen.

Gonna have a wank to take the edge off.

14th December / le 14 décembre

I've never been someone who enjoys a narrative. I find them suffocating, unlikely, linear, often missing out key parts of the picture – rewritten to amp up or downplay the pain, or the drama, or the emotion we've decided that story will tell.

My best bits are in all the minging bits that would never make it into a book or a film. Like when you love the smell of a crusty new piercing or when you pick your earwax and eat it and realise it tastes horribly bitter.[8]

'I bet Kerouac never wrote about cheesy piercings,' I said to a friend's boyfriend who idolises Kerouac (wtf?). And he said that he explored baseness in ways that could metaphorically mean that he was exploring those things.

Then I told him to fuck off.

15th December / le 15 décembre

I had my first argument with Ace today.

We were on Oxford Street, Christmas shopping, and I was talking about how different things feel this year versus last year: last year I was swaddled in three duvets, seeing nobody, in New York, eating pitta breads in bed and

---

8 Or when you wank over being gangbanged by the original cast of *Rent*.

wanking on a loop. I was talking about how much changes in a year for the individual but how so many parts of society that virtue-signal for change are actually the slowest to do the things they say. Journalism is a perfect example: it writes about us, or asks us to mine our trauma to get the clicks, but it doesn't hire us. Same with publishing, or making movies, or theatre.

I was churning over and over how culture isn't deemed to be culture until some middle-class, highbrow man reviews it, getting louder and louder, angrier and angrier, and then I accidentally smacked him in the face while I was violently gesticulating about men who violently gesticulate.

He got really mad, which was fair: told me I was so spatially unaware and inconsiderate, and I said he was entitled and then we both walked off in different directions.

And then, after he'd had a coffee and I'd had a full Five Guys burger and fries,[9] we met outside the flower shop at Liberty where I'd bought him the most expensive bunch of peonies ever and he had got me a can of Diet Coke which, while cheaper, was much more thoughtful because, you know, it's the little things. And as he approached I inhaled sharply, and was reminded, as I am every time I re-see his face, of the wonder of him.

I apologised, as did he, and we both admitted we were both wrong and then we kissed by the flower shop, the posh Tudor backdrop of Liberty illuminating the street, people looking – some in disgust, some in support, and I couldn't help but recall the Christina Aguilera 'Beautiful' video, the

---

9 Eating my feelings as per, stunning. xxx

one that made me realise I was gay. And it had all come full circle, without ever being a circle at all. I felt full.

17th December / le 17 décembre

Today was Wally Christmas, or Walmas, or Queermas – we never settled on a name, we're all so indecisive. But that's queer so it's fine.

Ellie organised it: she's a stickler for organised fun so, while we all tried to help, she got carried away and we let her run with it. We started out with a fashion show runway reveal at Stepney City Farm. Prizes were awarded for the best walk, the best look, and the best overall performance. Ace did a tri-reveal, un-layering three times, ending his sashay by sitting on a pig, as we all yelped, 'Work that pig, mama!' in utter exultation. He won, of course, and prizes were doled out after we were forcibly removed from the property for our inappropriate pig use.

'But the pig loved it!' we protested. No luck.

After that we arrived home to prepare Queermas dinner. As can be expected when planning a dinner with nearly twenty queers, nobody brought what they were assigned by Ellie – which would have made for the perfect, all-rounder Christmas dinner. What was brought in the end, by friends who'd rushed from all over town, some even from other countries, was far superior to any Christmas dinner I'd ever had.

On the menu we had:

- Ellie's sweet potato with marshmallows. Two bottles of rosé fizz.

- Cecily's duck, which wouldn't fit in the oven,
  so we had to ask the kebab place next door if
  they could fire it up for us, to which they sweetly
  obliged.
- Lily's brick of Marlboro Lights from the airport:
  'Twenty packs of twenty – I want to get through
  them all, bitches, smoke up! It's Queermas!'
- Glamrou's inhaler.
- Aphrodite's homemade cheese sticks.
- Ace's really stunning salad dressing, a Lady Gaga
  picture cake from Asda, and a cheese grater because
  ours had been used (and subsequently broken) to
  support one corner of the washing machine as the
  floor had somehow become warped in the kitchen and
  the washing machine was literally moving about a
  metre and a half every time a cycle was completed.
- Elektra's famous apple cake, which she actually buys
  from the bakery and takes all the credit for.
- Cora's news that she's moving to London!
- Amnah's magnum of cheap prosecco, some Patrón
  Café and a dildo for 'Stick the Dildo on Dolly
  Parton' – much like 'Pin the Tail on the Donkey',
  but queer.
- Savannah's whiskey and weed for everyone to share.
- Pak's disappointment at the lack of food, followed
  by twelve pizzas from Deliveroo over which Cecily
  shredded the duck.
- Violet's boyfriend, who was dressed in a rugby shirt,
  which we all made him change for a glitter halter.
  'Much better!' Violet rejoiced.

- Allegra's copy of Susan Sontag's *Notes on 'Camp'*, with which she posed like a seductive lecturer as she read a passage to us in place of grace.
- Jessie's camera and a bottle of Babycham.
- Hatty's decorations: the house was like a neon sex dungeon, plus tinsel curtains, and a homemade Christmas tree, made out of wire hangers, to which we made endless, obvious, *Mommie Dearest* jokes.
- My make-up, and some bondage tape for lapdance hour.
- A suitcase full of Rina's really beautiful clothes, which we all throw on and off throughout the day.
- Jacob's leftover spare ribs from a meal he'd just had with his dad in Chelsea, and his social media presence.
- Chris's playlist full of niche Swedish dance tracks that none of us know, plus his iconic brand of yuletide bitterness.
- Leyah's four pale ales and a bunch of petrol-station flowers: 'What? I'm broke!'
- Shirley's high heels and wigs, for those who put in low effort on the costume front.
- Everyone's avid desperation to drench the holidays with as much queerness as possible.

And it was drenched. A tasting menu. A far cry from last year in New York.

The night rolled on, and we got through eleven of Lily's packs of cigarettes, all of the pizza and every drop of booze. We rattled through games, sat around stewing in gloriously nostalgic stories from our collective years of friendship, and pulled queer crackers – just average crackers, but pulled with our ass cheeks, so that makes them queer.

The day drifted into the perfect Queermas night: over-full, drunk, full of the best people. We all began to drift off: strewn in full drag over mismatched dining-room chairs, covered over on the floor by thin veils of orange and green chiffon, five to a bed on the second floor, four to a bed in the basement, Amnah and Chris still smoking and chatting and cackling about being 'over thirty' on the roof.

Collecting glasses from across the house, I thought about going home for Christmas and how full up that made me feel, for the first time in years. I wandered round the corridors of my tiny queer life, looking at my glorious friends and remembering the hunt I undertook to find them, for us to find each other. I heard shouting outside, but being in here gives new meaning to the term safe as houses.

I thought about family: my chosen family, and my bio-logical family, and for a moment I stop and thank anything that is holy that I'm all the things I am, and that those things brought me to this day with these people.

In the middle of the night I was awoken by the drum of lorry-hour outside my window. It wasn't dark in the house, because it never gets dark from all the neon lights of east London. I lit a cigarette, and was stood looking out the win-dow when I heard muttering from the kitchen downstairs.

I padded down in the nude to find Hatty, Ace and Leyah chatting away, all unable to sleep, discussing identity poli-tics as per.

I sat down, and Ace and Hatty took a seat on each of my knees, and Leyah sat on the washing machine. The kitchen is so small that we were all huddled. We embraced so tightly.

'What do you want for Christmas, kids?' I asked them, like Santa.

A moment, the air becomes unusually sincere for a bunch of nude queers at Christmas.

'This.'

'This.'

'This.'

'This.'

We all say it one after the other, glimmers of happy tears in our eyes. And we all, really, mean it.

18th December / le 18 décembre

I've been keeping a diary on and off for as long as I could write. Through it I developed an honest dialogue with empty pages – seeking and finding solace in times when I desperately required it.

As we get older, as I find myself on stages or social media or penning a piece for a magazine or newspaper or in an awkward conversation at a dinner party, that honesty has served me well, and it always starts with the diary.

When I visualise the process of writing things down in here I see what's in my head as confused mulch, which percolates out onto the page, allowing me to make sense of the messiness of what's been locked beneath my wigs or my crown of ever-changing multicoloured hair.

By putting things into words you allow yourself a moment to take your mess and tidy it up – not that I give a shit about tidiness – but over years writing to myself has allowed me to solidify my identity, explore my opinions, relieve my heart of its lonely aches and untie the tangled knots of worry in my stomach.

This year has been one in which I've figured out many things: what I want to do with my life, at least for a bit; how to keep friends and not really make any more – something I used to be obsessed with; how to function in a relationship – and how to have one, get engaged and then press control alt delete on it; how to connect the ways I've changed to the place in which I started; how to appreciate my wobbling body; how to say 'yes' in sex rather than just 'if you want to'; how to shatter dreams and decide that failing was always the better, more exhilarating option; how to be in love with the people in my life, how to get an overdraft extension. I'm not going to say how to love myself because that's dull as fuck.

The process of keeping a journal has provided me a chance to wade through the messiness of the world. It was on these pages that I first wrote down that I was gay, that I wanted to become a drag queen; I plundered whether I was perhaps trans and found when I explored myself I felt most authenticity as a non-binary femme. It was in here, somewhere, that I figured out my body belongs to me, not gender, not diet culture, not even the fat that bubble-wraps it. It is here I stowed away the parts of me I had to destroy in order to survive as a queer person, only to revisit them and reclaim them when I was stronger – and there's lots of that left to do. It was here I sketched a map of my drag persona: her looks, her humour, her acerbic wit and obsession with smut-ridden jokes. It is here I wrote about the most beautiful jewels in the crown – my friends, my lovers, my family, my community. It is here I was allowed to make and unlearn mistakes. It is here I found a place to excoriate every single stare, word, scream, fist, or lemon squeezed into my eyes, so that it wouldn't settle on or beneath my skin, so that I escaped a life of internalised shame and hatred, pointing it, instead, back out to the world. It is here I worked out what it actually means to go home.

It is here I found someone to share with when I was small and afraid, and exercised my duty to myself to love radically and live powerfully in ways that allowed me to become giant and fearless and formidable again.

It is here that I fell in love, smoked thousands of cigarettes, made messes of my life and cleared them up. It is here that a thirteen-year-old me wrote letters to myself telling me that it was all going to be okay. It is here that I realised it was going to be better than okay: it was going to be glorious.

It is here, when things got particularly bad, I would promise myself that I would be a star.

It is here I realised that life is always going to be messy. It is here that I realised that I am so many things, and I proclaim them with honour all the time: queer, working class, a drag queen, non-binary, femme, fat. It is here that I worked out that all of those labels are the names of the things that I love about myself the most – they started as sites of violence and blossomed into beautiful, fuchsia, flowering trees with so much potential inside them to give and to learn.

But beyond the words I write – the delineations, the affirmations, the things that I am, and the things I've done that make me – it is here I've come to realise that I can be found in the things in-between: the messy bits, the ugly bits, the stinky bits, the bits where all of our identity Venn diagrams collide into a chaotic mess so big I can't fathom its enormity, I can't put it in words because language could never do me, or anyone else, justice.

I have spent a long time trying to understand the rabbit warrens of identity, mine and others', and the intersections that create communities, behaviours – both positive and negative. I'm invested hugely in this world view: understanding identity and the structures around them has allowed me to unlearn harmful things I thought about myself, and others, for the longest time.

A war rages on outside. One against our impossibly beautiful identities, and, as we should, we'll continue to figure out how to unpick and blow open the structures that started the war in the first place, all in a lifelong fight to be allowed the simplest things.

But it's between that figuring out, that integral unpacking and vital critique where real magic, real pleasure, real euphoria, real utopia, real radical love actually happens. It's where the Venn diagram crosses over, when we are all together, that just being, when allowed – in your most gleaming state – can take place.

While I'll most likely keep journalling in order to work out how to survive, I'm landing on the idea that it's perhaps in the bits that can't be described in words that makes the world worth surviving in. And that's where you'll likely find me – a fat, femme, non-binary, queer, working-class drag queen – along with some of the most beautiful, radical, love-filled siblings on the planet.

Acknowledgements

First of all, thank you for reading this. If you've got here, then I hope you got your life; if you're reading this in a book shop, then please buy it.

First I must thank Zoe Ross, my agent: this book is in so many ways down to you and how fervent you are in your support and championing of my voice. You are a wonder, and I am so lucky to work with you. The same goes for Kitty Laing, who, when I don't feel it, reminds me that I'm a star.

Sara Cywinski, Michelle Warner, and the whole team at Ebury – thanks for taking a chance on the little book that could, and on me. I hope it does you proud. It has been such a pleasure.

To the editors who empowered my voice, and told me my words were valid – Sarah Raphael, you are so deeply generous; Lynette Nylander, you were the first person who told me, and so many others, we could do it. Thank you.

My parents. Mum, thank you for teaching me how to love unconditionally, to stand up for myself, and for teaching me that the people in life are the most important. Dad, thank you for always telling me that it's the effort that counts, and for showing me that sensitivity isn't weakness. You are both the loves of my life. Danielle, James and Harry: for teaching me wit and humour, strength in the face of bullies. I love you all so very much. Grandma, you helped me find glamour and beauty when I couldn't. You are, really, an icon, and although you'll never know it, it was you that taught me to be gay. My nieces and nephew – don't read this 'til you're thirteen. Can't wait to give you your first cigarette. You're all amazing.

To Wally: for giving us a place to make mistakes, to love radically, and to ash on the floor.

My friends, my other family. To Shughie: you have shown me what it means to feel full, and to value myself by valuing me. You are the true queen, I love you. Hatty, you taught me queerness and I am forever in your debt. Can't wait to spend forever with you. Leyah, for your patience and kindness, for your strength and for always rolling me a cigarette. To Emily, for always giving your honest opinion, and for showing me gay culture. To Jacob, for being the best drag twin-baby ever, and for showing us all the radical power of glamour.

Amrou, you are a second mother/sister/daughter to me, and my world is expanded so greatly by your presence in it. I hope I can do the same for you.

Thurstan: thank you for always letting me be myself, for always being so proud of me, for teaching me work ethic, and for loving me when so many people love you. You are one of the world's real gems.

To Amnah, you always hear me, and tell me my emotions are important.

To Emma, for always telling me my work is valid and for all our early morning breakfasts and late nights falling asleep together.

Talia, thank you for showing me that weird is wonderful.

The Denims: you refashioned my idea of family and I owe you, in so many ways, a lot of my life.

To Allegra, for teaching me how to write way back in my bedroom in Lancaster. Amelia – thank you for the brilliant advice, and for being someone to laugh about it all with. To Sadhbh, for always analysing the niche with me.

To my other friends, without whom this book, and this life, wouldn't be possible: Daphne, Rina, Jessie, Eve, Charlie H, Claudia, Decca, Ellie K, Chris, Harry P, David, Tamara, Harriet, Kai, Will, Sarah L, Sarah S, Nick, Lettice, Liam H, Theo, Claire and Temi. To Sarah and Norman for giving me a home to start in, and for being so constantly interesting.

To my bezzaz, you make me laugh like no other, and you pushed me through some of the toughest years of my life. You're all so, so iconic. I love you all so much.

Celine Dion, for teaching me to be a queen.

To the north – for teaching me the value of kindness. To the drag community – for teaching me the value of community, of power, of self-love. To the LGBTQIA+ community wider – for teaching us all resilience. I am so proud, and so grateful, to be a part of you.

And, finally, thank you to my butthole – you've really been through the wringer, and yet you're the strongest thing I know.